Good Housekeeping

THE ULTIMATE
STRESS-BUSTER

Good Housekeeping

THE ULTIMATE
STRESS-BUSTER

A complete guide to help you relax
and enjoy life to the full

Dr Sarah Brewer

Ebury Press
London

First published in 1999

1 2 3 4 5 6 7 8 9 10

Text © Ebury Press 1999

Illustrations © Ebury Press 1999

First published in the United Kingdom in 1999 by
Ebury Press

Random House, 20 Vauxhall Bridge Road, London SW1V 2SA

Random House Australia (Pty) Limited
20 Alfred Street, Milsons Point, Sydney,
New South Wales 2061, Australia

Random House New Zealand Limited
18 Poland Road, Glenfield, Auckland 10, New Zealand

Random House South Africa (Pty) Limited
Endulini, 5a Jubilee Road, Parktown 2193, South Africa

Random House UK Limited Reg. No. 954009

Papers used by Ebury Press are natural, recyclable products made from wood grown in sustainable forests.

A CIP catalogue record for this book is available from the British Library.

ISBN 0 09 186876 9

Designed by Jerry Goldie

Cover design by Senate

Printed and bound in Great Britain by Butler and Tanner Limited

Note: Although every effort has been made to ensure that the contents of this book are accurate, it must not be treated as a substitute for qualified medical advice. Always consult a qualified medical practitioner. Neither the Author nor the Publisher can be held responsible for any loss or claim arising out of the use, or misuse, of the suggestions made or the failure to take medical advice. In particular, do not use aromatherapy or herbalism if you are pregnant, or if you have high blood pressure or epilepsy, without seeking medical advice.

CONTENTS

Introduction:

WHAT IS STRESS?

Stress is a modern term that simply means you are experiencing an abnormal amount of pressure. A certain amount of pressure is essential to help you meet life's challenges, release your creativity and fuel your continued personal growth. Once pressure falls outside the range with which you feel comfortable, however, it can lead to the unpleasant physical and emotional symptoms associated with distress.

Different people are comfortable with different amounts of pressure, and how you cope varies from person to person and even from time to time. One day you may feel totally calm and laid-back, able to cope with everything thrown your way, while on another occasion the slightest extra pressure will overwhelm you, turning you into a crumbling, tearful wreck. Sometimes you may even feel stressed because of insufficient pressure to drive your life forward. Being stuck in a boring rut with little stimulation can be just as frustrating and unpleasant as being loaded with too many tasks and not enough time. In some experiments performed in the 1950s, researchers put volunteers in a totally stress-free environment with no external stimulation of any kind. Within a short while some started to experience hallucinations and most felt disoriented — unsure of where they were and when. After three days, no amount of financial inducement could persuade the volunteers to continue staying in the totally stress-free, unstimulating environment.

Most musicians recognize that they perform better after feeling nervous before a concert starts, and Olympic athletes and professional actors normally need the presence of a live, interactive audience to achieve their full potential. When controlled, stress generates feelings of challenge, excitement and motivation. When uncontrolled, however, it produces extreme physical and emotional discomfort, bizarre behaviour, serious disease and ultimately premature death. It has been said that finding the right balance is like adjusting the strings of a musical instrument: too loose and the tune will be ruined; too tight and the strings will break. Just right, and the instrument will sing with a unique and lovely harmony that fills your mind, body and soul.

Why we feel stressed

Pressure is so important for survival that your body is programmed to produce a stress response known as the fight-or-flight reaction. It is this reaction — due mainly to the effects of adrenaline — that produces most of the physical and emotional feelings you experience when distressed. If your body did not produce adrenaline, feelings of stress would not occur, but as you would also not respond appropriately to the tasks and dangers of everyday life, you would not last long in the corporate and urban jungles of modern existence.

Adrenaline (also known as epinephrine) is produced by the adrenal glands, of which there are two — one above each kidney. The outer regions (cortex) of these small, triangular glands produce hormones that affect the metabolism while their inner parts — known as the medulla — form part of the body's sympathetic nervous system. This branch of the nervous system is designed to act as the body's first line of defence during times of stress.

When you are confronted with a stressful situation that may require increased physical activity, nerve signals from the brain trigger the release of adrenaline from the adrenal medulla directly into your bloodstream. As a result, stress increases blood levels of adrenaline by as much as a thousandfold

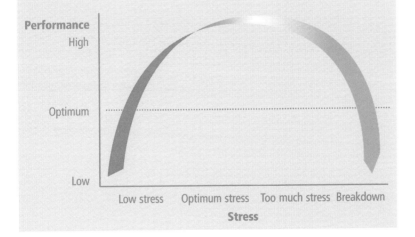

HOW THE AMOUNT OF PRESSURE YOU ARE UNDER AFFECTS YOUR PERFORMANCE

Too little pressure: In this situation there is insufficient challenge for you to achieve a sense of personal accomplishment. Skills are under-used. Lack of stimulation leads to boredom. There is a lack of purpose or meaning in life, which may lead to stress.

Optimum pressure: Life is balanced and, despite ups and downs, is perfectly manageable. Job satisfaction and a sense of achievement enable you to cruise through daily work without much problem, pleasantly tired at the end of the day.

Too much pressure: There is a constant feeling of having too much to do every day. Despite emotional and physical exhaustion, you feel unable to take time off to rest and play. You are in permanent overdrive but not achieving as good results as expected. You are feeling stressed.

Breakdown: If stress continues, you may develop severe physical or mental illness. In other words, your response to excess pressure is making you ill. You are extremely stressed.

Performance

High

Optimum

Low

Low stress   Optimum stress   Too much stress   Breakdown

Stress

QUESTIONNAIRE

THE BODY OF A STRESSED PERSON IS AFFECTED BOTH PHYSICALLY AND MENTALLY. ASK YOURSELF THESE TWELVE QUESTIONS TO FIND OUT JUST HOW STRESSED YOU MAY BE:

☐ 1. Are you finding it difficult to concentrate and make simple decisions?

☐ 2. Has your voice become more high-pitched and shrill, or do you suffer from a stiff jaw?

☐ 3. Have you increased your intake of nicotine or alcohol?

☐ 4. Are you over-breathing, which may show up as chest pains, tingling sensations, palpitations or asthma?

☐ 5. Do you feel nauseous and suffer from ulcers, heartburn or indigestion?

☐ 6. Do you sweat excessively or do you suffer from skin dryness or rashes?

☐ 7. Is your immune system less efficient?

☐ 8. Do you have difficulty in swallowing or does your mouth go dry?

☐ 9. Does your neck ache, or do you suffer from backache, muscle tensions, fatigue, or muscle pains?

☐ 10. Do you have high blood pressure? Is your heart pumping faster or do you have palpitations?

☐ 11. Do you suffer from tiredness, lethargy or sleep problems?

☐ 12. Do you experience the need to urinate frequently, or suffer from diarrhoea?

Your score: For each YES, score 1 point; for each NO score 0 points.

1–3: You appear to be coping well with your everyday life and are not displaying any significant signs of stress

4–9: You are showing some signs of stress. To help, make sure of Points 3–7 to reduce your stress levels before they get too great.

10–12: This signals an unduly high stress factor and you are advised to make large changes to your lifestyle to prevent illness.

within just one minute. Adrenaline then produces an instant response in different parts of the body, so your whole system goes on to red alert.

- Your pulse rate, blood pressure and the force of contraction of your heart increase so more blood can be pumped to your muscles and brain.
- Your circulation diverts blood away from the intestines towards your brain (for quick thinking), skeletal muscles (for exercise) and skin (for rapid cooling on exertion). Reduced blood flow in the intestines can cause feelings of 'butterflies', while extra blood in the skin can make you flush with fear.
- Your sweat glands are switched on, ready to cool your body during sudden exercise; you literally sweat with fear.
- Your muscles tense ready for action — you stiffen and tremble with fear and your voice becomes high-pitched and shaky.
- Your breathing rate goes up and your airways widen to bring extra oxygen into your body — you may breathe in suddenly and deeply, described as catching your breath.
- Your sugar levels increase as the body's stores are raised to provide instant energy for extra power, strength and speed.
- Your pupils dilate to improve your field of vision — your eyes can literally widen with fear.
- Your bowels empty (nervous diarrhoea) to make you lighter for running; under severe stress, you may even be sick, too.
- Chemicals are released into your blood that make it clot more easily, and cause damaged blood vessels to constrict to reduce bleeding from wounds.
- In males, the stress reaction also draws the testicles up towards the abdomen, for safe keeping.

These effects of adrenaline prepare the body for running away or for combat when you are under threat or pressure. This is the first stage of the stress reaction — known as the fight-or-flight response — in which energy is mobilized within the body. In ancient times, this helped the caveman survive in hostile surroundings, by giving him extra

RELATIONSHIP OF RESTING PULSE RATE TO FITNESS AND STRESS

Your resting heart rate – measured after you have been sitting quietly for at least fifteen minutes – is a good indication of how fit you are, but will also relate to how stressed you are feeling at the time. Feel for your pulse in the inside of your wrist on the same side as your thumb, or at the side of your neck.

50–59 beats per minute: Excellent fitness (trained athletes) and stress-free.

60–69 beats per minute: Good fitness and stress-free.

70–79 beats per minute: Fair level of fitness and relatively stress-free.

80–85 beats per minute: Poor level of fitness or under some stress.

86 plus beats per minute: Very poor level of fitness or under a high degree of stress.

If your resting pulse rate is high – either through lack of fitness or high stress – it will help to take regular exercise such as walking briskly, jogging, cycling, swimming or doing aerobics/step at least three times a week. NB Your pulse rate may be affected by certain drugs (for example, betablockers) and illnesses (for example, fever). If your pulse rate is high or irregular, it is worth asking your doctor to check your cardiovascular system.

speed, power and energy to run away from predators such as sabre-toothed tigers or hunters from neighbouring settlements. The effects of stress hormones would then be used up in vigorous exercise during fighting or fleeing which would soon neutralize the stress response and bring the body systems back into normal balance. This is the second stage of the stress reaction, in which energy is consumed. Nowadays, the need to fight or flee rarely occurs so the effects of stress build up to make you jittery, taut and trembling inside. This build up of stress then develops into the third stage of the stress reaction – the potentially harmful stage – in which energy is drained from the body.

Exercise itself will also trigger the fight-or-flight reaction as an appropriate response to prepare your body for intense activity – a response which will naturally power down as exercise comes to an end and another branch of the nervous system – known as the parasympathetic nervous system – reverses the stress reaction and brings the body back to normal function. As exercise is designed to accompany and neutralize the fight-or-flight response, one of the best stress-busting tactics is to increase your level of activity and burn your tension away when you feel the pressure building up. (See Chapter 4: Take exercise and relax.)

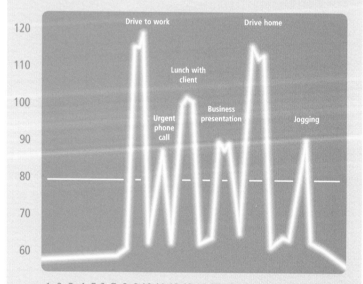

STRESS AND YOUR HEART RATE

Your heart rate will vary during the day depending on your level of stress and how active you are from time to time.

Heart rate per minute

120

110

100

90

80

70

60

Drive to work

Drive home

Lunch with client

Business presentation

Urgent phone call

Jogging

1 2 3 4 5 6 7 8 9 10 11 12 13 14 15 16 17 18 19 20 21 22 23 24
Time (24-hour clock)

During sleep, the pulse is at normal resting rate. It goes up on waking and in response to stressful situations and periods of activity during the day

Other stress hormones

As part of the short-term stress response, the adrenal medulla also produces another hormone, noradrenaline (norepinephrine). Noradrenaline helps to maintain a constant blood pressure by stimulating certain blood vessels to narrow when blood pressure falls, which helps to stop you fainting from shock. This mechanism doesn't always work however, and some people may find they swoon under extreme pressure.

If stress continues for any length of time, the adrenal glands also increase their output of the steroid hormone, cortisol, from the outer cortex. This rise in cortisol seems to be essential for survival, for if it does not occur (for example, if the adrenal glands are surgically removed) even slight stress may lead to sudden death unless steroid injections are given. Exactly how and why this happens remains unknown. It may partly be related to the fact that cortisol is needed to activate the rest of the sympathetic nervous system, helping to maintain blood pressure and to prevent the other physical effects of stress from becoming excessive. It may also be due to its role in releasing extra fatty acids into the circulation to act as an emergency energy supply. In the short term, this increase in cortisol levels is therefore potentially life-saving. If stress continues, however, so cortisol levels remain persistently high, it can lead to harmful and disruptive symptoms. Any stimulus that increases secretion of cortisol from the adrenal cortex is described as a stressor. It is helpful to know what these stressors are, and the causes of stress are discussed further in Chapter 1.

Positive pressure versus negative stress

Short-term positive pressure is a healthy part of everyday life. It gives you the energy and reserves you need to rise to the challenges of existence, helping you strive to achieve your best. By psyching yourself up and preparing physically and mentally for particular situations, positive pressure improves your performance and motivation so you are more likely to meet your goals. It also allows you to feel a wonderful glow of satisfaction when the pressure is over, the energy mobilized has been consumed, you have prevailed and your body powers back down to its normal settings.

Excessive or long-term pressure has a negative effect, however, and keeps the fight-or-flight response switched on to drain you of energy — especially if it is not accompanied by physical activity. This is best thought of as negative stress to differentiate it from positive pressure. Negative stress is due to persistently high levels of adrenaline and can lead to stress-related problems such as tension headaches, digestive disorders and muscular cramps. Ultimately it can also lead to depressed immunity, high blood pressure and other potentially serious health threats if the negative stress is not addressed.

Thinking positive

The power of mind over body should never be underestimated and is largely responsible for determining whether the adrenaline stress you experience has a positive or negative effect on your life.

When you think about it, there is obviously a vast difference between the enjoyable, anticipatory stress of excitement linked with positive thinking, and the worrying, down-dragging stress associated with negative emotions such as fear and anxiety. The same physical stress reactions are occurring in your body due to the release of adrenaline, but the way you respond to them is determined almost exclusively by your state of mind.

Imagine two people who have each been asked to give their first-ever speech to a large audience of over a hundred people at a work-related conference. Both face the same challenge, and experience the same stress reactions in their body — but one person feels in control, while the other feels terrified. The positive thinker looks on the task as a wonderful challenge, a chance to prove themselves at work, to gain experience in public speaking and to earn recognition and approval from those who are important for the advancement of their career. They picture the event in their mind and see themselves giving a flawless speech that holds the audience enthralled and impressed. The negative thinker, on the other hand, looks on the task with abject horror. Fear of failure, of getting muddled or tongue-tied and of making a fool of themselves takes over and they quake in their shoes, almost wishing they were dead. They picture the event in their mind and see themselves tripping up the steps, dropping their notes and fumbling their words. They just know they can't possibly do it properly and will end up being thought of as a complete idiot.

Both people experience the same stressful physical reactions in their body. The difference is how they mentally respond to them. The positive thinker responds to the high stress in a positive way and decides to prepare and practise thoroughly, so they will perform at their best. In contrast, the negative thinker responds to the high stress by becoming increasingly anxious, irritable and snappy. They feel trapped — there's no point in making any effort towards the coming disaster and no way to improve the outcome. They try to put the event from their mind and to survive through denial — perhaps they will even call in sick on the day.

When the big event arrives, both speakers feel the same nervous butterflies in their stomach, trembling hands, sweating and loose bowels. The positive thinker mentally rises to the challenge and copes brilliantly, however. Thanks to their careful preparation and the power of positive thought, they give an excellent speech that is well received. Afterwards, flushed with success, they bask in the glow of the limelight and can't wait to be asked to speak again. They have responded well to the positive stress and a new life skill has been learned.

The negative thinker experiences the humiliation of a self-fulfilling prophesy. They know they won't perform well, and they don't. They mumble their unpractised lines, fail to speak up so people can't hear at the back, and gabble through their talk too quickly, impressing no one — least of all themselves. The way they responded to the stress has adversely affected their performance and they have failed to cope. They have not learned a new skill and instead have learned to fear public speaking — the very thought of it will in future bring on a stress-related panic attack.

The way you think has a major effect on whether the stress you experience is beneficial or harmful. Some people are lucky and have learned a positive outlook on life from an early age. Others need to work hard to change the way they think, but this is a wonderful stress-busting strategy that will work for you time and time again throughout life. By thinking positive rather than negative thoughts, you can look on a stressful and difficult situation as a wonderful chance to learn new skills and acquire new experiences rather than seeing it through the fear of failure.

Try always to look for opportunities, not threats, as recent medical research suggests that negative emotions can be fatal. Over 300 men and women with heart disease were assessed and classed into negative thinkers (tendency to experience negative emotions and not to express emotions) and non-negative thinkers. They were then followed for six to ten years and it was found that the risk of premature death was nearly four times higher in those who had negative thoughts (27% compared to 7%) — this effect was independent of other risk factors such as whether they also had high blood pressure or raised cholesterol levels and may well be related to the increased negative stress associated with negative thoughts. Inspector Dreyfus in *The Pink Panther* certainly had the right idea when he repeated his own positive personal mantra: 'Every day, in every way, I get better and better…' To help you think more positively, see Chapter 6: Develop self-esteem.

Coping with stress

Although your stress response is largely automatic, you can consciously exert some control over two of its main features — your pattern of breathing and the amount of tension building up in your muscles.

When the body powers down from a high pressure situation, fight-or-flight is switched off and an opposite reaction is triggered called the rest-and-digest response. You can consciously help to switch off your stress response by altering your breathing pattern and by relaxing your muscles with a relaxation exercise. This starts to reverse some of the changes produced during the fight-or-flight reaction to stress so that digestion restarts, your breathing and heartbeat slow down and the tension in your muscles slowly recedes. To learn how to press your automatic reset button, see Chapter 4.

How you respond to stressful situations

Although it sounds like an obvious statement, it is worth emphasizing that whether or not you feel positive pressure or negative stress in a particular situation depends largely on the way you respond psychologically to that situation, or in other words, the way you interact with your environment. This is known as the 'interactional' model of stress, in which stress is thought to result from an imbalance between the demands being made on you (which may be real or perceived) and your ability (either real or perceived) to cope with them.

Some situations almost always cause stress for most people and are usually those that over-stimulate the senses such as excessive noise, extreme heat or cold and extreme physical exertion. Lack of stimulation — i.e., boredom — can also be stressful, as discussed earlier on page 6.

Some situations are stressful for the majority, but not for a lucky few. Examples include public speaking and taking an examination such as a mathematics paper. In these cases, a few people who are natural extroverts or who are trained orators will enjoy taking the podium, while those who are gifted with numbers will enjoy doing the maths and find it exhilarating rather than a high-pressure situation. Turn the tables, however, and put the boffin on television, and the TV presenter in a university examination on which his future career depends, and they will each find the alternative situation stressful in the extreme.

The way you respond to stress depends on a wide range of factors, including:

- Your personal circumstances (for example, how your love-life, finances and career are going).
- Your natural talents (for example, communication skills, intelligence, ability with numbers).
- Your previous experiences and expectations (particularly of the currently stressful situation).
- Your ability to recognize you are stressed and to quickly do something about it (see Chapter 1).
- Your self-esteem and perception of how you will cope (see Chapter 6).
- Your diet and how healthy it is (see Chapter 3).
- Your physical fitness (see Chapter 4).
- Your ability to relax (see Chapter 4).
- Your use of alternative therapies (see Chapter 5).
- Your organizational and time management skills (see Chapter 7).
- Personality traits (see below).

Stress and personality

Whether or not you respond to the normal pressures of life in a stressed or non-stressed manner depends largely on your natural personality type, although you can learn how to change harmful behaviour traits. People with certain personality types are more prone to experiencing high levels of stress and to have adverse effects as a result. These are the so-called Type A personalities who are easy to recognize as they are highly competitive, always setting tight deadlines for themselves and continually striving to get ahead even in the little things of life. Type As usually look tense and distracted — often with hair awry from running their hands over their head. Despite the hype they generate about doing everything better than anyone else, Type A people are secretly quite insecure and need constant praise and reassurance.

On the other hand, Type B personalities are self-assured, relaxed and pleasant to be with. They are equally motivated and get on with their tasks in an efficient, calm manner, using all the time they need. They wait patiently for attention, make excellent listeners and are rarely offensive. Type B can achieve just as many goals as Type A and be just as ambitious, but the major difference is their lack of panic, lack of aggression and lack of stress while they do so. They are working to please themselves rather than others and therefore do not need to seek outside approval. As a result, they may sometimes seem quite unambitious although this is not necessarily the case.

Type As tend to live to work, while Type Bs tend to work in order to live. They have many more outside interests and hobbies and therefore tend to be more interesting, well-rounded — and pleasant — people.

Which are you?

The distinction between Type A and Type B behaviour patterns is not clear cut, but forms a sliding scale. Most people will recognize character traits from both personality types in themselves and are likely to fall somewhere between the two

PERSONALITY TRAITS

TYPE A PERSONALITIES

- Schedule more and more into less and less time.
- Constantly work against the clock, doing two things at once – often against real or imagined opposition from others.
- Deny feeling tired.
- Measure success in terms of numbers (for example, numbers of clients seen or items sold).
- Believe that if you want something done well you have to do it yourself.
- Become impatient watching others do things they feel they could do better or faster.
- Are obsessed with punctuality.
- Are angry, aggressive and impatient with delays and queues; hostile to anything or anyone getting in the way of their progress.
- Have difficulty coping with sitting down and doing nothing.
- Talk a lot, particularly about themselves and often in an explosive way.
- Swear a lot.
- Don't listen to other people's conversation or impatiently try to finish what others are saying for them.
- Make angry stabbing motions and other gesticulations with their hands.
- Click their tongue, nod their head, clench their fist, suck in air or pound the table when talking.
- Frequently jig their knee, drum their fingers or click their pen.
- Blink or lift their eyebrows rapidly.
- Fail to notice the beauty of things around them.
- Are very competitive and always play to win.

TYPE B PERSONALITIES

- Manage time and only book in what can reasonably be achieved in the time allowed.
- Never suffer from time urgency, and are therefore happy to do one thing at a time.
- Are able to work without agitation.
- Measure success in terms of quality of work and the pleasure derived from completing it properly.
- Delegate certain tasks to those more suited to them.
- Don't feel they have to impress others with their achievements unless the situation demands it.
- Feel pleased for others' success and tell them so.
- Are not bothered by lack of punctuality in themselves or others.
- Wait patiently in queues and adopt a philosophical approach to delays or mistakes.
- Don't have any free-floating hostility.
- Are happy to sit down and relax, doing nothing during quality time without guilt.
- Listen readily to others, giving them all the time they need to have their say.
- Rarely feel the need to swear.
- Tend to hold their body in a relaxed manner, with no obvious tension when talking.
- Readily appreciate the beauty of nature and art.
- Are pleasantly competitive – good losers who are always happy to see others win.

PERSONALITY QUESTIONNAIRE

Score each of the following questions as: Always = 5,
Usually = 4, Sometimes = 3, Rarely = 2, Never = 1

☐ Are you ambitious?

☐ Do you always play to win and hate to lose?

☐ Are you on-the-dot punctual and hate being late?

☐ Are you eager to get things done as quickly as possible?

☐ Do you feel rushed?

☐ Do you get aggressive if frustrated?

☐ Are you impatient and angry when kept waiting?

☐ Do you tend to anticipate what others are going to say and finish their sentence for them?

☐ Do you interrupt others rather than waiting for them to have their say?

☐ Do you try to do too many things at once?

☐ Do you think ahead to the next things you have to do?

☐ Do you speak in a rapid, forceful manner?

☐ Do you eat or walk quickly?

☐ Do you gesticulate when you talk?

☐ Do you jiggle your knee, tap your fingers, click your pen or have to have something on the go rather than sitting quietly and relaxing?

☐ Are you a slave-driver who pushes yourself and others too hard?

☐ Do you want a good job, well done by yourself, to be recognized as such by others?

☐ Do you hide or suppress your feelings?

☐ Does your whole life revolve around work and home, with few hobbies or outside interests?

☐ Do you feel you have to do everything yourself and find it hard to delegate to others?

Score over 80: Driven Type A

You always put more pressure on yourself than necessary in your striving for success. In the long term, this will contribute to high stress levels and increase your risk of ill health if you don't take steps to change your behaviour patterns.

Score 65–80: Moderate Type A

You are a moderate Type A and need to watch that in striving for success, you do not push yourself too far. Ease back a little and make things easier on yourself. Take more time out for relaxation, and try to keep in touch with your inner self.

Score 56–64: Mixed Type A/Type B

Your personality displays a combination of Type A and Type B behaviour. You potentially have the best of both behavioural traits but need to ensure the Type A behaviour does not start to dominate as your ambitions grow. Continue to let pressure wash over you as much as possible so that it does not lead to physical or emotional symptoms of stress.

Score 40–55: Towards Type B

You have a healthy approach to life and are likely to achieve great things without harmful levels of stress. You are unlikely to suffer from stress-related illnesses.

Score below 40: Laid-back Type B

You have a totally laid-back approach to life and are rarely stressed by very much. You need to keep you eyes on your life's goals to ensure you achieve them in your allotted time-span. Assuming you are sufficiently ambitious, you can achieve great things without panic and are unlikely to succumb to stress-related illnesses.

ASSESSING DIFFERENT SITUATIONS

1. AN UNTAXING SITUATION

Perceived demand

Perceived ability

Ability is not tested so
the experience is
unstimulating

Stress Level

2. A TAXING SITUATION

Perceived demand

Perceived ability

Ability matches demand
so the experience is
stimulating

Stress level

3. POTENTIALLY STRESSFUL SITUATION: TYPE A

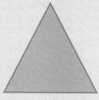

Perceived demand

Perceived ability

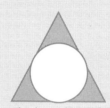

The demand is much
greater than ability to cope
and as failure is personally
unacceptable, the experience
is highly stressful

Stress Level

4. POTENTIALLY STRESSFUL SITUATION: TYPE B

Perceived demand

Perceived ability

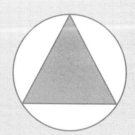

The demand is great
but the ability to cope
expands and even if failure
occurs it does not really matter
– as they've tried their best

Stress level

TYPE B IS MORE ABLE TO COPE WITH STRESS THAN TYPE A PERSONALITIES

extremes. Answering the questionnaire on page 17 will help you determine whether you currently have a predominantly Type A, Type B or mixed personality. The word *currently* is important here, as it helps to underline the fact that you can learn new behaviour patterns and learn to lose those that are harmful and gain those that will help you to cope with excess pressure.

Why do personality traits matter?

The Type A personality is linked with high levels of stress, because these people naturally put enormous pressure on themselves to succeed. They have unusually high expectations of themselves — and others — and tend to be perfectionists. Failure is not a word that fits easily into their vocabulary and this constant striving for success at the cost of a fulfilling personal and social life inevitably leads to enormous levels of stress. In other words, Type A personalities create a significant amount of their own stress. If they could only relax a little, take a more philosophical approach to life, set themselves less daunting standards of perfection and more realistic deadlines, their levels of stress would fall significantly. Another important factor is their insecurity and deep need for recognition of their worth and reward for their efforts. When they feel unsure about their ability to cope with a particular task, their level of stress automatically increases as shown in the box opposite.

Ways of reducing Type A behaviour

If you recognize you have Type A characteristics, try to become aware of the effect your behaviour has on others, who may see you as overly hostile. A number of strategies, detailed later in this book, will help you learn to move away from Type A behaviour so you become more of a Type B personality. It is also helpful to select a Type B friend and adapt your own excessive behaviour traits to match their less aggressive approach to life. Or you can use the structured steps listed below. These changes should be made slowly over a period of time until they became part of your normal behaviour pattern: don't attempt to assimilate them quickly in your usual harassed manner.

1: Realign your priorities and aim for things worth being rather than things worth having.

2: Aim to stop being an idealist or perfectionist — accept that things can and often will go wrong without it necessarily being the fault of yourself or others. Don't automatically look for someone to blame.

3: Don't keep looking for excuses to be disappointed — start looking for excuses to say 'well done' or 'thank you' to others.

4: Try being more relaxed and positive in your approach to life. Realize that Type B personalities may be just as ambitious as Type As, but they manage to reach their goals without seeming to panic.

5: Avoid other Type A personalities as much as possible, and when you are with them try to complement them rather than always having to compete.

6: Force yourself to listen to what others have to say — and let them finish their sentences. Rather than butting in, stop and ask yourself whether you really have anything important to say, whether anyone would want to hear it, and if so whether this is really the time to say it.

7: Learn to laugh at yourself rather than at other people.

8: Learn to prioritize your tasks by making a 'To Do' list and seeing what can wait until tomorrow rather than having to be done today.

9: Learn to delegate appropriate tasks, even if you think you can do the job better alone.

10: Make decisions in unhurried circumstances — they are more likely to be good decisions than those made in haste.

11: Don't make unnecessary appointments or table unnecessary meetings.

12: Learn to be patient. Try talking more slowly, and practise waiting in a queue without getting frustrated.

13: Practise driving more slowly and being courteous on the roads — let that other pushy so and so in front of you for a change.

14: Take regular 'time-out' breaks during your day where you relax and meditate — a personal mantra or mandala will help (see Chapter 5).

15: Take up at least one non-competitive hobby such as learning to play a musical instrument or to do Japanese flower arranging (Ikebana).

16: Put aside one evening a week for personal pleasure — to visit the theatre, for example, or read a good book while listening to a relaxation tape.

17: Start taking regular non-competitive exercise to reduce your levels of stress — brisk walking, gentle jogging, swimming or cycling are ideal. Avoid squash.

18: Stop watching the clock: try not wearing a watch and taking the clock off the wall. Try missing a few less important deadlines to convince yourself that the whole world won't come to a grinding halt. In many cases, a deadline can be extended with little risk of disaster.

ALTERNATIVE REMEDIES FOR TYPE A PERSONALITIES

BACH FLOWER REMEDIES

- Chicory (*Cichorium intybus*): for those who are obsessive or overly concerned with others; those who are demanding or full of self-pity; those who need others to conform to their own standards and ideals.

- Vervain (*Verbena officinalis*): for those with strong opinions, those incensed by injustice, the over-enthusiastic, argumentative and over-bearing.

- Vine (*Vitis vinifera*): for the strong-willed with a tendency to be ruthless, domineering, dictatorial or inflexible.

- Beech (*Fagus sylvatica*): for the critical and intolerant, those who seek perfection and are continually finding fault.

- Rock Water (*Aqua petra*): for those who are overly strict with themselves, hard taskmasters with a severely disciplined lifestyle.

AROMATHERAPY OILS

- camomile
- coriander
- eucalyptus
- geranium
- petitgrain
- rosemary
- sandalwood

19:Practise doing only one task at a time and completing it before moving on to the
   next.
20:Practise telling people how you feel: talk about your emotions rather than bottling
   them up.

Some Type As have the right approach to life
Not all Type A personalities will develop stress-related illnesses, and psychologists investigating this phenomenon have discovered that those who escape are more
likely to have:

● A sense of personal commitment.
● A belief that they can influence or control events (i.e., low sense of imposition).
● An understanding that change is a challenge to be welcomed rather than a threat to
  be feared.

These traits reduce the sense of stress that is felt and mean that pressure tends
to have a positive rather than a negative effect on success and health. Research
has also shown that developing relaxation skills, performing breathing exercises
and taking time out to meditate can help reduce the impact of Type A behaviour
patterns enough to reduce high blood pressure and lower the risk of stress-related
coronary heart disease. In other words, adapting their belief systems and
behaviour patterns can successfully help Type A personalities cope by reducing
some of the pressure on them and the sense of stress they experience.

Learning to cope

Everyone will feel stressed from time to time, whatever their lifestyle. Short-
term stress is not harmful, and if you use it positively it will help you out in
tricky situations. Challenges add zest to life and propel you on to greater
achievements. Stress is only a problem when it makes you feel distressed. The key
to successful stress management is to obtain the right balance between pressures
you can handle and the overload that drags you down. In this respect, the crucial
balance is not usually that between actual demands on you and your actual capa-
bility, but between the way you perceive these demands in relation to how you
think you can cope. The power of mind over matter can sway the balance between
successfully coping with a stressful situation and in knowing you will fail before
you've even begun.

   Coping with stress is not a lucky trait some people are born with and others
not — it is a skill that can be learned and perfected, just like any other in

life. Those who cope best with stress are those who see challenges as a normal, positive part of life; who feel in control, are committed to their work, hobbies, social life or family, and who see challenges as opportunities rather than threats.

The very fact that you are reading this book suggests your life is out of balance and you feel under abnormal pressure right now. Think of this as an opportunity to re-evaluate your life goals – where you are now, where you want to be and how you are going to get there. The seven chapters of this book make up an ultimate stress-buster plan that will show you how to relax, improve your coping skills and help you enjoy life to the full.

Slow down, eat a balanced diet, take more exercise, cut out the smoking and excessive use of alcohol, and make a start on a relaxation programme. There are many techniques to choose from, so dip into the selection and find what suits your temperament and your lifestyle best – in that way you will reap the benefits and continue to manage your stress.

Adaptation

The fact that you are prepared to make changes in your behaviour shows that you are willing to adapt to help cope with the excess stress you are experiencing. Adaptation is vital to survive and cope with longer term stress. There are two ways of adapting, however, and one is successful, the other not. It is therefore important to make sure the adaptive moves you make are going to work.

Unhelpful defence mechanisms

Defence mechanisms are subconscious ways of distorting reality and are rarely helpful in coping with prolonged or excessive stress. These include the well-known ostrich-head-in-the-sand approach: pretend it isn't there and it will go away. While this can be helpful for short periods of time, to allow you to gradually accept the truth, it becomes counter-productive if it persists and you start distorting reality in different ways to maintain the fiction. Unfortunately, the source of stress rarely goes away, and even if it seems to, the anxiety that it will return continues to lurk and provoke feelings of inadequacy and doom. Interestingly, dangerous concepts that have been tucked away and ignored will often reveal themselves in so-called Freudian slips.

Samantha's boss is often away and her work is managed by another partner. One morning, Samantha is told that she must handle the extra work load when her boss is away, herself, as the other partner is now too busy. Samantha has to deal with constant interruptions and several unpleasant calls from irate customers. She has no time for lunch, and becomes so stressed she fails to complete her own tasks and several important documents miss the post. By the end of the day she is totally stressed out. The thought of being in charge again fills her with dread, but she puts it out of her mind and tries to forget the experience, rather than asking for extra training and advice on how to cope. When Samantha next overhears her boss arranging a trip away, she calls in sick when her boss leaves, so she won't have to deal with it. When her boss tells her he will be away again a week later, Samantha unthinkingly says, 'Oh, I won't be able to help as I'll be off sick that day, as well.'

Another common defence mechanism is to always blame everyone else when things go wrong — by projecting the problem on to others, you automatically lose the need to feel responsible yourself.

Louise and David have been married just under a year and both are in high-pressure jobs. Louise persuades David to arrange a weekend away to spend some quality time by themselves. David agrees, but says he's too busy to make plans, so Louise picks the venue, books the hotel and buys tickets to see a show. David comes home late from work feeling stressed and in a foul mood. They leave late and get to the hotel after last orders have been taken in the dining-room. David blames Louise for choosing a hotel that stops serving food at 9.30 p.m. He finds fault with everything — the bed isn't hard enough, the weather's too cold, and the show is lousy. He refuses to choose where they should eat the next night and then finds faults with the French restaurant Louise eventually selects. David is too tired for sex and the whole weekend is a bickering disaster. David blames Louise, and fails to see that his sulky mood meant he would find excuses to criticize everything. And by leaving all the decisions to Louise, he ensured that nothing that went wrong could possibly be his fault.

Yet another favourite defence strategy is to rationalize everything away and to find acceptable excuses for things that really are quite unacceptable.

Jane works in an office and has a nine to five contract. She rarely manages to get away before 6 p.m., however, and often leaves later, which makes it difficult as she teaches the piano several evenings a week as a hobby. Her boss always gives her last-minute typing to do, which he says has to catch the evening post. She feels she can't afford to refuse as jobs are not easy to come by, and in any case, he always asks her so charmingly. One Friday evening, she says she has to leave at 6 p.m. as she is giving an extra lesson to a pupil preparing for a piano exam the next day. Her boss gets angry, accusing her of being unreliable and inflexible, then demands she gives up her piano teaching in the evenings as it is obviously interfering with her job. Jane cannot afford to lose her job, so she meekly agrees to give up her evening hobby. She rationalizes that her boss has the right to expect first call on her time, and that things will improve once the office business picks up.

You may also try to cope by isolating problems and talking about them in a cold, clinical and unfeeling way.

A GP is exhausted from working long hours and feels helpless to help some of his patients with incurable conditions. He puts up an emotional barrier and rather than showing empathy and compassion, learns to detach his inner feelings from the suffering he sees around him. As a result he comes across to his patients as cold and uncaring. This makes him unpopular, which stresses him even more, with the result that his bedside manner deteriorates further.

Sublimation – the substitution of acceptable for unacceptable activity (for example, channelling aggression into playing sport) is the only defence mechanism that has a chance of being successful. If the sport involved is a competitive one, however, then stress levels may not improve as a result of increased physical activity, as the pressure to win may overwhelm any enjoyment that might be obtained from participating.

Adaptive coping mechanisms

Adaptive coping mechanisms are explained in detail in Chapters 3 to 7. These are deliberate ways of adjusting to stress in a positive and constructive manner. They include recognizing when you are experiencing negative stress; developing self-esteem, eating wisely, taking exercise; relaxing; exploring alternative therapies; and streamlining your life.

How stressed are you?

It is hard to be objective about your own levels of stress as they can vary significantly from day to day and week to week. And challenges that are highly stressful for one person may be quite comfortable for others. The key is how well you are coping with your current stress levels and their effects on your quality of life. Even though you may not be aware of the physical, emotional and behavioural symptoms of stress, it is still possible to work out whether or not you are stressed by considering the questions in the box below.

QUESTIONNAIRE: HOW STRESSED ARE YOU?

Score the following questions A (not at all), B (sometimes, but not enough to be a major problem) or C (yes, very much so):

- ☐ Do you worry about your physical health?
- ☐ Do you worry about your emotional health?
- ☐ Do you worry about the future?
- ☐ Are you under financial strain?
- ☐ Is your motivation failing?
- ☐ Does your workload seem heavy?
- ☐ Do you feel uncomfortable with your job?
- ☐ Do you feel your work colleagues could be more supportive?
- ☐ Do you feel exhausted at the end of the day?
- ☐ Are you late for work?
- ☐ Have you been off sick from work?
- ☐ Do you feel uncomfortable with your social life?
- ☐ Do you feel your family and friends could be more supportive?
- ☐ Do you worry about the amount of alcohol you are drinking or feel you ought to cut back?
- ☐ If you smoke, has your need to do so increased?
- ☐ Are you sleeping badly?
- ☐ Do you get irritable or lose your temper?
- ☐ Do you feel trapped with no way to escape?
- ☐ Are you so busy you do not have time to relax?
- ☐ Do you wish you could drop everything and escape to a desert island?

INTERPRETATION

Mostly As: You are so laid-back that life seems too perfect for words. Either life is passing you by with few challenges and little room for personal growth, or there are very few goals left that you want to achieve in life. Re-evaluate where you are in comparison to where you want to be and assess whether a little more pressure might actually be beneficial. If not, then congratulations. You probably do not need to continue reading this book!

Mostly Bs: You are in the lucky situation of having achieved a balance between the challenges in your life and your ability to cope. Stress is not a major problem for you – yet – but you need to keep it that way. The following chapters will help you maintain your equilibrium in life.

Mostly Cs: You are under excess pressure and if this continues, stress will affect your health if it hasn't already done so. You cannot go on like this. It is imperative that you take a well-earned break and closely follow the advice given in the rest of this book. Once you have assessed the physical, emotional and behavioural symptoms of stress and worked out exactly how stressed you are, consider making significant changes to your work and lifestyle – or by the time you have achieved your ambitions in life you may no longer be fit to reap the benefits.

SPOT THE SIGNS OF STRESS

As we have already seen, short-term positive pressure is beneficial, but prolonged or excessive negative stress is harmful. When you experience excess pressure, it affects your whole being and produces a variety of physical, psychological, emotional and behavioural symptoms:

1. STRESSFUL SITUATION.
▼
2. PHYSICAL, MENTAL AND EMOTIONAL SYMPTOMS OF STRESS DEVELOP.
▼
3. STRESS RESPONSE FAILS TO IMPROVE THE SITUATION.
▼
4. STRESS BECOMES LONG-TERM.
▼
5. DEVELOPMENT OF PHYSICAL AND/OR MENTAL ILLNESS.

Excess stress affects different people in different ways at different times in their life. Your ability to cope will depend on several factors, such as your overall health, whether you are personality Type A or B; whether you tend to think positive or negative thoughts; the way you've learned to cope in the past; and the number of stressful events you have recently experienced, one after the other, without sufficient time to recover in between. Your overall health is particularly important because if you are already experiencing physical or emotional stress due to the symptoms of another illness, your reserves of coping will already be partly used up. Even a little additional external stress may mean you are unable to cope any more. Women also have the additional disadvantage that their menstrual cycle can cause symptoms of internal stress regularly each month (see page 112), and in middle age around the time of the menopause (see page 115). If you are anxious about change, have poor self-esteem or feel you are losing control of a situation, this will automatically make your symptoms of stress seem worse.

In many ways, your ability to cope can be compared to a metal spring. Piling on the pressure causes the spring to expand and stretch in response to the strain it is under. Once the strain is removed, the spring can usually bounce back to its original size and shape. If the strain it is under becomes too great, however, it reaches a point where the spring suddenly gives way. This causes permanent damage so that the spring never fully regains its original elasticity nor its original size and shape. Stress can produce a similar effect in you – you can cope with a surprising amount of strain, but a point is eventually reached when even just a little more pressure can result in physical and emotional collapse.

By learning how to spot the signs of stress, you are more able to take steps to reduce the pressure you are under before stress sets in long-term and your physical or emotional health starts to suffer. Stress affects different people in different ways. Some are more likely to develop physical distress, some experience serious psychological or emotional problems while others show worrying behavioural changes. It is useful to consider the symptoms of stress in the following categories, which broadly represent increasingly severe reactions:

- **Level 1:** Early warning signs.
- **Level 2:** Psychological symptoms.
- **Level 3:** Emotional symptoms.
- **Level 4:** Physical symptoms.
- **Level 5:** Behavioural symptoms.
- **Level 6:** Breakdown.

You can experience symptoms from different levels of stress at the same time. These five

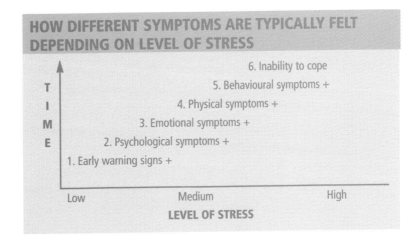

HOW DIFFERENT SYMPTOMS ARE TYPICALLY FELT DEPENDING ON LEVEL OF STRESS

T
I
M
E

6. Inability to cope
5. Behavioural symptoms +
4. Physical symptoms +
3. Emotional symptoms +
2. Psychological symptoms +
1. Early warning signs +

Low   Medium   High
LEVEL OF STRESS

levels tend to represent a natural gradation, however. Those under less stress are likely to experience more of the psychological and emotional symptoms of stress, while those under greater levels of stress are likely to experience more of the physical symptoms of stress. By the time you reach the stage of breakdown (which hopefully you never will) you might experience most of the symptoms associated with each level of stress all at the same time.

Your personal stress-buster attack plan

Self-awareness is the most effective way to deal with stress. By learning to recognize your own stress signals that result from adrenaline and from over-breathing (hyperventilation) you can take steps to reduce the amount of pressure you are under by building up your own personal stress-buster attack plan.

There is no one point at which positive pressure can be said to have turned into negative stress. The symptoms of one tend to blend with the symptoms of the other to form a continuous gradation of experiences. Feelings usually creep up on you until you suddenly realize you feel anxious, tense and irritable, perhaps with a slight tightness in your throat, stiffness in your shoulders and neck or a nervous sensation in your stomach. Most people know intuitively the point at which the limit of their ability to cope with the perceived pressures they are under has been reached. Listen to your inner self and take note when you start to receive the first clues that your stress response is starting to run out of control. By learning to recognize when this point has been reached, you can often alleviate the problem before your symptoms develop too severely.

Everyone will have experienced these early warning signs at some time. You may notice that you are becoming clumsy or restless, pacing up and down, fiddling with jewellery or – men especially – jingling coins in your trouser pocket. Your speech may be affected, so you find yourself hesitating, speaking too fast, too quietly/loudly or even stammering and stuttering. You may also find yourself putting things off – avoiding facing issues that may prove difficult (this is

LEVEL 1: EARLY WARNING SIGNS

When you feel stressed, you are usually aware of excess pressure and may describe yourself as being (tick the ones that apply to you):

☐ uneasy
☐ on edge
☐ tense
☐ hassled
☐ flustered
☐ uptight
☐ under pressure
☐ taut
☐ overloaded
☐ about to explode
☐ without your sense of humour
☐ at the end of your tether

known as avoidance behaviour). Most of all, however, you will probably notice strong emotional feelings such as irritability, anger, impatience and that you are constantly looking for – and finding – faults in others. You are likely to start feeling tired and irritable, to develop tension headaches and to notice some disturbance of your normal sleep patterns.

Quick tips to stop stress in its tracks

When you realize you are starting to experience the early warning symptoms of negative stress:

- Stop what you are doing and inwardly say, 'Calm!' to yourself.
- If you are sitting down, stand up and gently stretch to your fullest possible extent.
- Take a deep breath in and let it out slowly, concentrating on the movement of your diaphragm. Do this two or three times until you start to feel more in control. One of the breathing exercises in Chapter 4 may also help.
- Shake your hands and arms briskly, then shrug your shoulders.
- If possible, go for a brisk walk, even if it is only briefly around the room or to the bathroom, to help get your circulation going again.
- If possible, go somewhere private and groan or shout as loudly as you can. This can be very therapeutic. Some people find it helpful to punch a soft cushion as hard as possible.
- Place a few drops of Bach Flower Rescue Remedy under your tongue.
- Inhale a personally chosen blend of aromatherapy oils made by adding a total of 15 drops of essential oils to 30 ml of carrier oil (almond and grapeseed oil are both good carriers). Select two or three oils to blend from the following: bergamot, cardamom, camomile, coriander, geranium, grapefruit, lavender, lemon, neroli, sandalwood.
- Keep a mandala on your desk and spend a few minutes concentrating on its patterns (see page 194).
- Choose an appropriate, personal positive thought (for example, 'I am feeling positive pressure, not negative stress') and repeat this regularly to yourself during a visualization exercise (see page 193).

Level 2: Psychological symptoms

Prolonged stress leads to depletion of mental as well as physical energy and can result in a number of psychological symptoms that in turn reduce your ability to cope with the original problem. When you start to experience the psychological symptoms of stress, you know that your ability to cope is under threat. At this stage it is important to practise the 'Quick tips' given on page 29 and to start introducing more long-term stress-coping strategies.

Attack plan to help reduce your stress levels

1. Make sure you are eating a healthy diet and that you do not skip meals. Have healthy snacks to hand such as dried or fresh fruit, rice cakes or oatcakes to help stop your blood sugar levels from falling and creating an additional internal trigger for the negative stress response.

2. If you are not taking regular exercise, now is the time to start (see Chapter 4).

3. Learn a breathing/relaxation technique to use when your mind starts to feel like cotton wool (see Chapter 4).

4. Cut back on any excesses such as alcohol intake, cigarette-smoking or reliance on recreational drugs.

5. Try listening to calming background music to help you unwind if this is practical.

6. Start learning assertiveness techniques – saying no to unreasonable demands will help to reduce the pressure you are under (see Chapter 6).

7. Start organizing your life and managing your time more effectively (see Chapter 7).

8. Award yourself a special weekly treat (for example, an aromatherapy massage) as a reward for coping and for being such a wonderful person.

9. Make a point of complementing others around you – if you make them feel good about themselves, the effects will wear off on you too.

10. Make a point of practising your 'Chinese inner smile' whenever you feel pressurized (see page 38).

**LEVEL 2:
PSYCHOLOGICAL SYMPTOMS**

Place a tick next to any of the following psychological symptoms of stress that you frequently suffer from. If the number is high then it is time to seek solutions.

❏ inability to concentrate
❏ difficulty in making simple decisions
❏ difficulty in making rational judgements
❏ muddled thinking
❏ tendency to become vague and forgetful
❏ tendency to lose perspective
❏ making rash decisions
❏ loss of self-confidence
❏ negative self-talk
❏ undue mental tiredness
❏ memory lapses
❏ undue feelings of being under time pressure
❏ frustration and helplessness
❏ depression
❏ lost sense of humour
❏ loss of sex drive

If you ticked three or more symptoms, you are likely to be experiencing a significant amount of psychological stress.

ALTERNATIVE REMEDIES FOR PSYCHOLOGICAL SYMPTOMS OF STRESS

BACH FLOWER REMEDIES

- Cerato (*Ceratostigma willmottianum*): for those who doubt their own ability to judge situations or make decisions.
- Scleranthus (*Scleranthus annus*): for the indecisive and those subject to energy or mood swings.
- Gentian (*Gentianella amara*): for the easily discouraged, those who hesitate, are despondent or self-doubting.
- Gorse (*Ulex europaeus*): for feelings of despair, hopelessness and futility.
- Hornbeam (*Carpinus betulus*): for 'Monday morning' feelings of not being able to face the day, tiredness, procrastination, and those needing inner strength.
- White chestnut (*Aesculus hippocastanum*): for persistent, unwanted thoughts, mental arguments, preoccupation with worry.
- Mustard (*Sinapis arvensis*): for deep gloom descending for no apparent reason, melancholy and heavy sadness.
- Holly (*Ilex aquifolium*): For negative feelings, for example envy, suspicion, revenge, hatred, for those needing more love.
- Elm (*Ulmus procera*): For those who overextend themselves, are over-whelmed or burdened with responsibilities.

AROMATHERAPY OILS THAT CAN HELP TO CLARIFY YOUR THOUGHTS

Select two or three of the following to blend and dilute:

- basil
- bergamot
- black pepper
- cardamom
- cedarwood
- ginger
- lemon
- peppermint
- rosemary

HERBS THAT MAY HELP TO CLEAR YOUR MIND

- garlic
- ginkgo
- ginseng
- St John's wort

Level 3: Emotional symptoms

When you experience emotional symptoms of stress, your ability to cope is under threat of being overwhelmed, and your energy reserves approach depletion. You may already have started to experience some of the physical symptoms of stress (see below), and if you do not take steps to reduce the amount of negative stress you are under, this will soon start to take a toll on your long-term health. Emotional symptoms include those listed in the box overleaf. When you start to experience any of these you know you are experiencing a significant amount of harmful pressure. At this stage it is important to continue practising your Level 1 and 2 strategies to help reduce the stress in your life, and to introduce more advanced strategies to help you reduce the tension you are under.

ALTERNATIVE REMEDIES FOR EMOTIONAL SYMPTOMS OF STRESS

BACH FLOWER REMEDIES

- Cherry Plum (*Prunus cerasifera*): for fear of losing control, uncontrollable rages, tempers, impulses, fear of causing harm to oneself or others.
- Aspen (*Populus tremula*): for vague fears and anxieties of unknown origin, sense of foreboding, apprehension or impending doom.
- Larch (*Larix decidua*): for those lacking in self-confidence, who anticipate failure and make little effort to succeed.
- Star of Bethlehem (*Ornithogalum umbellatum*): for mental and emotional stress following traumatic experiences, for example grief.

BALANCING AROMATHERAPY OILS THAT MAY HELP

- basil
- bergamot
- geranium
- lavender
- lemongrass
- neroli
- rose
- sandalwood

Attack plan to help reduce your stress levels further

1. Work out what situations or people are causing you stress and why, then see if you can formulate sensible strategies to overcome the problem.
2. Keep a stress diary (see page 124).
3. Learn how to prioritize tasks so you can deal with pressures one at a time.

LEVEL 3: EMOTIONAL SYMPTOMS

Place a tick next to any of the following emotional symptoms of stress that you frequently suffer from:

- ❏ overwhelming feelings of anxiety and panic
- ❏ irritability
- ❏ angry outbursts
- ❏ increased cynicism
- ❏ feeling isolated from colleagues and friends
- ❏ defensive and over-sensitive to criticism
- ❏ fear of rejection
- ❏ fear of failure
- ❏ feeling of hopelessness
- ❏ feeling of hostility
- ❏ feelings of guilt
- ❏ undue aggressions
- ❏ resentment or animosity
- ❏ panic attacks
- ❏ feeling of depression
- ❏ nightmares
- ❏ a feeling of impending doom

If you ticked three or more boxes, you are likely to be experiencing a significant amount of emotional stress.

4. Practise positive thinking techniques or visualization to help boost your flagging self-confidence.

5. Develop more hobbies and interests to help you relax and take your mind off your worries.

6. Watch a favourite comedy film, comedian or humorous play and try to laugh as much as possible – laughter is a wonderful antidote to building stress. Similarly, if you feel like a good cry, then have one and get it out of your system. We are the only animals who cry, and shedding tears does seem to act as an emergency reset button to help relieve excess tension.

7. Treat yourself to an extra aromatherapy massage, facial or other body treatment to make you feel better in yourself.

8. Consider enrolling in a yoga or t'ai chi class.

9. Use visualization to help you achieve a more relaxed state of mind.

10. Consider having a few days' holiday relaxing at home so you can recharge your internal batteries.

Level 4: Physical symptoms

The physical symptoms of stress have their origin in the fight-or-flight reaction discussed on pages 7-11. In the short term, these symptoms help you to mobilize energy and prepare you for a sudden burst of intense exercise. If the energy is not consumed, however, it will build up and start to drain your energy reserves. While short-term physical symptoms of stress are common when the fight-or-flight reaction is initiated, they become more persistent and severe if you experience long-term negative stress.

If you have persistent physical symptoms, you have excess adrenaline and other stress hormones circulating in your bloodstream. If allowed to continue, this state of affairs may have a significant detrimental effect on your long-term health. Long-term high levels of stress damp down your immunity and are linked with an increased risk of a number of important illness, including coronary heart disease and possibly even some cancers. At this stage it is important to continue practising your Level 1, 2 and 3 coping strategies and, if necessary, to introduce more advanced strategies to help you reduce the stress in your life.

LEVEL 4: PHYSICAL SYMPTOMS

Place a tick next to any of the following physical symptoms of stress that are persistent and that you feel you frequently suffer from:

- ☐ sweaty palms and cold fingers (clamminess)
- ☐ dry mouth
- ☐ muscle tension
- ☐ shaking hands
- ☐ stiff jaw
- ☐ high-pitched voice
- ☐ difficulty swallowing
- ☐ lump in the throat
- ☐ knot in the stomach (butterflies)
- ☐ jelly legs
- ☐ cramps
- ☐ flushing

- ☐ palpitations
- ☐ rapid pulse
- ☐ dizziness
- ☐ faintness
- ☐ ringing in the ears
- ☐ erratic breathing
- ☐ hyperventilation
- ☐ pins and needles
- ☐ trembling
- ☐ panic attacks
- ☐ restless leg syndrome
- ☐ insomnia
- ☐ physical tiredness

- ☐ numbness
- ☐ headache
- ☐ chest pain
- ☐ indigestion/heartburn
- ☐ abdominal pain (for example, peptic ulcers)
- ☐ nausea
- ☐ diarrhoea
- ☐ frequent urination
- ☐ sexual difficulties such as impotence

If you ticked three or more symptoms, you are likely to be experiencing a significant amount of physical stress.

Advanced attack plan to help reduce your high stress levels

1. Review your stress diary regularly to help identify your main causes of stress so you can formulate sensible plans to overcome them.

2. Consider having a few days' holiday at home.

3. Learn how to meditate so you can find an inner spot of calm when all around you is in a state of tension or chaos (see page 190).

4. Surround yourself with calming colours (see page 175).

5. Take special care to eat a healthy, wholefood, organic diet.

6. Take a good vitamin and mineral supplement providing around 100% of as many vitamins and minerals as possible. You may need extra B-group vitamins if you are feeling tired all the time.

7. Take an additional antioxidant supplement so you are obtaining at least:
   - 500–1,000 mg vitamin C per day (ester-C is best as it is non-acidic – check labels to find it)
   - 400 IU vitamin E daily.

8. Consider taking coenzyme Q10 to help boost oxygen usage by your cells and to improve your energy levels.

9. Take evening primrose oil (at least 1,000 mg daily) to help correct any hormone imbalances resulting from increased stress.

10. Consider taking an adaptogenic herb such as American, Korean or Siberian ginseng (See pages 143-5). Take ginseng for six weeks initially, then continue on a two weeks on, two weeks off cycle.

Level 5: Behavioural symptoms

Someone under severe stress will make changes in their behaviour in an attempt to avoid or mask their problems. These changes are often subconscious and are easily recognizable as a sign that they need urgent help. Although in many ways behavioural symptoms represent a self-protective mechanism, they never solve the problem and soon become a source of additional stress in their own right. Once you start exhibiting such symptoms, you know that your ability to cope has been overwhelmed and that you have reached a stage where your health will suffer sooner rather than later. Behavioural symptoms of stress vary from person to person, and can include any or all of those listed opposite.

The fact that your stress levels are linked with behavioural changes should sound a loud warning bell. You need to reduce your levels of stress NOW because they lead to a total inability to cope – a condition commonly described as a nervous breakdown. Continue practising your Level 1, 2, 3 and 4 coping strategies and also take steps to address the behavioural changes you have adopted.

Attack plan to help reduce your behavioural symptoms of stress

1. Make plans to cut back on your alcohol intake (see page 190).

2. Take steps to cut back on the number of cigarettes you smoke. Once you feel stronger in yourself you can attempt to stop altogether (see page 87).

3. Seek help to rethink unhealthy behaviour patterns and learn new ones — hypnotherapy may be helpful (see page 187).

4. Cut back on your working hours and build regular rest or exercise breaks into your day. Make a point of doing at least one activity you enjoy for at least thirty minutes each day and preferably longer.

5. Arrange to have a therapeutic massage at least once a week.

6. Address absenteeism by taking a planned holiday (preferably at home) then starting back at work with a promise to yourself that you will continue going in, no matter what. If problems at work need addressing, raise issues with the appropriate manager.

LEVEL 5: BEHAVIOURAL SYMPTOMS

Place a tick next to any of the following behavioural symptoms of stress that you frequently suffer from:

- ☐ increased reliance on alcohol and/or smoking cigarettes and/or tranquillizers
- ☐ changes in eating patterns: increased or decreased food intake that affects body weight (or that leads to bingeing/purging in an attempt to control weight)
- ☐ avoidance of certain people and places
- ☐ social withdrawal
- ☐ phobic avoidance of certain situations or things
- ☐ becoming a workaholic with no time for relaxation or pleasurable activities
- ☐ absenteeism
- ☐ hair-pulling (trichotillomania)
- ☐ obsessive or compulsive behaviour, for example frequent hand-washing, checking and re-checking you have switched off lights or locked doors

If you ticked three or more symptoms you are likely to be displaying significant behavioural symptoms of stress.

Feeling tired all the time

Occasional tiredness is normal, and affects everyone, but increasing numbers of people admit to feeling tired all the time — usually shortened to TATT. This is one of the commonest physical symptoms to accompany prolonged excess pressure and tends up creep up on you, making you feel washed out and exhausted for much of the time. Interestingly, more women than men are affected, perhaps because women are much more likely to juggle different aspects of their life — looking after the home, working, raising children, organizing meals — and have less time to sit down, put their feet up and look after their own health. Surveys suggest that as many as three out of four women feel constantly tired, with the majority naming stress as the major cause.

When TATT is persistent and affects the quality of your life, it is important to learn to control it. TATT can often be overcome by improving your diet, improving the quality of your sleep and increasing the amount of exercise you take.

Self-help

- You'll be surprised how much better you will feel if you eat a healthy, low fat diet full of wholegrain cereals, fresh fruit and vegetables (see chapter 3)
- Lack of vitamins and minerals can make TATT worse. The B-group of vitamins are especially important:

    vitamin B1 – thiamin – is needed for burning carbohydrate and making amino acids

    vitamin B2 – riboflavin – is known as the 'exerciser's friend' as it is essential for the production of energy by burning fatty acids inside your cells

    vitamin B3 helps your cells absorb glucose from the bloodstream and burns energy stores (glycogen and fatty acids)

    vitamin B5 – pantothenic acid – is another one that's essential for obtaining energy from carbohydrates, fats and protein and for making new sugar and fat molecules in the body. It increases the amount of energy your cells can produce in relation to the amount of oxygen they consume

    vitamin B6 is needed for burning glycogen as an emergency fuel in muscle cells

    folic acid and vitamin B12 are needed in the formation of red blood cells and for preventing certain types of anaemia.

COMMON CAUSES OF TATT IN WOMEN

- stress
- overexertion
- anxiety
- following a too-strict slimming diet
- lack of exercise
- pregnancy
- breastfeeding
- looking after young children
- high-pressure job
- poor-quality sleep
- low blood-sugar from irregular meals
- possibly food allergy

- Make sure you obtain enough iron in your diet. One in three women are anaemic due to menstruation, pregnancy, poor diet or poor ability to absorb and store iron (see page 140).
- Avoid excess caffeine. Many people who feel tired and stressed are making their symptoms worse by drinking too much tea, coffee or other caffeine-containing drinks (see page 70).
- Lack of sleep increases feelings of TATT as sleep is a time of rest, repair, rejuvenation and regeneration. It allows your body to rest and your muscles and joints to recover from constant use during the day. Cell turnover rate increases and more red blood cells and immune cells are made. These processes are mainly controlled by the increased nocturnal secretion of growth hormone. Hair growth mainly occurs during sleep and protein in all parts of the body – especially the skin, eyes and brain – is replenished. Tiredness

MEDICAL CONDITIONS THAT CAN MAKE YOU FEEL TIRED ALL THE TIME

Only one in ten sufferers of TATT are likely to have a medical cause for their symptoms, such as:

- anaemia – especially iron-deficiency anaemia
- underactive thyroid (hypothyroidism)
- overactive thyroid (hyperthyroidism)
- depression or seasonal affective disorder (sad)
- side effects of medication
- poorly controlled diabetes
- uncontrolled high blood pressure
- irregular heartbeat
- heart failure with fluid retention
- infection – especially glandular fever, or long-term grumbling infections

- chronic inflammatory disease (for example, rheumatoid arthritis)
- auto-immune disorders
- disease of any organ system (for example, lungs, kidneys, liver, adrenal glands)
- post viral fatigue syndrome (myalgic encephalomyelitis or ME)
- serious illness such as cancer (less than one in 100 people with TATT)
- carbon monoxide poisoning is worth considering, especially if the tiredness is accompanied by headache, and if symptoms rapidly clear on breathing fresh air

therefore has knock-on effects on your appearance, causing sallow skin and puffy, bloodshot eyes. Your memory and concentration also suffer. Lack of good-quality sleep is a major cause of feeling tired all the time (see page 72 for tips on getting a better night's rest).

- Exercise regularly, as it is important to get fit. Apart from encouraging your body to become overweight, lack of exercise can cause lack of energy and feeling tired all the time – and can also lower your mood. If you take the time and trouble to exercise regularly, you will soon notice increased feelings of energy, more stamina and a more positive outlook on life. Exercise boosts your metabolism to burn more fat and release more energy for your cells to use.

- Find time for relaxation. Treat yourself to a massage, a facial, or a soak in an aromatherapy bath. Just sitting down quietly and listening to music by candlelight, or finding a quiet spot to read a book will help. Encourage the family not to disturb you during your relaxation period. Learn how to say no, so that you're not put upon and overloaded with tasks either at home or work. There are times when you must put yourself first, and if you're tired all the time, this is one of them.

If you feel tired all the time for longer than two weeks, despite increasing your exercise levels, eating a healthy diet and improving your quality of sleep, consult your doctor. Many illnesses start off with tiredness as one of their first symptoms. Whilst most people who feel tired are unlikely to be seriously ill, it's still worth having a check-up just in case. This is especially important if you have also noticed other symptoms such as weight loss, cough, shortness of breath, urinary problems or thirst.

Irritability

Everyone becomes irritable from time to time when they are tired, especially if they haven't eaten properly or skipped a meal and their blood-sugar level is low. Irritability can also be a feature of premenstrual syndrome (see page 112), menopausal symptoms (see page 115) and other forms of internal or external stress. When you realize you are being irritable, try to take steps to improve your mood before it gets any worse.

Tips to overcome irritability

- Consciously practise your 'Chinese inner smile' (see box below).
- Say 'Calm!' quietly to yourself and practise a breathing exercise.
- Keep a pack of dried fruit or rice cakes at hand and have a healthy snack if irritability is likely to be linked with low blood sugar levels.
- Take a brief break from what you are doing, even if it is just to visit the bathroom – exercise will help to boost your circulation so your brain receives more oxygen, energy and vital nutrients.
- Visualize the person or situation that makes you irritable passing right through you and leaving you unaffected – don't allow them to get to you.
- When all else fails, count silently to ten.
- Consider it a major achievement to remain smiling, sweet natured and pleasant no matter how irritating you find the people or situation surrounding you.

Longer-term solutions

- Try to identify people or situations that regularly tend to irritate you and work out why.
- Realize that the problem is not necessarily with others but with the way you personally react to situations and people.
- If you really can't stop feeling irritable, then take control by expressing your feelings openly. Practise saying, 'This really irritates me because...'

CHINESE INNER SMILE

A Chinese technique known as the 'inner smile' can help you relax when you are feeling tense and irritable:

1. Sit comfortably with your back straight and your arms relaxed at your sides.
2. Imagine something that readily makes you smile, for example someone telling you how much they love you.
3. Let yourself smile inwardly so the smile is only felt by you.
4. Let the smile spread all over your body until it shines out of your eyes.
5. Then concentrate on an area just below your navel – the Chinese call this the *tan tien* and believe it is the seat of your constitutional essence, or *jing*.
6. Continue feeling the smile radiate within you so you feel warm, calm and relaxed.
7. Now continue what you were doing, having shed your feelings of irritability.

- Eat regular meals — never skip breakfast or lunch, no matter how busy you are.
- Avoid excess caffeine or nicotine, which can make your irritability worse, especially if you get withdrawal symptoms.

Anger

Anger is a potentially destructive emotion that results when stress and frustration build up beyond your ability to cope. Anger uses up a lot of energy and triggers a high level of internal emotional and physical stress, which stops you thinking rationally. Anger often results when:

- you feel frustrated at not being able to do what you want, when you want
- you can't get your own way
- people do not do what you expect them to do
- you cannot find the words to express yourself properly
- communication breaks down.

Some people bottle up their anger, while others let it out. The effects on your health are the same, in that all forms of anger are stressful and unhealthy. When anger becomes too great, it can lead to aggressive behaviour and even violence. Anger comes from your thoughts, and learning to think in a different way is an effective method of defusing your anger response. It also helps to become more assertive — so you are not put upon — and to learn how to express your emotions more fully. By allowing someone else to make you feel angry, you are giving them power over you. To remove this power, you need to take responsibility for your own anger and realize that you are in control of it, nobody else. To help yourself do this, use 'I' language — 'I am angry because…' rather than 'You/They/ This makes me angry because…'. The first statement acknowledges that you are in control, the second says that someone or something else is in control of you.

Tips to help you control your anger

- Keep an anger diary to record exactly when you feel angry and why. If you can work out the triggers that arouse your emotions, you can help to circumvent them at an early stage. For example, if someone makes you angry when they don't do something, remind them in advance that the task needs completion by a certain time otherwise it is likely to make you feel angry.
- Try to delay your anger rather than acting immediately as this starts letting you feel in control of it. If possible, try to reduce its level, so you let yourself feel dismayed or disappointed rather than angry.

- Express your feelings and take ownership of them. Practise saying, 'I feel angry with this situation/you because…' Avoid accusing statements such as, 'You/this makes me feel angry because…'

- Accept that anger results from your own rigid beliefs. For example, if you feel angry because your partner is untidy when you feel they should clear up after themselves, try looking at this from a different point of view, for example, 'He/she may be untidy but they are also very supportive and loving — we all have our good and less good qualities and I shouldn't let this wind me up so much' or, 'His/her priorities in life are different to mine — that's partly why I fell in love with him/her'.

- Accept that you do not have a right to expect other people or things to be exactly how you want them to be — we live in an imperfect world and therefore need to be flexible and accept compromise.

- When you feel anger rising, practise a slow breathing exercise and consciously try to relax. This is your personal equivalent of biting your tongue or counting to ten.

- Use an appropriate personal affirmation such as, 'I will not feel angry, I will stay in control' or, 'Keep cool, calm and collected', and keep repeating this to yourself when appropriate.

- If you are too angry to think straight, then say 'I'll discuss this later' and move away from the situation temporarily — take a brisk walk, go somewhere private to scream or groan loudly, hit a cushion or throw a ball to help diffuse your tension. When you feel in control again, go back and address the issue — don't avoid it.

- When you are on your own, pretend the person or situation that made you feel angry is present and describe out loud exactly how you feel. Say all the things you want to say to that person or in that situation, to get them out of your system.

- Accept your attempts to overcome anger as a challenge and a learning experience — you will become a better person once you can control your emotions.

Tips to help you deal with someone else's anger

Dealing with someone else's anger can be just as stressful, but do not make it your problem, and do not let it affect your health.

- Remember, you are not responsible for someone else's anger.

- Acknowledge their anger by saying 'I can see you are very angry because of… I will discuss it with you when you have calmed down and are more in control.'

- Acknowledge how their anger is affecting you, for example, 'I feel angry or upset because of your behaviour.'

- Visualize their anger as a grey cloud that washes over you, leaving you untouched.

- If you are too upset to deal with the situation immediately, say so and walk away. You have the right to withdraw from someone who is shouting or has lost control.

- Don't ignore what has happened or pretend it never occurred. Deal with the situation when you have both calmed down.

Reasons why people may choose to display anger

1. It gives them power and control over others.

2. It draws attention to themselves.

3. It makes them feel/look important.

4. It helps them to avoid looking as if they have lost an argument.

5. It makes you feel guilty so you are more likely to do what they want in the future.

Anxiety and panic attacks

Anxiety is one of the main symptoms of stress and is associated with feelings of apprehension, dread, panic and impending doom. While short-lived anxiety is appropriate in some situations (for example, when going for an interview), those with morbid anxiety worry excessively about trivial matters and frequently experience other typical stress symptoms such as restlessness, palpitations, tremor, flushing, dizziness, hyperventilation, loose bowels, sweating, muscle tension and insomnia.

Anxiety often results from internal sources of stress and typically develops between the late teens and early thirties when it may also be associated with excess intakes of caffeine, alcohol or illegal drugs. Anxiety occurring later in life may be part of a depressive illness. In eight out of ten cases, anxiety due to internal stress is self-limiting and resolves within a few weeks following reassurance and emotional support such as counselling, behaviour therapy or relaxation techniques. In some cases, however, anxiety becomes worse and may develop into panic attacks.

Panic attacks are surprisingly common. They are a natural response to anxiety and extreme stress. Many of those who suffer can remember the exact occasion when they experienced their first attack, such as in a crowded supermarket or following a series of stressful events at work. If you suffer from panic attacks but cannot remember any particular trigger, some psychologists believe your fear may date from an event in early childhood which is stored in your subconscious memory.

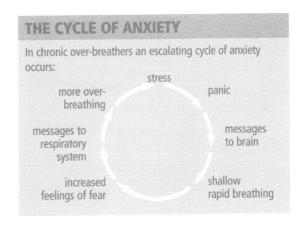

THE CYCLE OF ANXIETY

In chronic over-breathers an escalating cycle of anxiety occurs:

stress

panic

more over-breathing

messages to brain

messages to respiratory system

shallow rapid breathing

increased feelings of fear

Over-breathing

Panic attacks are now thought to be triggered by over-breathing — a condition known as hyperventilation syndrome. During times of extreme stress, your breathing pattern changes as part of the fight-or-flight response, so you take quick, irregular, shallow breaths that help to draw in more oxygen more quickly. This in turn means you blow off more carbon dioxide — a waste acid gas produced by your metabolism. If you continue hyperventilating, you will soon exhale so much carbon dioxide that your blood loses acidity and becomes increasingly alkaline. This affects the transmission of nerve signals and causes physical symptoms of dizziness, faintness and pins and needles. These symptoms heighten your sense of panic so you tend to breath even faster, blowing off even more carbon dioxide, to trigger a panic attack. The classic advice to breath in and out of a paper bag is designed to ensure you re-inhale some of your lost carbon dioxide to replace acidity and relieve your symptoms.

Lump in the throat

Many people under stress feel as if they have a lump in their throat and develop difficulty in swallowing. This is known medically as *globus hystericus*. It used to be thought that this was due to abnormal muscle contraction in the oesophagus (gullet) but researchers have now found this sensation can be brought on in most people just by over-breathing. Hyperventilation changes the ratio of different gases in the lungs and affects blood acidity, which in turn interferes with muscle contraction. It therefore seems that people under stress who develop this symptom have been over-breathing. Rebreathing air you have just blown out into a paper bag will help to correct the situation.

Panic attacks

The most common symptoms experienced during a panic attack are:

- extreme anxiety
- non-specific fears of losing control, embarrassment, rejection or failure
- fluttering in the stomach
- nausea and/or diarrhoea
- rapid pulse
- sweating, especially on the palms
- difficulty breathing or a choking sensation
- pins and needles, especially around the mouth and in the fingers

- blurred vision
- ringing in the ears
- clamminess
- faintness or swooning.

People who habitually hyperventilate sometimes experience frightening physical symptoms, including chest pain, palpitations, visual disturbances, numbness, severe headache, insomnia and even collapse. It is important to seek medical advice if these occur — don't make the diagnosis of panic attack yourself or it is possible that a more serious problem (for example, a heart condition) may be missed.

Who suffers

An estimated one in twenty people suffer from panic attacks on a regular basis, and it can be reassuring to know that other people feel the same way. Panic attacks seem to be more common in women than men and researchers have found that middle-aged housewives are the main sufferers. The reasons are not clear, but it is thought that women who have devoted a major part of their life to being a wife and mother may no longer feel worthwhile once their children leave home, their husband is working long hours and they are home all day on their own. Boredom can lead to feelings of no longer existing as a real, separate individual — something psychiatrists refer to as depersonalization — which can produce extreme anxiety.

Some women find they are more likely to suffer a panic attack just before or during a period. This may be linked with low blood sugar levels so that symptoms of faintness and light-headedness trigger feelings of anxiety and panic.

QUICK TIPS TO HELP STOP A PANIC ATTACK

- Concentrate on breathing slowly, deeply and quietly to prevent hyperventilation.
- When you feel panic rising say, 'Stop it!' quietly to yourself.
  1. Breathe out deeply, then breath in slowly to fill your lungs.
  2. Hold this breath for a count of three then breathe out gently, letting your tension go.
  3. Continue to breathe regularly and gently: imagine a candle in front of your face — as you breathe the flame should flicker but not go out.
- While continuing to breathe gently, consciously try to relax so that all your tense muscles unwind.
- If panic continues to rise, cup your hands over your nose and mouth so you breathe back some of the excess carbon dioxide gas you have blown off.
- If you are somewhere private, breath in and out of a paper-bag instead.
- Don't escalate the panic by worrying about what is going to happen.
- Try to distract your thoughts by studying your surroundings as you wait for the attack to pass — symptoms usually subside quickly.
- Stay in the situation if practical and you are in no physical danger — if you run away rather than facing your fear, it will be more difficult to cope and to avoid another panic attack when you experience the same situation again.

The breathing exercises in Chapter 4 will help, too.

How panic attacks progress

A panic attack is most likely to occur when you are feeling physically or emotionally exhausted and your ability to cope is reduced. It is such an unpleasant experience that you hope never to go through it again. This instills a fear that feeds on itself — the more you worry about having another attack, the more anxious you feel and the panic starts to build up so it becomes a self-fulfilling prophesy.

At first, you may only feel panicky when you are in a particular type of stressful situation (for example, the supermarket, or after a conflict with your boss at work). But once you are sensitized to the feeling of fear itself, just thinking about what stresses you can bring on an overwhelming sense of panic. You may feel you cannot face entering a supermarket again for fear of having a panic attack, or call in sick to avoid your boss at work.

If you suffer from panic attacks, talk to someone about your worries, either a valued friend or a professional counsellor, to help off-load your feelings so they don't build up inside. And if you are going somewhere or doing something stressful which has previously caused a panic attack, ask a trusted, sympathetic person such as a close friend or relative to go with you for moral support

Behaviour therapy

If your symptoms are debilitating, you may benefit from anxiety management training with a behaviour therapist. You will be taught how to reduce your anxiety through relaxation, distraction and reassuring affirmations such as, 'I can cope'. If panic attacks are becoming troublesome, ask your GP for advice about joining a therapy group or receiving individual psychotherapy.

Longer-term ploys to help avoid panic attacks

- Talk to someone about your worries, either a valued friend or a professional counsellor.
- Work out what makes you stressed and why — change those situations that can be changed and, where practical, avoid others (for example, shopping in the supermarket at the busiest times).
- If you are going somewhere or doing something stressful which has previously caused a panic attack, ask a trusted, sympathetic person such as a close friend or relative to go with you for moral support.
- Take regular exercise such as swimming, walking or cycling to help burn off stress hormones.
- Avoid excessive caffeine — limit your intake of tea, coffee and caffeinated soft drinks to three cups per day or switch to decaffeinated brands.

- Take a good multinutrient supplement containing as many vitamins and minerals as possible at around 100% of the recommended daily amount (RDA).
- Eat little and often to keep your blood sugar levels up — never skip a meal, especially breakfast.
- Cut back on sugar, salt, saturated fats and processed or convenience foods.
- Watch your alcohol intake and try to limit yourself to a maximum of one or two alcoholic drinks per day.
- Try to keep your mind as active as possible by developing several interesting, distracting hobbies — either around the home (for example, crochet, gardening, writing your memoirs) or outside (for example, voluntary work, bird-watching, line dancing).

Alternative therapies to help overcome panic attacks

Acupressure

This is similar to acupuncture but involves massaging points on the body rather than stimulating them with needles. This is thought to help balance the flow of energy (*chi*) through special channels in the body known as meridians. Acupressure can help many stress-related problems such as insomnia, headache, general tension and panic attacks.

Flower remedies

These are often highly successful at helping to overcome a panic attack. They include:

- Bach Rescue Remedy which contains five flower essences preserved in brandy: cherry plum, clematis, impatiens, rock rose and star-of-Bethlehem.
- Emergency Essence, which contains six flower essences preserved in brandy: camomile, lavender, red clover, purple coneflower, self-heal and yarrow.

When you feel a panic attack coming on, add five drops of Rescue Remedy or Emergency Essence to a glass of water and sip slowly every three to five minutes, holding the liquid in your mouth for a while. Alternatively, place five drops directly on your tongue.

Herbalism

This uses natural anxiety-reducing substances to help you achieve calm without the side effects associated with drugs. Valerian is one of the most calming herbs available and can help to relieve anxiety and muscle tension, and promote calmness. It is often used together with another calming herb, lemon balm, to ease nervous anxiety, headache, insomnia and to help avoid a panic attack. Adaptogenic herbs such as Siberian ginseng, Korean ginseng, gotu kola and reishi can also help you cope with stress and change so you are less likely to have a panic attack (see page 142).

Hypnotherapy

This involves helping you to achieve deep relaxation and then changing your thought or behaviour patterns, for example, by telling yourself your feelings of panic have been packed up, tied to a balloon and allowed to float permanently away.

Reflexology

This involves massaging areas known as reflexes on the feet and hands and can help to reduce stress-related problems such as headache, hyperventilation, digestive symptoms and panic attacks.

Visualization

This can help to relieve your distress when you feel a panic attack coming on. Sit down, close your eyes and instead of focusing on your panic, try to imagine yourself in one of the following situations:

- Walking through a sunlit forest glade with the sound of gently running water and bird song surrounding you while a cool breeze ruffles your hair.
- Swimming in a warm tropical ocean next to a deserted white-sand beach.
- Sitting in the sun on the veranda of a log chalet high up on a snow-covered mountain – breath in the cool air and hear the soft drip of snow melting from the surrounding fir trees.

Phobias

A phobia is a disorder associated with anxiety in which a morbid fear of certain objects or situations develops that is out of all proportion to the threat the object or situation really presents. Typically, someone with a phobia will go to any length to avoid exposure to the object or situation feared. It is estimated that as many as one in four women and one in six men have a simple phobia which, although mild, may be sufficient to interfere with some aspects of their work or lifestyle.

When you are under extreme stress, even a simple phobia can escalate until you start to hyperventilate and develop a panic attack. This is such a frightening experience that you may then develop a fear of having another if you are exposed to the same situation again in the future. Eventually, this fear may broaden until you reach a stage where you cannot face meeting new people (social phobia), visiting any crowded place or even going out alone (agora-phobia). In many cases, these fears are not so much the fear of open, crowded spaces or of people themselves, but the fear of having nothing interesting to say, not being able to cope or of looking foolish by having another panic attack in public.

Many phobias stem from events in childhood such as being barked at or bitten by an angry dog, or from seeing a parent react in a terrified way to a storm, mouse or spider. Even though the fear is irrational, the object triggers an inappropriate fight-or-flight response that does not lessen with time. The main factor that feeds a phobia is avoidance of the object or situation provoking it, and this failure to confront your fear must be addressed in order to overcome it.

COMMON PHOBIAS
● spiders
● snakes
● mice
● dogs
● heights
● needles
● flying
● thunder and lightning
● open spaces
● crowded or small spaces
● social contact with others

Therapy

A simple phobia can be treated with behaviour therapy in which gradual desensiti-zation slowly exposes the sufferer to the object feared. In the case of a spider phobia, for example, this may involve initially just looking at a picture of a spider and will progress to holding the picture. Once you can cope with bigger and bigger pictures, the object itself is introduced, for example, a dead spider in a glass jar. This is slowly brought closer and closer until you are able to handle the jar confi-dently. Eventually a jar with a live spider will be introduced and finally, the spider will be set free. The first exposure to the feared situation is obviously very stressful and will make you feel very anxious and stressed. If you

DIFFERENCES BETWEEN A SOCIAL PHOBIA AND AGORAPHOBIA	
SOCIAL PHOBIA: FEAR OF	AGORAPHOBIA: FEAR OF
● being introduced	● being alone
● being watched	● crossing the street
● being teased	● unfamiliar places
● using the telephone	● using public transport
● meeting people in authority	● crowds
● having visitors to your home	● leaving home
● eating out	● visiting a large or small shop
● talking in public	● open spaces

stay in the situation and try to view it rationally, however, your anxiety will slowly decrease. Each time you confront the fear again, you will usually find your level of anxiety decreases and you recover your composure more quickly.

Another technique involves prolonged exposure in which the sufferer is exposed to their intense fear and has to remain in the phobic situation without means of escape for at least two hours until they acclimatize. This can be extremely distressing and the person needs to be very motivated to undertake this form of treatment.

Tips to help conquer your phobia

- Try to recall where the fear came from so you can understand its roots — can you or your relatives remember you having a bad experience as a child? Could you have learned your phobia from another close family member who has a similar fear?

- Try to realize that the situation or object you fear is relatively harmless. Write down all the worst things you fear might happen to you if you faced your fear. Go back over each of these and plan how you could cope with each of these situations in a cool, calm and collected manner.

- Learn a breathing exercise (see page 153) so you can say, 'Calm!' quietly to yourself and slow your breathing when you feel afraid. This will help to stop you triggering a panic attack.

- Close your eyes, relax, then slowly visualize yourself in the situation you fear. Try to stay with the image for longer and longer each day, then imagine yourself confronting the fear, calmly walking past it and leaving it totally behind.

- Obtain a picture of the situation or object that you fear and practise looking at it and handling it for longer and longer periods each day.

- Write about or draw the situation or object you fear to help get it out of your system. Then take a pair of scissors and cut the paper into small pieces, or tear it up by hand. Imagine that what you are dividing up into small pieces is your fear, which you can then put in the garbage and send packing from your life.

- Discuss your feelings and fears openly with other people and listen to theirs — this form of group therapy can be very helpful.

- Arrange to expose yourself to the fear with someone you trust — a best friend, partner or close relative. It is often easier to face your fears initially while holding someone else's hand for moral support.

- Develop positive statements of self-worth (see page 203).

Alternative therapies that can help

See the suggestions for panic attacks in the previous section. Hypnotherapy (see pages 187-8).is especially effective for treating phobias. In a typical group session you will be helped to achieve a relaxed state and shown how to use visualization and auto-suggestion to help overcome your irrational fear.

Depression

Few people are blessed with a happy mood all the time. One day you may feel cheerful, energetic and lively, while the next you feel gloomy, listless and withdrawn, especially if you are under pressure. These mood swings are a normal part of everyday life, but sometimes they can get out of hand and if your mood swings too low, mild depression can occur.

Depression is often associated with long-term periods of excess pressure, and as many as one in eight men and one in five women will suffer from severe depression at some time during their life. It is one of the commonest reasons why people consult their doctor, yet it is estimated that only half of all cases are diagnosed, since many sufferers either do not realize they have a depressive illness or are unwilling to seek help. This is especially likely in those under severe stress who may perceive emotional symptoms as a sign of weakness and inability to cope.

Depression is caused by an imbalance of the chemical messengers in the brain that are responsible for passing signals from one brain cell to another. If levels of one or more of these fall too low, the brain does not function properly and a variety of psychological and physical symptoms can occur including:

- a general slowing down
- nervousness, anxiety and agitation
- constant feelings of tiredness or exhaustion
- headache
- difficulty concentrating
- loss of self-esteem and lack of confidence
- preoccupation with your health
- low sex drive
- loss of interest in life
- low mood with crying and sadness
- loss of interest in everyday life.

These symptoms are similar to those occurring during times of extreme stress, and the two conditions are often closely linked. With more severe depression, additional symptoms such as poor appetite, weight loss, difficulty sleeping and early morning waking (typically between 2 a.m. and 4 a.m.) develop.

Mild depression may eventually get better on its own, but your mood may dip even lower until you are suffering from a full-blown depressive illness. People suffering from moderate to severe depression are unlikely to snap out of their low mood without treatment with counselling and/or antidepressant therapy. If you think you are depressed, it is important to consult your doctor.

Tips to help overcome a low mood

- Make a 'To Do' list of a few simple tasks to achieve each day, even when you don't feel like doing much at all.
- Take care of your personal appearance — even though there may seem little point, try to take pride in having clean hair, clean, ironed clothes, polished shoes and clean fingernails. Men should aim to shave every day while women should try to apply a little light make-up such as lipstick and mascara.
- Combat loneliness by talking to as many people as possible during the day; writing letters and making phone calls will help too.
- Consider getting a pet to bring some extra interest and companionship into your life — but only if you know you have the commitment to look after it properly. Contact your local dog and cat home to find out what having a pet will entail. If you can take in a stray, you may well be saving their life. Owning a cat may be easier, as they are better at looking after themselves; but owning a dog will encourage you to exercise regularly.
- Take regular exercise as this triggers the secretion of natural antidepressant substances in the brain and will help to lift a low mood
- If you find yourself thinking negative thoughts, turn them instantly into positive ones (see page 203).
- Keep a diary and at the end of each day write down what you have achieved, what you have enjoyed, and what you would like to do tomorrow to bring more happiness into your life.

Diet tips for depression

- Eat plenty of fresh fruit, vegetables, wholegrain cereals, nuts and seeds.
- Get at least half your daily calories from complex, unrefined carbohydrates such as brown rice, wholegrain cereals, wholewheat pasta and brown bread.
- Eat little and often to stop your blood sugar level falling too low — semi-dried fruit (for example, apricots, dates, figs, prunes) makes an ideal healthy snack.
- Limit your intake of fats, alcohol, salt and caffeine as much as possible.
- Increase your intake of foods rich in the B group vitamins such as yeast extract, wholegrains, soya, walnuts, oily fish, green leafy vegetables, avocado, bananas, walnuts.

ALTERNATIVE REMEDY FOR DEPRESSION

St John's wort extracts can lift low mood and improve alertness and concentration, providing relief from feelings of anxiety, agitation, disinterest, insomnia, headache and despair.

Poor memory

Your memory is a personal storehouse of information. When you are under stress, however, it is natural for your memory to become less like a filing cabinet and more like a sieve. Anxiety interferes with memory storage and recall: your concentration goes and you're distracted by worry and preoccupied with personal thoughts.

Researchers believe there are three main types of memory:

- Sensory memory briefly remembers facts for a split second.
- Short-term memory stores facts for around five minutes.
- Long-term memory can store facts for as long as a lifetime. This can further be divided into 'habit memory', for example learned skills such as driving a car, riding a bike or playing the piano, and 'recognition memory', for example storage of general knowledge and personal experiences.

Scientists are still unsure exactly how memory is stored. Most believe that new connections (synapses) are laid down between brain cells (neurones), and that new

HOW GOOD IS YOUR MEMORY?

SHORT-TERM MEMORY

- Do you forget whether you've locked the door or turned off the oven?
- Do you walk into a room and forget why you're there?
- Do you start a sentence then forget what you wanted to say?
- Do you read something, forget what it said and have to read it again?
- Do you keep repeating yourself?
- What did you have for breakfast?
- Do you keep losing your umbrella?

MEDIUM-TERM MEMORY

- Can you remember what you did last weekend?
- Do you start telling a joke, then forget the punchline?

- Do you get lost on a journey you've made before?
- Do you forget to pick up the dry-cleaning or to buy an item you need for supper?
- Do you plan to watch a TV programme then forget it's on?

LONG-TERM MEMORY

- Can you remember what you were doing when you heard that John Lennon was shot/ Elvis died/ Margaret Thatcher resigned?
- Can you remember your last address and post code?
- When was your first kiss, and with whom?
- Who was Prime Minister when you voted for the first time?

WHAT IS YOUR SHORT-TERM MEMORY SPAN?

Ask someone to read the following numbers out loud to you, one at a time.

After each line, try to repeat the number digit for digit. Continue line by line until you come to a number you cannot repeat from memory. The most number of digits you can remember correctly is your memory's digit span.

- 3
- 56
- 865
- 7319
- 34721
- 948735
- 3583827
- 43672181
- 972568647
- 1726834956
- 53749427312

The average person's short-term memory can hold around seven unrelated facts at any one time (for example, a seven-digit number).

protein molecules are made to store information. It is possible that spare genetic material – DNA not being used to hold the genetic code – is involved or that electrical circuits play a part.

Sensory memories can be retained and registered as short-term memories. Without repetition, short-term memory only lasts for around thirty seconds. If the information is important enough, a short-term memory can be converted into a long-term one by studying and repeating it. If the memory can be linked with another remembered fact, a visual image or even a smell, it will be easier to store and retrieve it.

The ease with which long-term memories can be recalled at a later date depends on how well they were encoded. If a memory is poorly stored it may remain elusive and frustratingly 'on the tip of your tongue'.

Tips to help boost your memory

- When you want to remember an important fact, keep repeating it silently to yourself.
- Write memory-jogging notes of things to do on post-it pads and stick them up where you will easily see them.
- Associate a fact to be remembered with a visual image, for example, when introduced to someone who is an artist, picture them holding an enormous paint brush. If their name is Baker, picture them eating a large loaf of bread. The more outrageous or unusual your images, the easier you will remember them.
- If you can't remember someone's name, try to remember where you met them, what they were wearing, any unusual physical characteristic or mannerism and what you talked about – this will often jog your memory.
- Try to think up a mnemonic involving the first letter of each word when remembering a list. A good example is the mnemonic used to remember the colours of a rainbow: Richard of York gave battle in vain (red, orange, yellow, green, blue, indigo, violet). It is easier to remember the sentence and work out the colours, than to remember the colours alone.
- If you keep losing something (for example, your keys), try to form a mental photograph of where they are every time you put them down.
- When trying to remember a number, use visual images (for example, a shoe for two, a gate for eight, a bottle of wine for nine).
- The more you stretch your brain, the better your memory. Keep your brain cells active by reading demanding books or doing crosswords and other puzzles that need concentration. Games such as

SOME DRUGS THAT CAN AFFECT YOUR MEMORY

- alcohol
- nicotine
- tranquillizers
- sleeping tablets
- some blood pressure tablets

Scrabble or Trivial Pursuit are excellent for testing your memory skills.

- Try to learn at least one new fact, or memorize a poem or lines from a novel every day.

- Smell is interpreted in part of the brain called the olfactory bulbs. These are embedded in the limbic system, which is closely linked with your emotions and memory. If you learn a fact when smelling a particular aromatherapy scent (in a diffuser or on a hanky), then you can recall this fact more easily when sniffing the same scent again. Use a different blend of oils for each learning process and only smell the same blend again when you need to recall that information. Try learning a shopping list when smelling a new mix of three or four oils. In the supermarket, smell the same scent on a hanky and see how well you remember the items you need. Try blending some of the following oils together:

  > basil for clarity
  >
  > bergamot for extra confidence
  >
  > rosemary for improved memory
  >
  > lemon for better concentration
  >
  > ginger to help overcome forgetfulness
  >
  > cardamom for clarity
  >
  > coriander for improved memory
  >
  > black pepper to overcome emotional blocks and mental exhaustion.

Helpful diet and lifestyle changes

- Eat a healthy, wholefood diet with plenty of fresh fruit, vegetables, cereals and fish — avoid processed foods containing additives as much as possible.

- Increase your intake of foods rich in thiamine (vitamin B1) such as brewer's yeast, brown rice, wheatgerm, wholegrain bread and cereals. Poor memory during times of stress is occasionally due to vitamin B1 deficiency, especially in people who drink excess alcohol. As well as thiamine, other B-group vitamins and the minerals potassium, magnesium, calcium, iron and zinc are vitally important for good memory function.

- Eat more fish: it contains phosphatidylcholine that helps memory. Supplements containing choline, lecithin or phosphatidylserine may also help.

- Eat more garlic and consider taking garlic tablets to improve blood-flow through small blood vessels in the brain.

- Consider taking extracts from the *Ginkgo biloba* tree, which improve blood-flow to the brain and can improve memory and concentration.

- If you smoke, try to stop.

- Cut right back on alcohol intake.

- Increase the amount of exercise you take to boost circulation to the brain.

- Make sure you get plenty of rest and sleep.

Cramp

Cramp is the popular name for a painful, excessive contraction of a muscle. This is usually felt in the leg, but any muscle can be affected. Cramps are linked with a build-up of lactic acid and other waste products of muscle metabolism — usually during or after physical exercise. They can also occur when you are stressed, however, and your muscles are held unusually tense for prolonged periods of time. When stressed and working long hours, cramps can also be related to sitting in an awkward position for too long, for example being cooped up at your desk all day.

Cramps can usually be relieved by vigorous massage, applying a hot or cold compress, or by gently stretching the affected muscle. Recurrent night cramps can often be relieved by taking supplements of calcium or quinine and by ensuring you drink enough fluids during the day.

Restless legs syndrome

Restless legs syndrome — also known as Ekbom's Syndrome — causes an unpleasant creeping sensation in the lower limbs accompanied by twitching, pins and needles, burning sensations and a sudden, irresistible urge to move your legs. This relieves symptoms only fleetingly before the irresistible urge returns. The muscles in your legs usually twitch or jump with tension too, although this is not always enough to notice. The desire to move your legs may keep waking you

TIPS TO HELP PREVENT LEG CRAMPS

- Ensure you drink enough fluids during the day.
- Increase your dietary intake of calcium (for example, low-fat milk, cheese, yoghurt, dark-green leafy vegetables) and magnesium (nuts, seafood, dairy products, wholegrains, dark-green leafy vegetables).
- Improve a poor circulation with garlic tablets, ginkgo extracts and omega-3 fish-oil supplements.
- Consider taking coenzyme Q10, which increases oxygen uptake in muscle cells, especially when circulation is poor.
- Rub St John's wort oil or eucalyptus oil into the affected muscle to dilate small blood vessels and help relax tense muscle fibres.

- Some nutritionists suggest combining one tablespoon of apple cider vinegar and one tablespoon of honey in a glass and drinking daily.
- Add five drops of rosemary essential oil to a warm bath and relax before going to bed.
- Warm up and stretch for at least fifteen minutes before starting exercise.
- Start exercising slowly and gradually build up your exertion.
- Take a good vitamin and mineral supplement that includes calcium, magnesium and vitamin E.
- Try taking the homoeopathic remedy, Cuprum metallicum 6c.

when you are tired and trying to drift off to sleep. Restless legs syndrome affects around one in twenty people regularly and tends to occur when you are suffering from fatigue, anxiety or stress. The exact cause is unknown although it is believed to be a form of nerve irritation that is often linked with lack of iron and folic acid.

- Take a vitamin and mineral supplement that includes iron, folic acid and vitamin E.
- Consider taking coenzyme Q10 – a vitamin-like substance that increases oxygen uptake in cells.
- *Ginkgo biloba* extracts and garlic tablets may help symptoms by improving your circulation.
- Just before going to sleep, try placing your feet in cold water for five minutes to help promote sleep.
- Avoid synthetic socks, tights and underwear as these seem to make the condition worse.
- Avoid alcohol and caffeine, which may make symptoms worse.
- A gel developed for tired legs, which contains extracts of seaweed, hazel, grape, butcher's-broom, pine, camphor and lavender, is said to improve symptoms in more than three-quarters of patients.

Loss of sex drive

Sexual problems are common among people experiencing excess pressure. Loss of sex drive is especially likely and affects at least 60% of adults under stress, 30% of middle-aged women and over 70% of post-menopausal women. Stress-related loss of sex drive is largely due to hormone changes produced as a result of a prolonged fight-or-flight response.

The sex drive or libido is normally the second strongest urge in humans, after sleep. It is controlled through complex interactions between sex hormones (for example, testosterone, oestrogen), some metabolic hormones (for example, prolactin), brain chemicals (for example, dopamine) and pheromones – volatile, odorless chemicals secreted in human sweat that have subtle effects on the sexuality of others. Psychological stimuli (sight, imagination), physical factors (smell, touch) and cultural customs also play a role. These interactions are further modified by factors such as levels of stress, exercise, drug and alcohol intakes, smoking habits, general health, fatigue and diet.

Stress is one of the most widespread causes of loss of libido, along with overwork, tiredness and lack of sleep. Excess stress is associated with a fall in testosterone and oestrogen levels, and an increase in secretion of prolactin – a hormone produced by the pituitary gland in the brain. Prolactin has a powerful negative effect on libido, and literally switches off the sex drive as well as reducing fertility. Low sex drive is in itself a powerful cause of stress in relationships, so a vicious circle sets up. It is therefore important to tackle low sex drive sooner rather than later.

Be your own sex therapist

Sexual exercises – known as sensate focusing, or pleasuring – can help any couple whose sex life is adversely affected by stress. You need to set aside around an hour at least once a week to explore each other's body and give pleasure through stroking and massage while telling each other what you like and how it makes you feel. Sensate focusing starts with non-sexual massage and touching that avoids obviously erotic areas such as the breasts and genitals. Make sure your bedroom is comfortably warm, then take it in turns to give and receive a loving massage.

Once both partners are comfortable with this, the erogenous zones can be included as well. Oral sex and mutual masturbation is allowed, but penetrative sex is initially banned to take away the stress of having to perform. This helps to show you that arousal can be pleasurable itself even when climax is not the main objective.

It is important to let your partner know with a sound, gesture or word when they do something you like – soon you will have enough confidence to take their hand and gently show them what to do, too. The next stage of pleasuring – which may not be reached for several weeks – involves penetration, but thrusting is banned. Finally, penetration with movement can occur when both partners feel comfortable with this.

Sensate focusing is surprisingly successful because both partners agree the boundaries in advance and therefore feel in control at all times.

Alternative treatments that can help sex drive

Herbalism

- Catuaba promotes erotic dreams in both men and women, followed by increased sexual desire within five to twenty-one days of regular treatment.
- Damiana produces localized tingling and throbbing sensations in the genitals and increases sensitivity of nerve endings.
- Muira puama stimulates desire through a direct action on brain chemicals, stimulating nerve endings in the genitals and by promoting the effects of testosterone.

- Korean and American Ginsengs can help the body adapt to physical and emotional stress and are widely reputed to have an aphrodisiac effect. Siberian ginseng is also noted for its aphrodisiac properties.
- St John's wort helps 60% of post-menopausal women become interested in sex again after three months of treatment.
- Tribulus terrestris — a plant widely used in Indian ayurvedic medicine — works by increasing the effects of testosterone, especially where reduced sexual activity is associated with stress, tiredness and fatigue.

TIPS TO HELP IMPROVE YOUR SEX DRIVE

- Start taking steps to lose any excess weight by eating more healthily (see Chapter 3).
- Exercise regularly to build up your stamina (see Chapter 4).
- Reduce your intake of alcohol to within safe limits (see page 90).
- Improve your self-esteem (see Chapter 6).
- With your partner, learn how to give each other a massage with a sensual aromatherapy oil or lotion (see page 188).
- Make sure you get a regular good night's sleep (see page 70).
- Take a vitamin and mineral supplement to help correct any deficiencies.

Homoeopathy

Homoeopathic hormones such as testosterone or oestrogen are used by some practitioners to normalize hormone imbalances associated with loss of libido, especially in those unable to take orthodox hormone replacement therapy. The following specific remedies should be taken at 6c potency twice a day for up to a week:

- For low sex drive linked with listlessness, lethargy, sluggishness or feelings of guilt about sex: Phosphoricum acidum.
- For low sex drive linked with anxiety and fear of failure: Arsenicum album.
- For low sex drive linked with physical exhaustion and mental fatigue: Cuprum metallicum.
- For low sex drive linked with anxiety, depression and other strong emotions, especially those that are suppressed: Natrum muriaticum.
- For low sex drive in those who are workaholic, stressed, irritable, over-active, have difficulty sleeping and indulge in excess alcohol, caffeine or cigarettes: Nux vomica.

Aromatherapy

The heavy, floral essential oils of geranium, rose, jasmine and ylang-ylang are among the most powerful aromatic aphrodisiacs. Other essential oils that can increase sex drive include black pepper, cardamom, cinnamon (for perfuming the air only — do not bring into contact with the skin) and ginger.

Impotence

Impotence – also known as erectile dysfunction – affects as many as one in ten men on a regular basis. It is especially common in men who are under stress, since anxiety interferes with the normal processes of arousal. It can also worsen the effects of other underlying physical causes of impotence such as diabetes, high blood pressure, reduced blood flow to the area, and the side effects of medicines to treat hypertension, depression, heart disease and gastric ulcers. Stress can also lead to smoking and the long-term abuse of alcohol or recreational drugs, which can also affect male potency.

As well as being a sign of stress, impotence is also a powerful cause of stress – one in five men with erectile dysfunction blame impotence for the break-up of their relationships, for example. This can set up yet another vicious stress circle, so it is important to seek help sooner rather than later.

Fortunately, more than nine out of ten men are able to regain potency with one of the many treatments now available such as psychosexual counselling, drug treatments (for example Viagra, testosterone replacement therapy, urethral pellets, penile injections), mechanical aids (vacuum pumps, implants) and vascular surgery to improve circulation.

ALTERNATIVE REMEDIES THAT CAN HELP IMPOTENCE

HERBALISM

Ginkgo biloba extracts can relax blood vessels to boost circulation to the brain, hands, feet and genitals. It is usually taken to improve memory but can also increase blood flow to the penis: half of previously impotent men have regained full potency after taking it for six months. Korean ginseng is also beneficial.

HOMOEOPATHY

The following specific remedies may be taken at 6c potency twice a day for up to a week:

- For impotence linked with low sex drive, lack of confidence, indecision or anxiety about size: Baryta carbonica.
- For men with impotence who do not really like sex: Graphites.
- For men whose impotence is linked with an enlarged prostate or physical tiredness that tends to come on in the afternoon and last until the evening: Lycopodium clavatum.

BACH FLOWER REMEDIES

Rescue Remedy can be helpful for men fearing impotence or poor performance.

AROMATHERAPY OILS

- black pepper
- clary sage
- ginger
- jasmine
- patchouli
- sandalwood
- ylang-ylang

Hair-pulling

Most people will have used the phrase, 'I'm tearing my hair out' when they are feeling under excess pressure. Few are aware that some people actually do this, however. The compulsive urge to pull out one's own hair forms a little known clinical condition known as trichotillomania. This is classed as an impulse control disorder in which there is:

- recurrent pulling out of one's hair resulting in noticeable hair loss
- an increasing sense of tension immediately before pulling out the hair or when trying to resist an attack
- pleasure, gratification or relief of tension when pulling out the hair.

Trichotillomania is closely linked with stress and is thought to affect as many as one in fifty people, making it as least as common as other, better known anxiety-related conditions such as panic attacks. Because sufferers are usually unwilling to talk about their condition through feelings of shame, hopelessness and embarrassment, few people seek help and few doctors are experienced in helping people with the condition.

People with trichotillomania may pluck hair from their scalp, eyebrows, eyelashes, legs or pubic area — anywhere, in fact, that hair is present. This leads to noticeable areas of hair loss and occasionally causes complete baldness. Most people with trichotillomania pull hair from more than one site on the body. Some may also bite their nails or pick at their skin, which may lead to scarring, disfigurement and chronic skin conditions. The hair is frequently eaten as well and can lead to a build up of a hairball (trichobezoar) in the stomach.

Often, this hair-pulling is absent-minded, done when the person is concentrating on something else such as reading or watching TV. At other times, however, the hair is pulled out with concentration and deliberation — usually when alone. Some sufferers describe entering a trance-like, almost meditative state where they lose all track of time and their surroundings. Others describe searching for the right hairs to pull because they feel wrong or different; the task demands attentive absorption. Some select a favourite area of their scalp to pluck from to produce soothing, comforting or pleasurable feelings. The length of an attack can vary from only a few minutes to several hours. During an extreme attack, a sufferer may clear her whole head of hair within five hours.

Symptoms frequently start around the time of puberty but can occur at any age. It is rare for someone to start pulling for the first time over the age of sixty, however.

In childhood, boys and girls seem to be equally affected. Trichotillomania starting at puberty is from five to ten times more common in females than males and in adults seeking help there are approximately twelve females for every male. Some people with tri-chotillomania have other symptoms of obsessive-compulsive disorder such as compulsive checking, hand-washing or cleanliness.

If hair-pulling can be stopped, hair may grow back normally with time. There seems to be a 50% chance that the hair will have a different colour or texture than non-pulled hair, however, and this change may be temporary or permanent. Occasionally, scalp scarring occurs as a result of ripping hair out, in which case hair loss may be permanent.

Habit reversal training involves learning a structured method to increase awareness of the hair-pulling activity and what might trigger it, and to replace pulling with a more acceptable behavioural response so that the urge to pull is controlled. Individual, tailored treatment with a behavioural therapist is usually important for success. Group therapy may also help.

> ## ALTERNATIVE TREATMENTS THAT CAN HELP YOU OVERCOME HAIR-PULLING
>
> **Hypnotherapy** can help you cast aside unhealthy behavioural changes.
>
> **Creative visualization:** Imagine yourself with a luxuri-ously full head of hair that has grown because you have successfully stopped pulling. This reality can become true if you let it.
>
> **Herbalism:** Calming herbs such as valerian, and mood lifting herbs such as St John's wort frequently help.
>
> **Bach Flower Remedies:** Rescue Remedy or Emergency Essence, or cherry plum (*Prunus cerasifera*) for fear of losing control, uncontrollable impulses, and fear of causing harm to oneself or others.
>
> **Medical hair design:** Covers the bald attack area with a special mesh to which individual hair-like fibres are knotted. This looks like real hair, so disguises the bald patch and also makes it difficult for sufferers to get their fingers at the hair roots (see Attention X in Resources).

How to stop pulling your hair

This method of reversing a habit can be used to help overcome several obsessive-compulsive disorders.

1. Concentrate on developing an awareness of when you are pulling your hair, especially if this happens in a trance-like state. Keep a record of exactly

- when hair-pulling occurs
- your feelings or emotional state before, during and after the attack
- what might have triggered it, if anything
- how long the bout lasts
- how many hairs were pulled

- how strong the urge was
- where the pulling occurred
- what you were doing at the time.

It is important to fill out the sheet immediately after the episode — don't try to rely on your memory later.

2. After a week of successful self-monitoring and sheet filling, learn a muscle relaxation and breathing exercise, for example using a relaxation tape. Most people become good at relaxing their bodies and regulating their breathing after around two weeks of daily sessions. The therapist will then often suggest using a relaxation tape to help you become relaxed quickly within a minute or two, which should be practised several times a day while learning Step 3.

3. Learn a muscle-tensing activity that is performed when the urge to pull is present, and which makes it impossible to tug at your hair. For example, make a clenched fist with the hand you usually pull with, then bend that arm at the elbow and push the clenched fist firmly into your waist. Hold the position for a minute, then relax and repeat for a total of ten times in quick succession. This exercise should be repeated regularly, at least three times per day initially.

4. Once you are keeping up-to-date hair-pulling records, have learned how to relax, to breathe properly from the diaphragm, and to tense your pulling arm, you are ready to integrate all three steps into a successful habit-reversal response. Whenever you get the urge to pull, or find yourself pulling, you should now be able to:

> 1. Quickly relax yourself.
> 2. Breathe from the diaphragm for one minute.
> 3. Then clench your fist and press it into your waist for one minute.

Repeat this process as often as necessary — before, during and after a hair-pulling episode. If you are driving at the time, practise the breathing exercise and clench the wheel firmly instead.

POSITIVE THINKING EXERCISE FOR HAIR-PULLING

Self-confidence can be enhanced by substituting positive, calming thoughts for those that are stressful and negative. Suitable thoughts to repeat to yourself include:

- I *am* good enough.
- I can stop pulling my hair.
- I can overcome the urge to pull.
- I can succeed if I try hard enough.

Say the most appropriate positive statements for you regularly as affirmations to counter negative self-talk and feelings. If you say them frequently enough they will automatically come to mind in an emotional emergency and have a profoundly calming effect. The word 'calm' itself can also be used as a personal mantra — an utterance whose vibration helps you relax during times of stress.

Patience is needed to become practised with this technique. Those who pull out their hair will have practised that technique many thousands of times — so don't give up on habit reversal training after just a few attempts. You may need to do this twenty, fifty or a hundred times or more until it becomes second nature to relax, breathe correctly and clench your fist to your waist rather than pulling your hair.

Alopecia

Alopecia is a common hair loss condition which can be linked with stress. It occurs when certain hair follicles stop growing, either in a small patch of skin, on one region of the body, or occasionally all over the body. There are four main types:

- alopecia areata, in which hair is lost in patches, usually on the scalp
- diffuse alopecia, in which patchy hair loss affects the whole scalp
- alopecia totalis, in which there is total loss of scalp hair
- alopecia universalis — loss of hair over the entire body, including eyebrows and eyelashes.

The exact cause of alopecia is unknown, but it seems to be related to abnormal activity of the immune system which attacks or switches off certain hair follicles. Stress plays a major role — both because stress can affect immune function, and because stress leads to tension and tightness of the scalp plus contraction of blood vessels in the area, which reduces blood supply to the hair follicles.

Everyone is born with around 100–150,000 hair follicles on their head. This number is fixed through life and no new follicles will develop after birth. Every scalp hair has its own life cycle made up of three stages:

1. A vigorous growth phase (anagen), which normally lasts 3–6 years,
2. A resting phase (catagen), which lasts from 3 to 6 months, in which the hair follicle shrinks and the hair loosens.
3. A hair-shedding phase in which the hair falls out (telogen), usually to be replaced by reactivation of the hair follicle and production of a new hair.

Because each hair has its own life cycle, hairs are continually being lost and replaced. At any one time, 90% of the hairs on your head are in the growth phase, and 10% in the resting phase. On average, you lose between 80 and 100 hairs per day through a process of natural shedding (telogen). These lost hairs are replaced by new hairs growing through. Every hair follicle is programmed to have around 25 cycles of hair growth during its natural life.

During times of stress, however, a strange thing can happen in that, rather than each hair life cycle occurring independently of those around it, all hair life cycles may synchronize so many more than usual enter catagen together. All these synchronized hairs will also enter telogen together, which means that they will all fall out together. This phenomenon is known as telogen effluvium and commonly occurs during times of great physical or emotional stress. This can produce a localized patch of hair loss, or a more diffuse pattern of hair thinning. One of the best known examples is the hair thinning that can occur around three months after the end of a pregnancy.

Tips for overcoming stress-related alopecia

- Try to reduce the amount of stress you are under.
- Massage your scalp with your fingers for 5–10 minutes per day to boost circulation.
- Lift handfuls of hair and use these to gently push and pull your scalp over the underlying bone to help loosen any tense tissues.
- Flower Essences: Take Rescue Remedy drops whenever you feel stressed; massage Rescue Remedy Cream into the bald areas of scalp.
- Homoeopathy: For alopecia linked with the break-up of a relationship: Natrum mur. 30c once a week.
- Herbalism: Massage with Arnica cream or use diluted tincture as a hair rinse; take 20 drops southernwood (*Artemisia abrotanum*) tincture three times a day and use diluted as a hair rinse (avoid in pregnancy).
- Aromatherapy: Massage the bare patch twice a week with essential oils of rosemary and lavender diluted with almond or jojoba oil (do not use aromatherapy if pregnant, or if you have high blood pressure or epilepsy without seeking advice).
- Occasionally alopecia is linked with lack of iron or an underactive thyroid — ask your doctor if you need blood tests to rule out these common conditions.

Increased susceptibility to infections

More than 200 different viruses can cause symptoms of the common cold. Not every infection with a cold virus results in being unwell, however. Researchers have found that high levels of stress double the chance of developing symptoms when exposed to a cold virus. This is most likely when you feel tired and 'run down' and is thought to be due to stress hormones interfering with immune function in some way.

Top tips for boosting your immunity

There are several ways in which you can help to boost your natural immunity when you are under stress:

- Eat a healthy, wholefood and preferably organic diet that provides at least five servings of fruit and vegetables per day (see Chapter 4)

- Eat as much fruit, vegetables and salad-stuff raw as possible to preserve their immune-boosting plant substances (phytochemicals).

- While diet should always come first, a good multinutrient supplement provides a nutritional safety net. Choose one containing around 100% of the recommended daily amount (RDA) of as many vitamins and minerals as possible. Even a relatively minor lack of some nutrients can lower your immunity. Depleted iron stores, for example, have been linked with an increased risk of recurrent candida (thrush) and herpes simplex (cold sore) virus infections, at levels that are not quite low enough to cause anaemia.

- Eat more Brazil nuts — these are the richest dietary source of selenium. Selenium deficiency is common and symptomatic viral infections are more likely in those lacking selenium, as high selenium levels seem to interfere with viral reproduction.

- Try to eat oily fish (for example salmon, mackerel, herring, sardines) at least once or twice a week. These contain essential fatty acids important for good immune function. If you don't like eating fish, consider taking an omega-3 supplement. Evening primrose oil capsules supply important essential fatty acids, too.

- Take vitamin C (at least 1,000 mg daily) with bioflavonoids to help to protect against viral infections, and if symptoms of a cold start to develop, suck throat lozenges containing zinc — these boost the action of white blood cells in the throat and can reduce symptoms of the common cold (see box opposite).

- Take regular exercise — see Chapter 4.

- Take time out to relax — see Chapter 4.

- Get a regular good night's sleep (see pages 70-4).

Herbal supplements

Many herbal remedies are known to boost immunity. Some act as adaptogens, helping the body to cope with the stress when low immunity is due to an underlying problem such as poor or irregular diet, hormone imbalance, stress or excess consumption of coffee, nicotine or alcohol. Results are often greatest when an adaptogen is used together with vitamin C and a vitamin B complex. Popular immune boosters include:

- aloe vera
- ashwagandha
- astragalus
- echinacea
- garlic powder tablets

- gotu kola
- Korean, Chinese, American and Siberian ginsengs
- lapacho
- propolis
- reishi and shiitake mushrooms
- schisandra.

See Chapter 3 for more information.

Treating a cold

If a cold develops, over-the-counter medicines will help to reduce cold symptoms but do not shorten the duration of illness. Nasal congestion can be relieved with decongestant tablets and sprays, while steam inhalation will help to loosen mucus so you can expel it more easily. Added essential oils such as menthol, eucalyptus or pine will also help you breathe more easily. Herbal products containing echinacea (purple coneflower), liquorice and essential oils can also help to relieve the symptoms of a cold gently and naturally, while simple painkillers such as ibuprofen, aspirin or paracetamol will help to relieve aching. Your pharmacist will advise on the range of remedies available and which would suit your symptoms best.

Cold sores

At least 12 million people in the UK are infected with the cold sore virus, Herpes simplex. The virus lies dormant in certain nerve roots and quickly reactivates when you are under stress and feeling run down. As viral particles travel down the nerve, many people notice a characteristic tingling, burning or itching sensation, known as the prodrome. These symptoms last for twelve to twenty-four hours and usually herald the onset of one or more blisters around the lips, nostrils or genitals. The blisters

VITAMIN C

Vitamin C is one of the most popular supplements for boosting immunity and relieving symptoms of the common cold. Taken at a dose of 1,000–6,000 mg per day it can reduce the duration of a cold by at least a day, and due to its anti-inflammatory effects also minimizes symptoms and hastens healing. For some groups of people – especially male students under stress, and those doing heavy physical exercise – regular vitamin C has also been shown to reduce the risk of catching a respiratory infection in the first place by as much as 30%.

Unfortunately, some people find vitamin C supplements give them indigestion since standard vitamin C is an acid known as ascorbic acid. Scientists have found a clever way round this problem in the form of ester-C. This super vitamin C contains the active break-down products that the body normally produces when metabolizing vitamin C. Ester C has a neutral pH (7.0, the same as distilled water), and as it is non-acidic cannot trigger indigestion. Ester C also has other advantages in that it is absorbed into the bloodstream more quickly than normal vitamin C and also stays in the body for longer. Ester-C is an ideal supplement for people under stress who may already have a tendency towards acid indigestion. It is now included in several mainstream brands of multinutrient supplement – just check the labels to find it.

develop quickly as viral particles spread from one cell to another, hijacking the cell's nucleus to make more virus and killing the cells in the process. The blister then bursts to form a shallow ulcer, which is particularly painful as underlying nerve endings are exposed. Eventually, the ulcers crust and scab over to heal after ten to fourteen days. Cold sores are highly infectious from the time they first appear until they are fully healed.

A variety of treatments are available over the counter, which contain soothing balms, local anaesthetic or antiseptics. Products containing natural extracts of melissa (lemon balm) or the antiviral drug, aciclovir may also help the cold sore heal more quickly. According to some herbalists, taking echinacea can prevent or shorten an outbreak and help to keep recurrences at bay. Take 25 drops tincture of echinacea in water every 2 hours for 4 doses, then take it 4 times a day while symptoms are present.

By lowering your stress hormones, you can reduce the number of cold sore recurrences you experience.

Tension headache and migraine

Headaches are one of the commonest symptoms of stress since blood-flow to the brain is affected by tension in the neck and scalp muscles, as well as by high levels of stress-related chemicals such as adrenaline.

Many people are unsure whether their stress-related symptoms are tension headaches or migraine. A tension headache tends to feel like a severe, continuous pressure on both sides of the head which may seem to centre over the top of the skull, over the back of the head or above both eyes. Some tension headaches feel like a tight, constricting band, while others are more like a non-specific ache. In contrast, migraine pain is severe and so much worse than a tension headache that it is usually described as a full-blown attack. The pain is usually only felt on one side of the head or is definitely worse on one side. There are two main types:

- Migraine without aura — or common migraine — consists of a severe, throbbing, pulsating or hammering headache on one side, usually with abdominal symptoms. These include loss of appetite, nausea, vomiting, dislike of food, constipation or diarrhoea. Nine out of ten sufferers experience this form of migraine.

- Migraine with aura — or classic migraine — includes visual disturbances as well as any or all of the symptoms of common migraine. Vision can be distorted with shimmering or flashing lights, strange zigzag shapes or blind spots. One in ten sufferers get this form of migraine. Migraine without aura is often misdiagnosed as a tension headache. If you think your recurrent headache may be migraine, it is important to tell your doctor.

ALTERNATIVE REMEDIES THAT CAN HELP MIGRAINE AND TENSION HEADACHES

Massage: gentle manipulation of muscles in the neck, shoulders and back can help to relax taut muscles and relieve tension headache.

Acupuncture: stimulation of acupoints on the stomach and large and small meridians plus use of moxibustion is often effective.

Homoeopathy: It is best to consult a practitioner for an individual diagnosis and treatment tailored to you. The following treatments are often used at a dose of 10c every ten minutes for up to ten doses:

- for blinding, throbbing or burning headache: Nat mur or Nux vomica
- for right-sided headache: Sanguinaria
- for left-sided headache: Spigelia or Ipecac

- for tension headache that comes on suddenly and feels like a tight band: Aconite
- for tension headache that brought on by emotional stress – a sharp severe pain in the side of the head accompanies the tight band sensation: Ignatia
- for a tension headache that feels bursting and crushing, with sharp pain brought on by the slightest eye movement: Bryonia
- for tension headache with muscular spasm and stiffness in the neck: Cimic

Aromatherapy: Essential oils that can help a tension headache (do not use during pregnancy) include: camomile, geranium, lavender, peppermint and rosemary (rosemary should not be used if you have high blood pressure).

Both migraine and tension headaches can be brought on by stress-related factors such as feelings of excess pressure, relief of stress (for example, at the end of a long, trying week), physical fatigue, lack of sleep, missed meals and extreme emotions such as anger and excitement. Migraine can also be triggered by certain foods — especially cheese, red wine and chocolate — and by hormonal changes, for example those that occur around the time of menstruation or that are associated with the oral contraceptive pill.

Tips to help avoid stress-related headaches

- Try to work out what factors trigger your attacks and, where possible, avoid them.
- Look out for signs of tension in the way you sit and stand. Try not to stoop when standing or sitting, and concentrate on keeping your back straight, your shoulders square and your abdomen lightly pulled in. This will help to reduce feelings of stress by helping you breathe correctly using your diaphragm and abdominal muscles.
- Avoid folding your arms tightly — let your upper arms hang loosely from your shoulders, and widen the angle at your elbows. Shake your arms and hands regularly to help release any tension.
- Avoid hunching your shoulders. Hold your shoulders straight yet relaxed, and circle them from time to time to relieve any built up tension.
- Avoid clenching your fists. Hold your hands loose with your palms open and your fingers curled lightly and naturally.
- Avoid clenching or grinding your teeth. Keep your mouth slightly open and try to relax your upper and lower jaws — every now and then open your mouth wide and move your jaw from side to side to check the muscles aren't clenched.

TMJ Syndrome

Stress is a common cause of TMJ syndrome, which affects the temporomandibular joint (TMJ) between the jawbone and skull. The TMJ is a modified hinge joint oiled with synovial fluid that helps to keep it moving smoothly. The joint is unusual in that it contains a disc of cartilage that provides a smooth internal articular surface and increases the range of movement of the jaw, so that as well as opening and closing it can also glide from side to side and protrude forwards and backwards during chewing and grinding.

TMJ syndrome is often linked with excess tension and spasm in the chewing muscles in people who are stressed, or who subconsciously clench their teeth when feeling under excess pressure. Some people also grind their teeth in their sleep — an activity known as bruxism. TMJ syndrome can also be caused by the habit of holding a telephone receiver between your shoulder and cheek, and by an incorrect tooth alignment.

TMJ syndrome is associated with a range of symptoms that may not all occur in everyone:

- headache
- tender jaw muscles
- dull, aching pain around the face, TMJ or ear
- difficulty in opening the mouth
- locking of the jaw
- clicking as the jaw is opened or closed (this is quite common and when it occurs alone does not necessarily mean you have TMJ syndrome).

Tips for overcoming TMJ syndrome

- Consult a dentist, who will check your bite, your muscles and your jaw's range of movement.
- Avoid stress as much as possible.
- Rest the joint, apply warmth and follow a soft diet to help reduce spasm of chewing muscles.
- Devices to prevent clenching or grinding the teeth at night are available — ask your dentist for advice.

Insomnia

Stress is the commonest cause of lack of sleep, and in turn, lack of sleep is a common cause of stress. Once you develop insomnia, stress and lack of sleep can keep feeding on each other to make each condition worse.

Sleep is a form of unconsciousness that is our natural state of rest. It is the strongest instinctive urge in humans, yet scientists still do not fully understand how or why we sleep. They do know it is essential for our continued physical and emotional well-being, however. We are designed to spend around a third of our life asleep, yet four out of ten people do not get a regular good night's rest. As a result, they wake up feeling tired, make more mistakes during the day, and may repeatedly fall asleep for several seconds at a time. These so-called microsleeps are a common cause of accidents, both on the roads and in the home.

Most people have suffered from insomnia at some stage of their life – usually when they are worried or stressed. Stress can cause difficulty in falling asleep, tossing and turning without finding a comfortable position, difficulty staying asleep, and waking up feeling unrefreshed. Recurrent lack of sleep leads to poor performance and achievement during the day. It is also linked with increased risk of serious stress-related illness such as high blood pressure, stroke and even a heart attack.

Stress-related insomnia may be:

- transient – lasting only a few days, for example as a result of jet lag
- short-term – lasting 1–3 months, for example as a result of bereavement
- long-term – lasting over 3 months, for example as a result of anxiety, depression, illness or alcohol abuse.

Even if you do not usually have

SLEEP

There are two main types of sleep:

- rapid-eye-movement (REM) sleep, in which the eyes are constantly on the move
- slow-wave (or non-REM) sleep, in which the eyes are relatively still.

There are four stages of slow-wave sleep, Stage 1 being the lightest. On first falling asleep, you rapidly pass through Stages 1 and 2, then spend 70–100 minutes in Stages 3 and 4 before sleep lightens and a period of around 10 minutes REM follows. This cycle repeats four to six times throughout the night, but as morning approaches more and more time – up to one hour – is spent in REM sleep.

Interestingly, people who only sleep five hours per night get a similar amount of slow-wave sleep as those who regularly sleep eight hours per night – additional time spent sleeping is spent in REM sleep, which is when dreaming occurs.

The average time a young adult spends in each stage of sleep per night:

- Stage 1 (light sleep): 5% of the night
- Stage 2: 50% of the night
- Stage 3: 5% of the night
- Stage 4 (deep sleep): 15% of the night
- REM: 25% of the night.

problems sleeping, you may find sleep difficult if your bed partner is under stress and tosses and turns all night. This may disturb your sleep, as can recurrent snoring – either in yourself or your partner.

Caffeine, stress and sleep

Caffeine – found in tea, coffee, chocolate, soft drinks such as colas, and some over-the-counter analgesic blends – is a stimulant drug whose immediate effect is to reduce tiredness and make the body feel alert. Coffee is often consumed in large amounts (eight to ten cups a day, for example) when you are under pressure, and this can make symptoms of stress even worse. Caffeine mimics the effects of adrenaline causing nervous tension, irritability and insomnia. As it is also a stimulant, it interferes with sleeping even more.

High intakes of caffeine may cause withdrawal symptoms such as irritability, cravings and increased stress when you try to reduce them. If you think you are drinking too much coffee, reduce your intake by switching to decaffeinated brands. If stopping caffeine suddenly seems to be making you jittery, gradually reduce your intake by replacing every other cup with a decaffeinated brand then slowly reducing your intake further. Cut back slowly, perhaps by increasing the amount of non-caffeinated coffee you drink, or by switching to tea, which has less caffeine.

Natural sleep remedies

Sleeping tablets are not a good idea at the best of times, and when you are stressed and vulnerable, it is even more easy to become dependent on them. It is also worth avoiding over-the-counter sleep medications containing antihistamines. These have been shown in sleep laboratories to give a poor night's sleep with an abnormal sleep architecture, leaving you more drowsy the next day. Fortunately, a number of alternative remedies can help diffuse away feelings of stress and encourage a natural and restorative sleep.

Acupuncture

Acupuncture frees blockages in the flow of energy (*chi*) and stimulates the release of natural, heroin-like chemicals in the brain that help you relax. It is excellent for relieving insomnia linked with stress. Acupressure or shiatsu is similar, but stimulates acupoints with firm thumb pressure or fingertip massage.

INSOMNIA

Do you have difficulty:

- Falling asleep?
- Staying asleep?
- Getting back to sleep after waking?
- Feeling refreshed?
- Waking early?

NB Early-morning waking is one of the biological signs of a depressive illness. This is linked with an imbalance of chemicals in the brain and usually needs treatment with anti-depressants. If you feel low in yourself, have difficulty getting to sleep, wake early – classically between 2 and 4 a.m. and find it difficult to get back to sleep, it is important to tell your doctor.

Is your insomnia linked with:

- Anxiety and depression?
- Personal stress?
- Shift work?
- Bereavement?
- Relationship problems?
- Looking after young children?
- Financial worries?
- Illness?
- Premenstrual or menopausal symptoms?

Herbalism

Supplements containing natural extracts of three herbs: valerian (*Valeriana officinalis*) lemon balm (*Melissa officinalis*) and hops (*Humulus lupulus*) can induce a refreshing night's sleep without the side effects associated with drugs.

- Valerian is one of the most relaxing herbs available and is commonly used as a sedative to relieve stress, anxiety and tension.
- Lemon balm has been used since ancient times as a healing, soothing herb with calming properties. It is widely used to help people suffering from insomnia.
- Hops have a powerful relaxant effect, easing tension and anxiety, and overcoming insomnia.

Herbal treatments are so effective that they can cause mild drowsiness, so do not take if you need to drive or operate machinery. Avoid if you are pregnant or breastfeeding.

Soothing herbal teas can also help you sleep. Try infusions of limeflower, lemon balm, fennel, rosehips, passionflower, nutmeg, cinnamon, camomile, valerian or skullcap. It is also worth investing in a herbal pillow filled with dried lavender flowers to place at the head of your bed.

Homoeopathy

Take a 30c strength tablet of one of the following remedies half an hour before going to bed and repeat every thirty minutes if necessary. Use for ten nights then stop and see if your normal sleep pattern has returned.

- if you are wide awake with an overactive mind and can't relax: Coffea
- for sleeplessness leaving you irritable and unrefreshed: Nux vomica

TWELVE TIPS TO HELP YOU WAKE UP FEELING BETTER

1. Avoid napping during the day as this will make it more difficult to sleep at night.

2. Take regular exercise, as active people tend to sleep more easily.

3. Avoid strenuous exercise late in the evening – a gentle stroll round the block is fine.

4. Eat a healthy, low-fat, wholefood diet with plenty of complex carbohydrates (for example, cereals, bread, pasta), and fruit and vegetables for vitamins and minerals.

5. Try to eat your evening meal before 7 p.m. and resist late-night snacks, especially of rich food.

6. Avoid over-indulgence in substances that interfere with sleep such as caffeine (coffee, tea, chocolate, colas), nicotine and alcohol – although alcohol may help you fall asleep initially, you are likely to have a disturbed sleep once the drugged effect has worn off.

7. Take time to unwind from the stresses of the day before going to bed – read a book, listen to soothing music or have a candlelit bath.

8. A warm, milky drink just before going to bed will help you to relax – hot milk with cinnamon or nutmeg is better than chocolate drinks that contain some caffeine. Don't drink too much fluid in the evening, however – a full bladder is guaranteed to disturb your rest.

9. Get into the habit of going to bed at a regular time each night and getting up at the same time each morning. Set a bedtime routine such as checking house security, brushing your teeth, bathing and setting the alarm clock to set the mood for sleep.

10. Make sure your bed is comfortable, and your bedroom warm, dark and quiet – noise and excessive cold or heat will keep you awake. A temperature of 18–24°C is ideal.

11. If you can't sleep, don't lie there tossing and turning. Get up and read or watch the television for a while. If you are worried about something, write down all the things on your mind and promise yourself you will deal with them in the morning, when you are feeling fresher. When you feel sleepy, go back to bed and try again.

12. Preserve your bedroom as a place for sleep (and sex) – don't use it for eating, working or watching television.

- if you are overtired physically and mentally and can't get comfortable: Arnica

- if kept awake by fear, shock or panic: Aconitum

- if you can't sleep and fear you will never do so again: Ignatia

- for nightmares that wake you: Phosphorus.

Bach Flower Remedies

Bach Flower Remedies are homoeopathic-like infusions of flower essences in brandy. Thirty-eight different essences can treat most negative emotions that lead to difficulty in sleeping. A practitioner will select the one most suited to your state of mind, for example:

- for vague fears and anxieties of unknown origin: aspen

- for feelings of not being able to face the day: hornbeam

- for total physical or mental exhaustion: olive

- for persistent, unwanted thoughts and preoccupation with worry: white chestnut

- for those who blame themselves for the misfortunes of others: pine

- for those who are overly strict with themselves: rock water.

Aromatherapy

Aromatherapy can improve sleep problems dramatically (only use under specialist advice during pregnancy). Add 5 drops of essential oil to 10 ml (two teaspoons) almond oil and pour into a deep, warm — not hot — bath. Relax in the fragrant water for 15–20 minutes, then sprinkle a few drops of the same essential oil on a cottonwool pad and tuck under your pillow. Choose your favourite fragrance from:

- camomile
- geranium
- juniper
- lavender
- neroli
- rose
- sandalwood
- ylang-ylang.

Mix several oils together in blends if you prefer. Vary the oils every four to five days, otherwise you will adapt to them and treatment will be less effective.

Chiropractic

Chiropractors manipulate the spine with rapid, direct thrusts to correct poor alignment. If sleep is difficult because of tension in your neck, or shoulder or back pain, a chiropractor can manipulate your back to realign muscles, tendons, ligaments, joints and bones to ease tension and help you to relax.

Hypnotherapy

A hypnotherapist will help to uncover subconscious fears and anxieties that are causing stress, then use suggestion to help you relax, lose your fears and sleep more easily. Suggestions can be taped and replayed when you go to bed.

Massage

There are many different types of massage that use a variety of rubbing, drumming, kneading, friction and pressure strokes. All are very relaxing. Therapeutic massage is particularly useful in helping sleep problems due to stress and muscle tension, especially when combined with aromatherapy essential oils.

Meditation

Meditation is a self-help technique in which the power of concentration is used to control thoughts, and calm the body. During meditation you learn to enter a trance-like state which tunes you into your body — some people can lower their pulse and blood pressure at will. Muscular tension drops, blood circulation improves and brain-wave patterns change. Meditation often leads to sleep.

Reflexology

Massage and tiny pressure movements over reflexes on the feet before bedtime will help you sleep — ask your partner to learn the technique!

Yoga

Yoga is excellent for improving joint suppleness, relieving stress and helping sleep.

Eczema

Eczema is an inflammatory skin disease that commonly appears on the hands, inside the elbows or behind the knees but may be found anywhere on the body. Around one in ten people are affected, and most find that symptoms flare up whenever they are under stress although the cause of worry may not always be obvious, especially in children. Eczema tends to run in families and can also be triggered by allergies, exposure to certain chemicals, and overgrowth of certain skin bacteria.

Eczema seems to be due to overactivity of immune cells in the skin. Scientists have recently discovered that when you are under stress, a chemical (calcitonin gene related peptide) released from nerve endings in the skin affects the activity of immune cells and makes eczema symptoms worse. So, while it isn't exactly caused by stress, pressure can bring symptoms on or make them worse. Eczema symptoms can also be a cause of stress themselves. Itching, for example, is often severe enough to keep sufferers awake at night, leading to exhaustion and worsening feelings of stress. Visible lesions on the skin can also cause emotional distress with anxiety, feelings of embarrassment and shame, lack of confidence and low mood.

The symptoms of eczema vary from mild to severe and can include:

- dry, scaly, thickened skin
- redness
- itching with excoriation
- blisters
- weeping sores which may become infected
- crusting
- flaky scalp.

Other alternative treatments to help treat eczema

Aromatherapy

Add four drops each of camomile, geranium and lavender essential oils to 50 ml carrier oil (for example, almond) and apply to affected area twice a day. (NB do not use during pregnancy except under specialist advice.)

Herbalism

Eczema brought on by stress can be helped by taking herbs such as echinacea, nettles, yarrow, skullcap, vervain and wild oats. Consult a practitioner for individually tailored treatment.

Homoeopathy

Take the remedy four times a day for up to two weeks.

- for dry eczema : Sulphur 6c
- for moist eczema with cracked skin: Petroleum 6c
- for moist eczema with a honey-like discharge: Graphites 6c.

Dead Sea salts

Dead Sea salts contain minerals such as magnesium chloride, potassium chloride, sodium chloride, calcium chloride, bromides and sulphates that can help a number of scaly skin problems such as eczema. Add to bath water and soak for at least twenty minutes to help you relax. Dead Sea mud packs can also be applied to skin for a more intensive treatment.

TIPS TO HELP RELIEVE STRESS-RELATED DRY SKIN

- Avoid excess stress.
- Take evening primrose oil supplements (1,000–3,000 mg daily).
- Eat more foods rich in essential fatty acids such as nuts, seeds and oily fish.
- Dilute a total of 12 drops aromatherapy essential oils (selected from fennel, camomile, geranium, sandalwood, hyssop, juniper or lavender) to 50 ml carrier oil and apply to affected area twice a day (avoid during pregnancy).
- Relieve eczema symptoms with marigold tea. Make an infusion by adding 30 g marigold flowers or petals to 600 ml boiling water. Drain after 5–10 minutes and drink throughout the day. May also be used to bathe skin lesions.
- Take a good vitamin and mineral supplement containing around 100% of the recommended daily amount of the following nutrients – lack of which have been linked with scaly skin problems: vitamins A, B2, B3, C, E, biotin, iodine, manganese, selenium and zinc.
- Use an emollient cream (for example, aqueous cream, emulsifying ointment, dry skin cream containing evening primrose oil) to moisturize skin.
- Use aqueous cream instead of soap: substitute by simply applying to the skin, massaging in lightly then rinsing off.
- Use a bath emollients to soothe, hydrate and soften the skin.
- For flaky scalp, wash hair regularly with a shampoo containing tea tree oil.

Psoriasis

Psoriasis is a skin condition in which skin cells are produced ten times faster than normal. New skin cells push to the surface in around seven days rather than the more usual twenty-eight. This causes a build-up of cells to produce silver-white thickened plaques with an underlying redness due to dilated blood vessels.

Psoriasis affects around one in fifty adults. It tends to run in families with skin lesions commonly appearing on the knees, elbows and scalp. Between 10 and 20% of people with psoriasis also develop a form of arthritis known as psoriatic arthropathy.

The exact cause of psoriasis is unknown, but flare-ups are closely related to stress. Many sufferers find their symptoms flare up when they are under stress, for example taking examinations, following bereavement, serious marital or financial problems or the shock of illness/accidents. It is also common for psoriasis to occur for the first time after a stressful situation, including infections, trauma and childbirth. Symptoms can also be made worse by smoking, drinking excess alcohol and, in some cases, by exposure to sunlight and cold weather.

Tips to help improve psoriasis

- Avoid stress as much as possible.
- Take evening primrose oil supplements (1,000–3,000 mg daily).
- Eat more foods rich in essential fatty acids such as nuts, seeds and oily fish.
- When applying topical therapy to the body, sit with the skin uncovered for at least fifteen minutes, then put on loose clothing so the preparation is not rubbed off. When waiting for medication applied to the skin to soak in, practise breathing exercises and other relaxation techniques (see pages 152-7).
- If the area needs washing (for example, hands, elbows, feet), give a topical agent enough time to penetrate (at least fifteen minutes) and use this time to

PSORIASIS SYMPTOMS

These vary from person to person but can include:

- bright red, scaly patches that may contain silver-white scales – plaques vary in size from a few millimeters to extensive, confluent plaques covering the body
- redness (erythema) due to dilated, tortuous blood vessels beneath the scales
- pustules (usually localized to the palms and soles) due to sterile collections of white blood cells
- thickening and pitting of the nails
- flaky scalp
- joint pains (psoriatic arthropathy)

Not surprisingly, visible skin lesions can cause extreme distress, with sufferers commonly feeling anxious, ashamed, embarrassed, lacking in confidence or depressed. Having to use messy, strong-smelling creams is also stressful for many people. Perseverance with medications is important to help symptoms resolve, however.

practise positive self-affirmations (see page 203).

- When applying treatment to the scalp, apply thoroughly at least an hour before going to bed so the medication doesn't rub off on to the pillow before having time to work; wearing a disposable shower cap for at least an hour helps treatment penetration. While waiting for treatment to soak in, practise a visualization technique (see page 193) in which you imagine your skin lesions melting away.

- Use an emollient cream (for example, aqueous cream, emulsifying ointment, dry skin cream containing evening primrose oil) to moisturize your skin.

- Use aqueous cream instead of soap: substitute by simply applying to the skin, massaging in lightly, then rinsing off.

- Use a bath emollient to soothe, hydrate and soften the skin.

ALTERNATIVE TREATMENTS THAT CAN HELP PSORIASIS

Dead Sea salts: The minerals found in Dead Sea mud, especially magnesium, calcium, bromide, selenium and zinc, slow the excessive production of skin cells in people with psoriasis. This can be highly effective, with complete clearance of skin in over half of people visiting the Dead Sea area. Home treatment using Dead Sea products is also helpful, but less effective without the unique UVA spectrum (320–400 nm) found in the Dead Sea area.

Herbalism: Aloe vera gel or cream can improve psoriasis lesions by over 80%.

Chinese Medicine: *Bian zheng shi zhi* herbal blend individually prescribed by a practitioner and drunk as a boiled infusion can significantly improve symptoms in over half of sufferers.

Homoeopathy: Individually prescribed remedies can be used as creams, tinctures or tablets. Found to be helpful in 37% of patients with psoriasis

Fish oils: in liquid or capsule form fish oil supplements seem to help in 15–50% of people with psoriasis.

Indigestion and heartburn

People under stress have increased activity in the nerve endings supplying the stomach. This can lead to increased secretion of acidic juices and churning sensations (butterflies) due to increased muscular contraction of the stomach. This is linked with symptoms of heartburn (acid reflux from the stomach up into the oesophagus) and peptic ulcers in the stomach or duodenum.

Indigestion and heartburn are common and unpleasant symptoms linked with eating and are especially common when you are under excessive stress. Symptoms include feelings of distension from swallowing air, flatulence from excessive wind in the intestines, nausea, abdominal pain and sensations of burning. Indigestion (or dyspepsia) is the term used to describe discomfort or burning felt centrally in the upper abdomen, while heartburn is the term used for discomfort felt behind the chest bone (sternum).

One of the commonest causes of heartburn is acid reflux, in which stomach contents reflux up into the oesophagus — the tube connecting the mouth and stomach. Normally this is prevented by a muscle sphincter, and by downward contractions of muscles in the gut wall. This protective mechanism may fail due to poor muscle coordination, weakness of the stomach sphincter, the presence of a hiatus hernia, or increased pressure on the stomach, for example due to excess weight or overeating.

Acid reflux causes a hot, burning sensation in the chest that may rise up into the throat. It usually comes on within thirty minutes of eating a meal and may be triggered by eating too much, taking exercise, bending or lying down. Meals containing fat, pastry, chocolate, acidic fruit juices, pickles, coffee or alcohol are the commonest culprits.

Quick tips to help prevent indigestion and heartburn

- Eat little and often throughout the day, rather than having three large meals.
- Drink fluids little and often, rather than large quantities at a time.
- Avoid hot, acid, spicy, fatty foods.
- Avoid tea, coffee and acidic fruit juices.
- Cut back on alcohol intake.
- Avoid aspirin and related drugs (for example, ibuprofen) if you are prone to indigestion — take paracetamol if necessary instead.
- Avoid stooping, bending or lying down after eating.
- Avoid late-night eating.
- Elevate the head of the bed about 15–20 cm (for example, put books under the legs at that end).
- Wear loose clothing, especially around the waist.
- Drink milk or take an antacid to help ease burning sensations.

Longer-term measures to help control your symptoms include losing any excess weight and not smoking cigarettes.

Irritable bowel syndrome

Irritable bowel syndrome (IBS) and stress are closely linked. Stress is not a recognized cause of IBS but it does make symptoms worse, and can bring on an attack in those who already suffer from the condition. IBS may therefore be a sign of excess stress in those who are affected.

During the body's fight-or-flight stress response, several powerful chemicals are released that affect the bowel. These include adrenaline, neuropeptide Y and somatostatin, which trigger bowel contraction. These effects stem from the need to rapidly empty the bowel to make you lighter for action. In people without IBS, these normal responses do not seem to trigger any unpleasant symptoms except for the expected diarrhoea. In those with IBS, however, the response seems to be accentuated and prolonged.

Irritable bowel syndrome is the most common condition to affect the gut and affects at least a third of the population at some time during their life, even if only mildly. IBS is a problem of bowel function rather than structure, and as a result there is nothing abnormal to find during investigations and no obvious clues to help with the diagnosis. Many sufferers find that their symptoms improve with time and disappear in later life.

Coping with irritable bowel syndrome

- Take regular exercise — as well as burning off stress hormones, this stimulates production of the body's own natural painkillers as well as relieving bloating and distension.
- Make a point of sitting down to eat rather than eating on the move.
- Don't rush meals — leave plenty of time to eat so you don't bolt down your food and swallow too much air.
- Try to eat little and often during the day rather than the traditional three large meals.
- Cut out all pre-packaged or processed foods and stick to a natural, wholefood diet which is as organic as possible.
- Eat more complex, unrefined carbohydrates that contain a variety of fibre types such as wholegrain bread, wholemeal pasta, brown rice and unsweetened wholegrain

COULD YOU HAVE IBS?

In order to diagnose irritable bowel syndrome, there must be:

At least three months' continuous or recurrent symptoms of abdominal pain or discomfort which is:

- relieved by defaecation
- and/or associated with a change in frequency of stool
- and/or associated with a change in consistency of stool.

Plus two or more of the following, on at least a quarter of occasions or days:

- altered stool frequency (usually taken to mean more than three bowel movements per day, or less than three bowel movements per week; different people, however, have their own individual sense of what is normal for them, and against which changes in bowel habit are measured)
- altered stool form (lumpy/hard or loose/watery)
- altered stool passage (straining, urgency, or feeling of incomplete evacuation)
- passage of mucus
- bloating or feeling of abdominal distension.

NB Never diagnose IBS yourself as its symptoms closely resemble those seen in other, more serious bowel conditions.

breakfast cereals such as muesli or porridge.

- Eat more fresh fruit and vegetables — especially nuts, seeds, figs, apricots, prunes, peas, sweetcorn and beans.
- Eat live bio yoghurt (containing a culture of *Lactobacillus acidophilus*), drink liquid yogurt containing *Lactobacillus casei* 'Shirota' (Yakult) or take acidophilus supplements to line your bowel with friendly bacteria.
- Bran fibre helps some people with IBS but not others — regularly alternate different fibre supplements such as bran, ispaghula, psyllium or sterculia as bowel bacteria quickly adapt to them and the beneficial effects may be lost.
- Cut back on your intake of red meat and eat more fish and skinless white meat instead.
- If wind is a problem, avoid beans, cabbage and any other foods which encourage bacterial fermentation and may trigger intestinal gas.
- Many natural herbs and spices contain substances that calm the bowels, relieve spasm and prevent a build up of wind. These include aniseed, camomile, lemon balm, dill, fennel, black pepper, marjoram, parsley, peppermint, rosemary and spearmint. Use them as a garnish on food or as soothing, herbal teas.
- Drink more fluids — especially bottled water or herbal teas. Aim to drink two to three litres of fluid throughout the day.

Alternative treatments that can help IBS

Acupuncture

This stimulates the release of natural painkillers that can help to reduce the symptoms of irritable bowel syndrome, including constipation, diarrhoea and cramping pains.

Aromatherapy massage

Abdominal massage can help constipation, wind and distension, as well as relieving pain associated with diarrhoea. Dilute a total of 10–20 drops of rosemary and/or marjoram essential oils in a carrier such as almond oil. Gently massage into your abdomen using firm, circular movements of one hand. NB substitute rose oil for rosemary oil if you have high blood pressure; do not use during pregnancy.

Herbalism

Take ginger to reduce flatulence, nausea, and colic. Peppermint or camomile tea can relieve mild intestinal cramps or flatulence. Garlic-powder tablets are helpful for diarrhoea, wind and indigestion. Aloe vera juice can relieve indigestion and constipation. Goldenseal helps to normalize bowel function, so is helpful for both constipation and diarrhoea. Ginseng is an adaptogen that can help you adapt to stress so symptoms become less troublesome.

Homoeopathy

Take one of the following every half hour for up to 10 doses:

- for constipation with spasm and strong urges to open the bowels: Nux vomica 6c
- for diarrhoea with flatulence or burning: Aloe 6c
- for diarrhoea with anxiety and stress: Argentum nit. 6c
- for simple diarrhoea associated with IBS especially if symptoms are brought on by drinking coffee: Psorinum 6c
- for bloating and distension, especially after eating or when constipated: Lycopodium 6c.

Hypnotherapy

This can significantly reduce abdominal pain and distension, encourage a regular bowel, and improve general well-being.

Reflexology

This is helpful for some people with IBS.

Visualization

When you feel an attack of pain coming on, try to visualize yourself relaxing, pain-free, swimming in a warm tropical ocean next to a sandy, deserted beach.

High blood pressure

High blood pressure is common and affects as many as one in five adults. The incidence increases with age, so it becomes more common in middle life and beyond, although it can develop earlier. High blood pressure is now thought to be linked with excessive levels of stress in some people. When you are under excess stress, your blood pressure goes up by an amount equivalent to carrying an extra forty pounds in weight, or an additional twenty years in age. Stress is intended to only produce a transient rise in blood pressure when adrenaline causes arteries and veins to constrict. In some individuals, however, the nervous system is over-active and is unusually responsive to levels of stress that would normally be associated with only a mild, temporary rise in blood pressure. This is probably an inherited trait. In people who are sensitive to the effects of stress, their blood pressure may show a tendency towards becoming high by varying considerably from time to time so it is sometimes high, sometimes low and other times normal. This is known as Gaisbock's syndrome and is a sign that if your lifestyle and levels of stress don't slow down, you may develop permanent high blood pressure

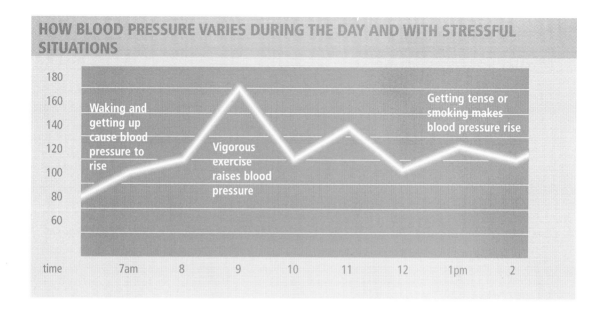

HOW BLOOD PRESSURE VARIES DURING THE DAY AND WITH STRESSFUL SITUATIONS

Waking and getting up cause blood pressure to rise

Vigorous exercise raises blood pressure

Getting tense or smoking makes blood pressure rise

time   7am   8   9   10   11   12   1pm   2

(hypertension) in the future. One of the commonest signs of this is so-called 'white coat hypertension' – blood pressure that shoots up on being measured in a stressful situation such as the doctor's surgery or hospital (often by someone wearing a white coat or uniform). If this happens to you, it can help to buy an automatic wrist blood pressure cuff so you can monitor your own blood pressure at home in less stressful surroundings.

If your blood pressure temporarily goes very high during a stressful situation, you will not usually notice any symptoms, although a few people develop a

ALTERNATIVE THERAPIES TO HELP HIGH BLOOD PRESSURE

Aromatherapy: Essential oils that can help lower high blood pressure (do not use during pregnancy) include: clary sage, geranium, lavender, lemon, marjoram, melissa and nutmeg.

Herbalism: Dandelion is a diuretic used to help flush excess salts and fluid through the kidneys. It is a useful treatment for high blood pressure as it can reduce fluid retention without also encouraging a build up of sodium. Garlic-powder tablets can lower high blood pressure, high cholesterol levels and blood stickiness enough to reduce the risk of a stroke by almost a half, and the risk of a coronary heart disease by a quarter.

Lemon balm is a healing herb with calming properties. It is widely used to combat the effects of nervous stress, to improve heart function and reduce high blood pressure.

Meditation

Floatation therapy

Yoga is excellent for improving joint suppleness, relieving stress and reducing high blood pressure.

pounding sensation in their ears or a tension headache. If your blood pressure stays high all the time and remains untreated, however, it will damage your circulation and contribute to hardening and furring up of the arteries. This in turn increases your blood pressure even more so your risk of a heart attack or stroke

SALT SENSITIVITY, BLOOD PRESSURE AND STRESS

As many as one in two people are now thought to be sensitive to salt, so that it increases their risk of high blood pressure. This sensitivity will magnify the harmful effects of stress and increase your risk of future coronary heart disease. It is therefore worth cutting back on salt intake. Ideally, you should take no more than 4–6 g salt per day. This is equivalent to 2–2.5 g sodium or about one teaspoonful of table salt (sodium chloride). Most people take much more than this in their diet. Just reducing salt intake from 9 g to 6 g is estimated to lower your risk of a stroke by 22% and your risk of death from coronary heart disease by 16%. Unfortunately, three quarters of dietary salt is 'hidden' in processed foods such as canned products, ready-prepared meals, biscuits, cakes and breakfast cereals.

Cut back on salt intake by not adding salt during cooking or at the table, and by avoiding:

- obviously salty foods such as crisps, bacon, salted nuts
- tinned products canned in brine
- cured, smoked or pickled fish/meats
- meat pastes, pâtés
- ready prepared meals
- packet soups and sauces
- stock cubes and yeast extracts.

Salt is easily replaced with herbs, spices, lemon or lime juice: it doesn't take long to retrain your taste buds.

increases. Persistent hypertension also damages small arteries in the circulation and can lead to changes in the eyes and kidneys. Even if your blood pressure is dangerously high, you may feel relatively well. Because of this, it's worth having your blood pressure checked on a regular basis. Early diagnosis and successful treatment of high blood pressure will help to keep you healthy.

Tips to help reduce your risk of high blood pressure

- Lose any excess weight – shedding as little as 3–4 kg in weight can be enough to bring a moderately raised blood pressure down to normal levels again.
- If you smoke, make a concerted effort to stop – chemicals in cigarettes damage artery linings, cause spasm and constriction of vessels, and raise your blood pressure.
- Reduce your overall consumption of fat so that it makes up no more than 30% of your daily energy intake – with saturated fat ideally making up no more than 15% of daily calories. Eat more of the healthy fats such as olive, walnut, rapeseed and fish oils instead, which help to keep the circulation healthy.
- Eat plenty of fresh fruit and vegetables for protective vitamins, minerals and fibre.
- Keep alcohol intake within recommended limits.
- Increase the amount of exercise you take.
- If you are diabetic, make sure your blood sugar levels are well controlled.
- Consider taking an antioxidant supplement which may protect against hardening and furring up of the arteries. The most important dietary antioxidants are vitamins A/betacarotene, C, E and selenium.

Chest pain

Severe stress can lead to chest pain which may be due to spasm of muscles in the chest wall or, more seriously, to spasm of the coronary arteries supplying blood and oxygen to the heart. This triggers heart muscle pain (angina) which is usually

- felt behind the chest bone
- described as tight and crushing – like a bear hug
- described as spreading through the chest and may radiate up into the neck, jaw or down the left arm.

Angina may also be brought on by exertion and relieved by rest if circulation to the heart is impaired by hardening and furring up of the arteries. If heart muscles cells die due to prolonged oxygen starvation, a heart attack occurs. Heart attack pain is similar to angina but:

- lasts longer
- is more intense
- is usually accompanied by sweating, paleness and breathlessness
- can come on at any time and is unrelieved by rest.

Sudden chest pain should always be taken seriously and medical assistance sought without delay.

The number of deaths attributed to coronary heart disease is slowly falling, however, as more and more people take stock of their life, reduce their stress levels, lose excess weight, take more exercise, stop smoking and follow a healthier diet.

HOW DIET AND LIFESTYLE CHANGES CAN REDUCE YOUR RISK OF CORONARY HEART DISEASE

FACTOR MODIFIED	REDUCTION IN RISK OF CORONARY HEART DISEASE
Stopping smoking	50–70% lower risk within five years
Exercise	45% lower risk for those who exercise regularly
Losing excess weight	35–55% lower risk if you maintain a healthy weight
Avoiding excess alcohol	25–45% lower risk for those drinking 2–3 units per day

Aromatherapy oils for coronary heart disease

Helpful essential oils include geranium, peppermint and rosemary (do not use during pregnancy or if you have high blood pressure without specialist advice).

Asthma

Asthma is a long-term inflammatory disease of the lungs. The number of sufferers has doubled over the last thirty years and it is now especially common in women of all ages – two out of three sufferers are female. The reasons for this are unknown, but one theory is that women are now under more stress from having to juggle work and family pressures.

When asthma is triggered, the airways go into spasm. This produces the symptoms of coughing, wheezing, tightness in the chest and shortness of breath. The other signs of inflammation – swelling and extra mucus secretion – take longer to come on and often result in a further bout of tightness and wheeze 6–8 hours later. In severe cases, airway narrowing and plugs of mucus can block the flow of oxygen into the lungs

Symptoms occur when the lining of the airways becomes red and swollen and produces increased amounts of mucus. Once irritation sets in, the airways become increasingly sensitive to a wide range of triggers such as exercise, strong emotions – including stress – and air-borne particles.

Some researchers believe that inflammatory diseases such as asthma may be linked with an imbalance of dietary fats. The polyunsaturated fatty acids (PUFAs) we eat are of two main types, omega-3 PUFAs derived from fish oils and omega-6 PUFAs derived from vegetable oils. Ideally, we need a balanced intake of omega-3s and omega-6s, but the average Western diet currently contains seven times more omega-6s than omega-3s. Eating more fish may be beneficial – aim for 100 g oily fish two or three times per week, or try omega-3 fish oil supplements.

YOU COULD HAVE ASTHMA IF YOU ANSWER YES TO ANY OF THE FOLLOWING QUESTIONS

❑ Do you cough, feel wheezy or have difficulty breathing when you are under excess pressure?

❑ Do you sleep badly with coughing, wheezing, or difficulty breathing?

❑ Does coughing ever wake you up?

❑ Have you stopped enjoying any sport because of chest problems?

❑ Do you get surprisingly out of breath if you run or hurry?

❑ Do you avoid smoky places because they make you wheezy?

❑ Do you have difficulty shaking off a cold?

Asthma has also been linked with low dietary levels of selenium, magnesium or B6 in some studies, while those with high intakes of antioxidants (vitamin E or vitamin C) seemed to have the lowest risk.

How asthma is treated

If you think you have stress-related asthma, you should be assessed regularly by your doctor so that adequate treatment is given. This can be life-saving, especially when you are under extreme pressure. Two main types of drug are used to treat asthma: relievers and preventers. Short-acting relievers (for example, salbutamol, terbutaline) relax smooth muscles in the airways so the tubes dilate. This quickly makes breathing easier, with the effect lasting from three to six hours. Relievers can only relax your airways, however. They cannot tackle the underlying inflammation that led to asthma in the first place. Because of this, if you need to use your reliever inhaler more than once a day, you should really use a preventer inhaler every day as well. Preventers (for example, cromoglycate, nedocromil, inhaled steroids) damp down the inflammation that leads to asthma, and when used regularly can prevent an attack by making your airways less sensitive. When inflammation is severe, however, they can take up to fourteen days to get symptoms under control.

The aim of asthma treatment is the total control of your symptoms, even when you are under stress. Ideally, someone with asthma should be given an asthma management plan individually tailored for them by their consultant, GP or practice nurse. This will show you how to match treatment with symptoms, for example stepping up the dose of a preventer drug or adding in another treatment when symptoms are worse. When asthma is under control again – perhaps when your stress levels are lower – treatment can be stepped back down.

One of the best ways to monitor how well your lungs are working is to use a peak-flow meter. This shows how fast you can blow out and is a measure of how constricted your airways are. Ideally, asthma treatment will keep your peak-low score within 20% of what is normal for someone of your age, sex and height who does not have asthma. Signs that your asthma is poorly controlled include:

- poor peak-flow readings
- waking at night (or in the morning) with symptoms
- having to use your reliever inhaler more than once a day
- having to make compromises in your life because of symptoms.

If this is happening to you, ask your doctor to review your treatment or refer you to an asthma clinic. Surveys show that under-treated asthma is common. Three out of four sufferers find their asthma restricts day-to-day activities – for one in five, it has a major effect on their life and is a significant cause as well as a result of stress.

Tips to help improve your asthma symptoms

- Stop smoking – and try to avoid smoky places.
- Wear a special mask when exercising near traffic.
- Keep the home as dust-free as possible. Dusting with a damp cloth and using a vacuum cleaner with a special filter will help. A spray that kills off dust mites is available from chemists. Spray on to beds, curtains and carpets every three months.
- Put special covers over your mattress, pillow and duvet to overcome bedmites.
- If you have asthma, avoid taking aspirin or ibuprofen, which can trigger an attack.
- Take your medication correctly, as prescribed.
- Ask the practice nurse or doctor to check your inhaler technique is good.

Alternative therapies that can help asthma

A modern alternative therapy known as Buteyko can help asthma by allowing you to control your breathing. The Buteyko method is based on the belief that people with asthma breath a greater volume of air than healthy people, which is in turn thought to affect immunity. By changing the basic breathing patterns, the Buteyko method seems to boost the immune system and damp down inflammation in the lungs (see Chapter 5 for more on alternative therapies).

Smoking and stress

During times of stress, it is common for smokers to increase the number of cigarettes they smoke. This is a subconscious behavioural response since nicotine produces a drug-like soothing effect on the nervous system. Nicotine also acts on nicotinic receptors elsewhere in the body, however, such as in skeletal muscle and in the gut, and can produce symptoms similar to some of those occurring in the stress fight-or-flight response such as muscle tension, tremor and jitteriness, as well as affecting bowel function. Smoking is also linked with sex hormone imbalances – smokers' fertility falls and women who smoke are likely to enter the menopause up to two years earlier than non-smokers – not to mention the fact that smoking is a powerful cause of premature skin ageing and wrinkles.

Cigarette smoke contains over 4,000 different chemicals, many of which are harmful and cancer forming. These chemicals damage the lining of arteries to increase the risk of them hardening and furring up, high blood pressure, coronary heart disease and stroke as well as affecting cell division to increase the risk of cancer. Smoking therefore maximizes many of the harmful effects produced by prolonged, excessive stress. If you are stressed and smoke, one of the greatest contributions you can make to your long-term health is to stop smoking. If you can give up:

- within twenty minutes your blood pressure and pulse rate will fall significantly as arterial spasm decreases
- within eight hours the levels of carbon monoxide in your blood drop to normal so that blood oxygen levels can rise
- within forty-eight hours the stickiness of your blood and the quantity of blood clotting factors present will fall enough to reduce your risk of a heart attack or stroke
- within one to three months the blood supply to your peripheries will increase, and your lung function will improve by up to a third
- within five years your risk of lung cancer will have halved
- within ten years your risk of all smoking-related cancers (for example, lung, mouth, throat, bladder) will have reduced to almost normal levels.

Giving up is easier said than done when you are also having to cope with excess pressure, however. Nicotine is addictive, which is why it is so difficult to quit. Withdrawal symptoms of tension, aggression, depression, insomnia and cravings can occur which will magnify the psychological and emotional effects of any stress you are under. You therefore need to take things one step at a time, and initially aim to cut down until you feel strong enough to stop smoking altogether.

A simple 'quit plan' to help you stop smoking is outlined here. Your doctor will be pleased to help you, too.

Tips to help you stop smoking

- Find support – giving up nicotine is easier with a friend or partner.
- Name the day to cut back or give up and get into the right frame of mind. If cutting back, cut out a number of cigarettes per day, starting with those you will miss the least. Then continue reducing your intake until you gradually stop, or until you feel ready to cut out the remaining cigarettes altogether.
- Get rid of temptation. Throw away all smoking papers, matches, lighters, ashtrays, spare packets, etc. before the day arrives.
- Take things one day at a time. Every morning, say to yourself, 'I just have to get

through today.' If you think longer term, you're more likely to give in.

- When you want to smoke, instead of saying, 'I must have a cigarette,' change your thought patterns and say instead, 'While I would like a cigarette, I don't need one because I no longer smoke,' then remind yourself of all the reasons you have decided to quit.

- Keep a quit chart and tick off every day you keep within your target level of consumption or have lasted without a cigarette. Plan a reward for every week of success.

- Learn to relax. Have a massage, practise yoga or meditation. You need something to replace the anxiety-relieving effects of nicotine.

- Find a hobby to take your mind off smoking – a habit that keeps your hands busy such as model-making, drawing, painting, embroidery or origami is best.

- Keep active with DIY jobs in the evening rather than sitting in front of the TV.

- Increase the amount of regular exercise you take as this can help to curb withdrawal symptoms.

- Identify situations where you would usually smoke and either avoid them or plan ahead to overcome them, for example practise saying, 'No thanks, I've given up,' or 'No thanks, I'm cutting down.'

- Ask friends and relatives not to smoke around you.

- Watch your diet. Avoid excess saturated fats and count calories so you don't put on weight. Chew sugar-free gum or drink water and unsweetened herbal teas instead.

- Save the money previously spent on cigarettes in a special anti-stress fund. Buy a luxury for yourself – or save it to spend on a happiness retreat or a stress-busting weekend break.

When you have a strong urge to smoke, try:
- sucking on an artificial cigarette or herbal stick (available in chemist shops)
- sucking on celery or carrot sticks
- eating an apple
- cleaning your teeth with strong-flavoured toothpaste
- going out for a brisk walk, swim, cycle-ride or jog
- taking a supplement containing oat straw (*Avena sativa*), which can reduce cravings
- take a flower essence, for example Rescue Remedy, Emergency Essence or agrimony (*Agrimonia eupatoria*); for those seeking solace in drugs or alcohol, crab apple (*Malus pamila*) helps to detoxify and cleanse
- use the aromatherapy device Logado, impregnated with nineteen essential oils (available from chemists), which can be sniffed or inhaled so cigarette cravings disappear for up to thirty minutes. In trials, one in three smokers using Logado regularly gave up, and a further one in four cut the amount they smoked by half.

Here's a useful relaxation exercise to stop your cravings for nicotine:
1. Breathe in deeply through your mouth and feel your rib cage expand to its fullest extent.

2. Hold your breath for three seconds.

3. Let out all the air slowly, until your lungs feel totally empty.

4. Hold your breath for a further three seconds.

5. Repeat this cycle twice more, so you have breathed in and out slowly a total of three times.

6. Now start to breathe normally again.

Nicotine replacement therapy

If you find it difficult to stop smoking, consider using nicotine replacement products such as skin patches, chewing gum, inhaler or spray. The quit rate with nicotine replacement patches or gum is at least double that of people trying to give up alone. Studies suggest that nicotine nasal sprays are three times more effective in helping people remain cigarette-free after one year. Don't be tempted to smoke while using nicotine replacement therapy, however, as this can trigger dangerous spasm of blood vessels and may even lead to a heart attack.

If you find it difficult to cut back, phone the national Quitline for help and advice (see Resources).

Alcohol and stress

When feeling stressed, it is common to feel 'I must have a drink' and for your alcohol intake to increase. Up to a certain point, alcohol seems to be beneficial, in that a moderate intake — especially of red wine — has been shown to lower a high blood pressure, reduce stress levels and decrease your risk of coronary heart disease by as much as 25–45%. This is mostly due to the powerful antioxidants found in red wine, and the thinning effect of alcohol on the blood. In fact, new research suggests that if you have high blood pressure and drink within the recommended limits, your risk of dying from a stroke is 40% less than for a teetotaller. These benefits of moderate intakes of alcohol are thought to be linked with the fact that those who drink are more likely to laugh and giggle than non-drinkers. Laughter helps to buffer the effects of stress and can also improve immunity and increase resistance to disease.

There is a cut-off point at which the benefits of alcohol intake are lost and excess alcohol intake is harmful to health, however. Once this point is reached, your risk of high blood pressure, coronary heart disease and stroke reverses and becomes significantly increased. At the same time, the risk of liver damage leading to cirrhosis also rises. It is therefore important not to let your

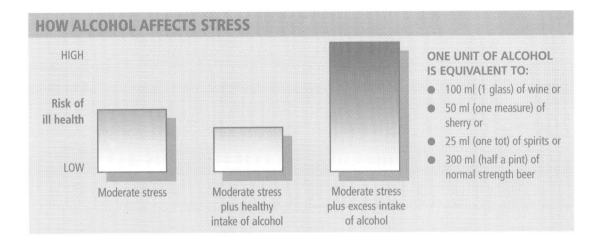

HOW ALCOHOL AFFECTS STRESS

HIGH

Risk of
ill health

LOW

Moderate stress

Moderate stress
plus healthy
intake of alcohol

Moderate stress
plus excess intake
of alcohol

**ONE UNIT OF ALCOHOL
IS EQUIVALENT TO:**

- 100 ml (1 glass) of wine or
- 50 ml (one measure) of sherry or
- 25 ml (one tot) of spirits or
- 300 ml (half a pint) of normal strength beer

alcohol intake rise above that which may be beneficial for health, no matter how stressed you feel, as this will magnify the harmful effects of the stress itself. Healthy drinking guidelines therefore suggest that:

- Men should aim to drink no more than 3–4 units of alcohol per day. Consistently drinking 4 or more units a day is not advised, however.
- Women should drink no more than 2–3 units per day and consistently drinking 3 or more units a day is not advised. Women who are pregnant or planning a baby should aim to avoid alcohol altogether.

You should also aim to have one or two alcohol-free days per week. For men, drinking more than 50 units of alcohol per week is considered dangerous, while for women, the equivalent figure is 35 units.

Most people tend to overestimate the strength of spirits and underestimate the strength of beer. It is important to realize that:

- someone drinking two pints of beer has consumed *four* units
- someone drinking two glasses of wine and a double vodka has also consumed *four* units.

Could you be drinking too much alcohol?

Do you:

- Feel you drink more than a normal drinker?
- Ever feel you should cut down on your drinking?
- Get annoyed if anyone criticizes the amount you drink?
- Ever feel guilty about the amount you drink?
- Always reach for a drink when you arrive home after a stressful day?
- Ever drink first thing in the morning?
- Regularly drink alcohol at lunchtime and in the evenings?

- Regularly drink more than the recommended safe maximum?
- Try to cover up the amount you drink?
- Ever neglect your responsibilities at home or work because of drinking too much?

If you answered yes to two or more questions, keep an accurate drink diary and record what you drink in a normal week. Don't try to cut back — carry on drinking as normal for this week while you are recording your intake, otherwise you will underestimate your regular intake. Write down what you drink straight away so you don't forget later.

At the end of the seven-day recording period, calculate how many units of alcohol you have drunk. If you have drunk more than the recommended weekly maximum, aim to cut back and work out the best way to tackle this. Some people decide not to drink before 6 p.m. in the evenings, for example.

If you are drinking dangerous amounts of alcohol or you find it difficult to cut back:

- Phone the national Drinkline number for help and advice (see Resources).
- Confide in your doctor so he can arrange a blood test to check your liver function and blood pressure.

Simple tips to help you cut your alcohol intake

- When drinking alcohol, sip slowly and keep putting your glass down rather than holding it in your hand — this will reduce the amount you sip out of habit, when talking.
- Savour each sip and hold it in your mouth for longer.
- Alternate each alcoholic drink with a non-alcoholic one.
- Many bars offer exotic, non-alcoholic cocktails that are delicious and full of nutrients.
- Drink mineral water with a dash of fresh lemon juice, or low-calorie drinks.
- Tonic water with ice, lemon and a dash of Angostura bitters is an excellent substitute for a gin and tonic.
- Mix chilled white or red wine with sparkling mineral water to make a refreshing spritzer.
- Elderflower cordial diluted with mineral water is an excellent substitute for white wine.
- Drink fruit/herbal teas — these are delicious, relaxing or stimulating depending on which you choose and, as they are drunk without milk, have the additional bonus of being calorie-free.
- Practise saying, 'No thanks, I'm cutting back for my health/blood pressure' or 'No thanks, alcohol and stress don't mix well together,' or, 'No thanks, I'm driving.'

There is no shame in wanting to cut back the amount of alcohol you drink and your firm stand may well help someone else decide to do the same.

Stress and disease

Excess stress can affect your general health and is increasingly recognized as a contributory factor in both minor and major illnesses. Although stress cannot be blamed for all the conditions listed below, it often plays a large contributing role. In fact, it is estimated that as many as 40 million working days are lost in Britain each year as a direct result of stress-related illnesses. Conditions in which stress is known to play an important role include:

- poor resistance to infection
- high blood pressure
- stroke
- coronary heart disease
- asthma
- eczema
- psoriasis
- migraine
- diabetes
- peptic ulcers
- insomnia
- anxiety
- panic attacks
- depressive illness
- cancer.

These stress-related illnesses cause a vicious circle of health-related worry that in turn leads to further illness. The important thing to realize is that everyone has it within themselves to take the necessary steps to manage their levels of stress and these will in turn go a long way towards helping to prevent short-term minor and longer-term more serious illnesses.

The existence of a link between mind, body and spirit has been recognized by alternative practitioners for thousands of years. In fact, Chinese medicine teaches that physical, emotional and spiritual well-being depends on the balance of *chi*, the invisible life-force which flows through the body during health. During times of stress, however, *chi* energy is weakened and its flow becomes blocked. This in turn is believed to reduce the body's immunity and increase the risk of developing many common illnesses.

The effects of stress — or blocked *chi* — often appear when least expected. It is common, for example, to come down with a serious cold just at the start of a holiday when you have begun to unwind. This suggests that you were able to cope for just as long as necessary — the adrenaline buzz kept you fighting or fleeing

— but as soon as the pressure lessened and you sat back to relax and digest, your weakened defences crumbled and the effects of long-term pressure caught up with you.

This concept has only recently been embraced by conventional medicine. Researchers investigating factors that increase susceptibility to the common cold, for example, have now confirmed that high levels of stress can double the chance of developing symptoms of upper respiratory tract infection when exposed to a cold virus. In other words, it confirms that stress lowers your resistance and increases your chance of an infection.

This and other findings have led to the development of a new branch of medicine known as psychoneuroimmunology (PNI) — the mind-body-link between psychology, brain chemistry and immunology that holistic therapists have long used as the basis for their techniques. This interaction between the state of mind and disease is probably mediated via the immune system. Scientists have already discovered a direct mind-body link between stress and skin disorders such as allergic eczema and psoriasis. A small protein, calcitonin gene related peptide (CGRP), is produced by nerves in the skin and transmits signals to nearby immune cells (lymphocytes) responsible for detecting and destroying infections. Secretion goes up during the fight-or-flight response, and affects the immune response, although why this should happen is unknown. CGRP is now thought to explain the way inflammatory skin disorders flare up during times of anxiety and stress. CGRP or similar substances may also explain the increased susceptibility to infection and malignant disease that occur during stress.

As well as lowering your immunity, stress causes wounds to heal more slowly and this may prove significant after surgery, for example.

The best way to cope with stress is to adapt to it in a positive, constructive manner.

Try to put situations into perspective, and analyse problems logically so you can make sensible plans to resolve them. The following chapters show you how to cope with excess pressure by:

- developing self-esteem
- eating wisely
- exercising to reduce stress
- relaxing properly
- breathing correctly
- exploring de-stressing alternative therapies
- streamlining your life at home and work, and learning the principles of time management

AREAS AFFECTED BY STRESS

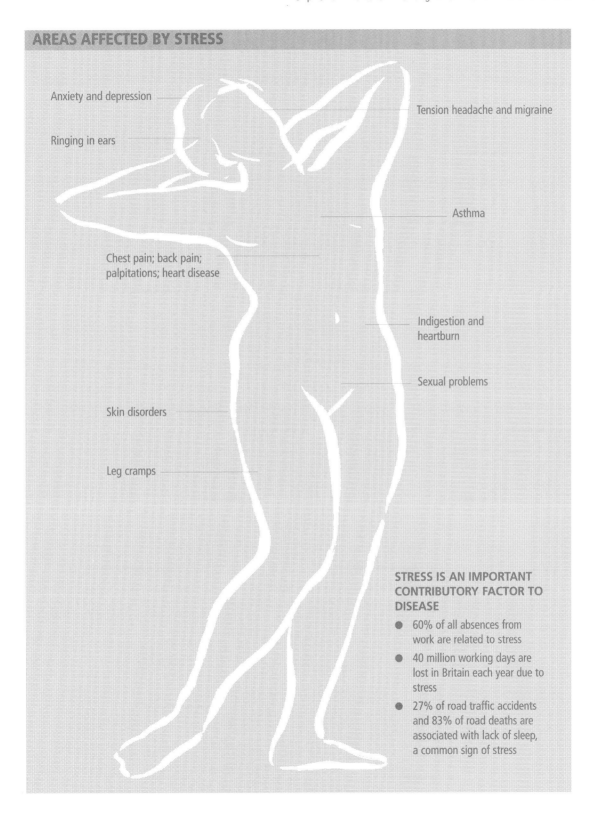

Anxiety and depression

Ringing in ears

Chest pain; back pain;
palpitations; heart disease

Skin disorders

Leg cramps

Tension headache and migraine

Asthma

Indigestion and
heartburn

Sexual problems

**STRESS IS AN IMPORTANT
CONTRIBUTORY FACTOR TO
DISEASE**

- 60% of all absences from
  work are related to stress
- 40 million working days are
  lost in Britain each year due to
  stress
- 27% of road traffic accidents
  and 83% of road deaths are
  associated with lack of sleep,
  a common sign of stress

DISCOVER THE CAUSES OF STRESS

As already discussed, some pressure in life is normal and necessary, and only becomes harmful when it is excessive or prolonged, at which stage the feelings you experience are known as stress. One of the most important steps in managing the various pressures in your life is to recognize the ones that are potential sources of stress for you. These are known as your stressors. Having recognized your stressors, you then need to weigh them up to see how severe a threat they really are compared with how bad you believe them to be. Your perceptions of threat play a key role in the way you react and it is a common tendency to over-estimate problems or — as the saying goes — to make mountains out of mole-hills. Feelings of stress feed on each other and can produce unpleasant sensations of panic. These can in turn lead to fears or phobias which may seem irrational on the surface but feel very real deep down. Surprisingly, it is often the people who appear most cool under pressure who are most vulnerable to anxiety and stress — this is because they fear losing control and this underlying fear magnifies many of the challenges they meet in life.

Internal and external causes of stress

This chapter initially looks at the internal and external causes of stress and shows you how to analyse the ways change affects you. A large part of the text is then concerned with looking at the most common causes of stress in more detail (see pages 102 to 122). Finally, a questionnaire and ways of recording daily

INTERNAL CAUSES OF STRESS

There are many internal causes of stress. These include certain personality traits, such as the competitive Type A discussed previously, uncertainty about your goals in life, and having a negative self-image. Have a look at the following internal causes of stress and tick all those that are relevant to you:

☐ The physical and emotional effects of working long hours.

☐ Inadequate time off for relaxation.

☐ Lack of sleep.

☐ Physical tiredness.

☐ Mental exhaustion.

☐ Menstruation.

☐ Menopause.

☐ Negative self-image.

☐ Negative thoughts.

☐ Lack of fitness.

☐ Disruption of bio-rhythms caused by such things as shift work, jet lag and insomnia.

☐ Physical or mental ill-health.

EXTERNAL CAUSES OF STRESS

Sources of external stress are mainly related to change, since anything new readily evokes a stress response to help you prepare for the unknown challenge. Change causes uncertainty, uncertainty leads to anxiety, and anxiety is a powerful trigger for stress. Different changes therefore set up a chain reaction of similar responses, whether they are related to changes in your relationships with other people, changes in family dynamics, or changes occurring at work. Have a look at the following list and tick all those where changes are currently happening in your life:

☐ Changes in your relationship with your husband/ wife/ girlfriend/ boyfriend.

☐ Changes in your job title/position.

☐ Changes in your working environment.

☐ Changes in your career prospects.

☐ Changes in your relationships with work colleagues.

☐ Changes in your hours of work.

☐ Changing from working to retirement or redundancy.

☐ Changes in your living accommodation.

☐ Changes in your health.

☐ Changes in your relationships with relatives.

☐ Changes in your social life/relationships with friends.

☐ Changes in your hobbies/recreations.

events show you how to start overcoming the stressful aspects of life.

Sources of stress rarely exist in isolation and it is common for several related events to combine to produce feelings of excess pressure. It is important to try to identify what these are so you can plan how to start removing them from your life. The sources of your stress can be either internal, within you, or external, caused by events outside you.

The speed of these changes will play an important part in determining whether or not you feel stressed. Slow changes give you a chance to gradually adjust and become familiar with new experiences. In this way you can acquire new coping skills without being aware of undue pressure. Rapid changes are the most stressful, since the goal posts seem to be moving in front of your eyes and it is difficult to fully assess what is happening, let alone prepare in advance for the impact these changes may have on your life.

Although external factors may be the stimulus for the stress you are experiencing, it is usually how you react to these changes that actually results in your feelings of stress. Type B personalities will react very differently from Type As, for example, so although you may feel your stress is totally due to pressures from outside you, most sensations of stress are in fact self-generated. The exceptions are environmental situations that tend to cause stress for everyone, such as excessive heat, cold, humidity or prolonged exposure to loud noise or bright lights.

Threats versus challenges

The way you respond to change depends largely on whether you perceive the changes as desirable or a threat. If you see the changes as desirable, the feelings you experience will remain on the level of positive pressure. If you see the changes as a threat, however, then you are programmed to start experiencing feelings of stress. The degree of stress you feel in turn reflects how well you think you can cope.

Chosen versus imposed changes

Changes that are perceived as desirable are often those you have deliberately instigated yourself — for example, moving house, changing jobs, or finishing an unrewarding relationship. If these same changes were imposed on you — having to move house because of your job, having your job description restructured or being deserted by your partner — the situation would be entirely different. Change plus the feeling that you have little control over a difficult situation causes frustration and strong negative feelings against the changes themselves and those who have instigated them. These will inevitable trigger feelings of stress.

Analysing change

It is often helpful to analyse possible changes in your life in terms of whether they are desirable or a threat, chosen or imposed, to work out in advance how stressful they are likely to be.You may think that few changes are likely to be both chosen and a threat, but in fact those who are most successful in life are often those who deliberately choose to face extremely challenging situations, such

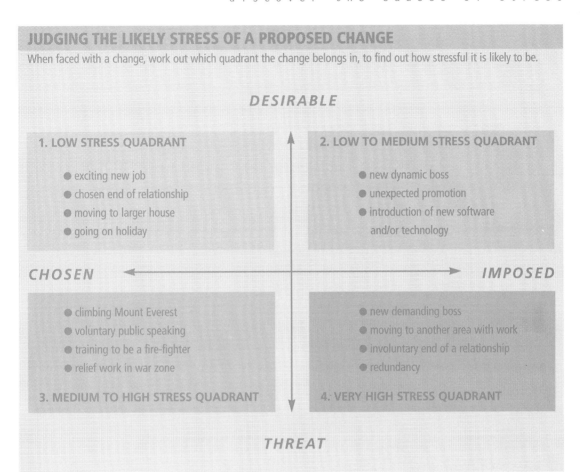

JUDGING THE LIKELY STRESS OF A PROPOSED CHANGE

When faced with a change, work out which quadrant the change belongs in, to find out how stressful it is likely to be.

DESIRABLE

1. LOW STRESS QUADRANT

- exciting new job
- chosen end of relationship
- moving to larger house
- going on holiday

2. LOW TO MEDIUM STRESS QUADRANT

- new dynamic boss
- unexpected promotion
- introduction of new software and/or technology

CHOSEN ⟵⟶ **IMPOSED**

- climbing Mount Everest
- voluntary public speaking
- training to be a fire-fighter
- relief work in war zone

3. MEDIUM TO HIGH STRESS QUADRANT

- new demanding boss
- moving to another area with work
- involuntary end of a relationship
- redundancy

4. VERY HIGH STRESS QUADRANT

THREAT

as climbing Mount Everest or even volunteering for public speaking. Success and the acquisition of new life-skills often comes from daring to do what others fear or refuse to do.

Go back to the list of changes you ticked above and see which quadrant of the box above each change fits into according to the following key:

1. Chosen, desirable changes (low stress).
2. Imposed, desirable changes (low to medium stress).
3. Chosen, threatening changes (medium to high stress).
4. Imposed, threatening changes (very high stress).

This will give some indication of the degree of stress you are likely to be under at present. The reality will depend on how accurate your perceptions are, however. People who choose to have a baby, for example, will usually see this as highly desirable. They may therefore assume that having a baby fits into the upper left-hand quadrant as a low source of stress. In reality, however, a baby is a threat in that your whole life has to change to revolve around the needs of the new helpless, demanding (yet adorable) addition to your family. Having a baby brings a number of other imposed changes such as lack of sleep, difficulty going out alone with your partner and less time for hobbies. You therefore need to be realistic about exactly how each change (chosen or imposed) is likely to impact on your life. Few changes or sources of stress exist in isolation and it is important to consider all the knock-on effects they will produce when assessing the degree of threat or desirable challenge they represent.

Example 1

Imagine you have seen an interesting job advertised and that, after careful consideration, you have decided to apply, been short-listed and are about to attend the job interview. You have researched the company beforehand and know as much about their products and work ethos as possible. The job is one you know you will enjoy and which, while it will be more challenging than the one you currently have, you are capable of doing well. You know you will create a good impression. You also know that if you don't get this job it is not because you are incapable but because another candidate was obviously more suitable at this time for whatever reason. In any case, another equally good job is bound to come your way eventually. You perceive the interview as a chosen, desirable challenge – not a threat – so while you experience a certain amount of nerves (positive pressure) beforehand, you do not feel particularly stressed.

Example 2

Now imagine you are about to attend the same job interview, but only applied because your husband/wife/mother/boss made you. You have only had time to find out a little about the company beforehand. You are not entirely sure what the advertised job will entail and are therefore worried it may be more than you can cope with. You have a poor self-image, lack confidence and are afraid you won't make a good impression. You are therefore secretly convinced you won't get the job because you simply aren't good enough. Although you would love to move away from your current boring job, you are convinced that good job opportunities are few and far between for talentless people like yourself. You therefore perceive the interview as an imposed threat, not a desirable challenge, and the fact that you will fail is a foregone conclusion in your own mind. You feel very stressed about the whole situation for several weeks beforehand.

Now consider the two ways in which you might have approached the same interview.

ASSESSING STRESS

TRAIT	EXAMPLE 1	EXAMPLE 2
Reason for interview	Chosen	Imposed
Preparation	Adequate	Inadequate
Belief in your personal ability	Good	Poor
Mode of thinking	Positive	Negative
Perception of interview	Desirable challenge	Threat

Which is the most beneficial for health? Which way do you think has the most chance of success?

Internal causes of stress are generally easier to deal with than external problems, because however difficult they may feel you also have a greater sense of control. When you are faced with a stressful situation, try looking at it objectively and deciding how you can influence the situation by changing the circumstances or your own attitudes and behaviour. If you perceive the problem as worse than it really is you will subconsciously be sabotaging your ability to cope.

Luckily, although the type of thinking illustrated in Example 2 is common, it is readily changed by learning how to think more positively, acquiring good self-esteem and changing the way you perceive challenges so they are more of a challenge and less of a threat.

Shifting relationships

Many causes of stress come from emotions triggered by your close interactions with your immediate family. Have a look at the list right, and tick those that have previously been a cause of stress in your life or which are affecting you now.

The advertising stereotype of happy smiling families is only a small snapshot on reality; although we are social animals, living closely with others causes frequent ups and downs. Everyone has their

YOUR FAMILY RELATIONSHIPS

☐ Committing to a partner either through engagement, living together or marriage.
☐ Becoming a parent.
☐ Family rows with parents, in-laws or siblings.
☐ Problems with babies, toddlers or young children.
☐ Problems with adolescents.
☐ Problems with step families.
☐ Children leaving home.
☐ Separation.
☐ Divorce.
☐ Extra-marital affairs.
☐ Mid-life crisis and the need to be free from others to 'find yourself'.

own way of doing things and these may sometimes conflict with those around us. One of the main causes of family problems, however, is lack of communication. Most families would benefit from talking to each other more and communicating in a direct, open and honest way. One of the biggest culprits in this respect is the television – after a hard day at work or school, it is easier to sit in front of the box and be entertained than to talk to the rest of the family and find out what has happened in their world while you were away.

If family dynamics are causing you stress, try to work out what the problems are and how many can be addressed by simply sitting down together and talking things through. A discussion aimed at addressing the root causes of relationship stresses needs to be frank and open, not hidden behind gestures, inferences, veiled comments, jokes or put-downs.

If a relationship has broken up, remember that time is your best friend. In two or three months' time you will feel very differently to when the relationship first ended.

HOW ARE YOUR FAMILY RELATIONSHIPS?

Do you feel that your family relationships would benefit from:

- ☐ More time talking rather than watching television?
- ☐ More time just being together?
- ☐ More time socializing?
- ☐ More time going on outings, walks or taking part in activities together?
- ☐ More honesty?
- ☐ More guidelines on what is acceptable behaviour and what is not?
- ☐ More privacy from each other?
- ☐ More flexibility?
- ☐ More fun?
- ☐ Sharing worries?
- ☐ Less time rowing?
- ☐ Appreciating one another more?
- ☐ More affection and being nice to each other?

TIPS ON HOW TO CLEAR THE AIR

- It is important to be clear in what you are saying, so think about what you want to say beforehand and how you are going to say it.
- Deal with the most important issue first .
- Be careful and sensitive in what you say.
- Don't express your feelings as a criticism or blame; use 'I' language – rather than saying 'You...' say 'I would prefer it if...'
- Avoid generalizations, for example, 'You never...' or 'You always...'
- Be positive – start off with a good point about the topic under discussion rather than going straight in with what is wrong.
- Try not to criticize each other, as it is then easier to work together to find a way round a problem.
- Try not to feel defensive or aggressive.
- Don't talk at the person you are talking to, give them a chance to respond.
- Don't bring up old grievances that are not relevant to the point under discussion.
- Stick to the point and try not to get sidetracked until the issue has been resolved.

Don't bottle up your emotions — express your feelings and don't be afraid to cry. Crying is a great reliever of stress. It is important to have someone close you can talk to or confide in — but it must be someone you trust, such as a close family member or an old friend. If you lack this sort of support system, remember that the Samaritans are always on the end of the phone to listen — just call 0345 909090.

Caring for the infirm, elderly or disabled

Caring for those who are very young, elderly, infirm or disabled is a rewarding task that can nevertheless be draining — physically and emotionally. It is important to help others maintain as much independence as possible but this will invariably lead to conflicting needs and demands, and a need for compromise that can be highly stressful.

Before you can care for others, you need to ensure you care for yourself. It is a common failing to ignore your own needs when those of others seem so much greater. You are not being selfish in taking the time for respite, however — you are ensuring that you — the carer of those you love — remain physically and emotionally equal to the task. Ask yourself what would happen if your health or strength were to fail too. Where would everyone be then?

- Take regular breaks from stressful situations.
- If you are caring for someone who is dependent night and day, make sure you have some nights off to allow you to sleep through.
- If caring for someone at home, seek advice to ensure you are receiving all the financial benefits you and the person you are caring for are entitled to.
- Go out socially at least once a week — even if it is only window shopping or for a stroll with a friend.
- Talk to other family members about how you feel and how you are coping — don't bottle your emotions up.
- If you need extra help, don't be afraid to ask for it. Practise your assertiveness skills. You may even find that friends and family have been holding back from offering to help for fear they may offend you.
- Keep up an outside hobby or interest such as gardening, writing to a penpal or researching a topic that interests you in the local library.
- Keep active — physical fitness is important. Take steps to lose any excess weight and consider joining a yoga class for relaxation, a swimming class for fitness or perhaps a rambling club to meet new people. If the person you care for needs constant super-

vision, ask friends, relatives, neighbours or self-help/charity groups to help
organize a rota that gives you regular time off each week for an outside activity.

- When stress builds up, use visualization, meditation, breathing exercises or a
relaxation technique to help you regain control.

Bereavement

Sooner or later everyone will have to cope with bereavement. Whether it is the
death of a parent, partner, child, family pet or close friend, the loss of a
loved one is a devastating experience that affects your whole life and causes an
enormous amount of stress. Everyone will react differently and every situation is
different, but grief is a painful and isolating experience. Try not to be alone,
however — even if you feel you want to shut yourself off from the outside world.
Company is important at this difficult time. The support of family and friends is
vital. You need to be able to talk about your feelings openly, without holding
back. If someone asks how you feel, it is no use saying 'all right' if you feel
absolutely awful. Take the opportunity to be honest about your emotions.

Emotional feelings

Anyone faced with death will feel unpleasant emotional symptoms such as shock,
panic and helplessness at first. The facts take time to sink in, and feelings of
unreality, such as 'It can't be happening to me' or, 'This isn't real' are

common. You may feel numb and find it difficult to cry — but it will help to let your emotions out and shed a few tears or even scream and shout. Time is your best friend: as the weeks and months pass, it gets easier to accept what has happened. You may feel guilty, that in some way you are to blame for what happened — again, this is a normal part of the grieving process. Later, you may feel angry at your loss, or jealous of others who have not had to go through what you have had to face. With time, you will start to accept what has happened and look to the future.

EMOTIONS COMMONLY FELT AFTER BEREAVEMENT

Are you experiencing:

- Numbness and feelings of unreality?
- Sadness and longing?
- Helplessness?
- Fear for the future?
- Anger and resentment?
- Loneliness?
- Disappointment and despair?
- Guilt or shame?
- Depression?

If so, don't worry. These are all a normal part of the grieving process and will soon mature into feelings of resignation, acceptance and hope for the future.

Sharing your feelings

When you are coping with the stress of bereavement, it is important to voice your feelings and share them with others as this is a powerful part of the healing process.

- Thinking and talking about the person who has died will help keep their memory alive for you. To begin with this can be painful as it will bring raw emotions to the surface, but sharing your feelings is healthier than bottling them up.
- Try talking with a close friend or relative — someone who also knew the deceased person, as this will help you both.
- Some people find it easier to talk to someone removed from the situation, however, such as an uninvolved friend, doctor or a priest. You may even feel that professional bereavement counselling is what you need. Do whichever you feel most comfortable with.
- With time, you will be able to talk about the person with pleasure, remembering all the good times you shared. This is not 'dwelling in the past' or 'failing to get over it'. It is a healthy way of coping with your loss.
- When you can smile again, you will know you are well on the way to recovery.

Everyone will eventually recover from the raw emotions, stresses and changes that result from a bereavement, but you will need to recover at your own pace and in your own time. Don't rush it as it is important to let the process run its natural course for you. There are no right or wrong ways to grieve, and everyone copes differently. Sometimes, people who have suffered a bereavement slowly sink into depression. Depression can creep up on you, until you are overwhelmed with feelings of sadness, loneliness and despair. If you start feeling that things are getting on top of you, that you can no longer cope, or that life is no longer worth living, it is important to seek help from your doctor. Depression is an important warning sign that the stress resulting from your bereavement is overwhelming and that you need professional help to come to terms with your loss.

Grief is an intense stress reaction in which you are likely to experience a number of stress-related emotional and physical symptoms. These are all part of the normal grieving process along with feelings of guilt, anger, depression, loneliness and — eventually — hope.

When a loved one dies, it is also common to develop sleep problems. It can be difficult to get off to sleep, and when you do manage to nod off, you may find that your rest is disturbed by unusual dreams or that you wake earlier than normal. Sleep is one of nature's best healers, so it is important to get a good night's rest. If it is your partner who has died, the bedroom will be associated with memories and it often helps to move into the spare room for a while or — even better — to stay with relatives or close friends. It can even help to phone someone and have a short conversation with a friend or relative before going to bed so you can voice any worries or thoughts that might otherwise stop you sleeping. For hints on how to get a better night's sleep, see page 72.

Major illness or injury

Serious illness either in yourself or those you are close to is a powerful cause of stress, especially when there is uncertainty — over the diagnosis, the best treatment or whether a full recovery is possible. Some illnesses and accidents have temporary effects from which, although it may be touch and go to begin with, a full recovery is usually made. This allows you to achieve a sense of closure on the episode, the stress recedes and you can carry on with life much as before. When an illness or injury has long-term consequences, however, your life will inevitably change from what it was. Major illness or injury can trigger a number of different causes of stress such as:

- worrying about the significance of various symptoms
- having to endure a series of tests
- waiting for results
- having to face a serious diagnosis
- feeling numb
- coping with pain
- coping with immobility
- coping with changes in certain bodily functions
- coping with treatments that may have unpleasant side effects
- having to face surgery
- fear of disfigurement
- frustration at infirmity
- anger — feelings of 'why me?' or 'why us?'
- guilt or remorse — feelings of 'if only'
- uncertainty and fear about the future
- changes in family income or outgoings — illness can be expensive
- worry about how loved ones will cope
- fear that things are being kept from you
- fear of loss of control
- coming to terms with your own mortality.

It is no good dwelling on what might have been or what you could have done differently. The best way to fight any illness is to face it head on, steel yourself for what lies ahead and make plans about the best way to cope. Negative thinking will drag you down and slow the healing process. When feeling stressed by illness or pain, it can help to practise a breathing exercise, a relaxation technique or to visualize yourself fighting the illness and becoming well again. The power of mind over body is phenomenal, and positive thinking will reduce pain, improve the body's ability to heal itself and help you cope as well as providing the basis for many modern-day miracles.

After a traumatic event, it is common to suffer from post-traumatic stress disorder in which you may experience anxiety, flashbacks, panic attacks, difficulty sleeping, depression, avoiding anything linked with the event, and feelings of guilt, remorse, anger or even shame. Don't bottle your emotions up — let them out. Talk about your feelings and once you have made a good recovery, try to get back to normal as soon as possible within the limits of your condition. If you feel you need extra help, however, don't be afraid to ask for it. Counselling is especially important if you are suffering the effects of post-traumatic stress, and your doctor can refer you if necessary.

Coming through a serious illness or trauma can be a strengthening experience once you are out the other side and realize you have coped — usually much better than you would have expected.

Financial problems

Money worries are frequently present in most families. Even people who seem to be doing well often have a shaky financial foundation with large overheads, an overdraft and a bank manager who, although outwardly friendly and accommodating, may have to change his priorities at short notice to protect his bank's investors.

No matter how tight or flush your finances, unexpected expenses can cause stress if you have not made suitable plans to cope with monetary changes: either in outgoings or in income.

Tips for good financial planning

- Record where your money comes from and where it goes to in up-to-date household accounts — keep everything together in one filing drawer, desk or concertina file so that everything is immediately at hand.
- If economies have to be made, it is surprisingly easy to pull in your horns and reduce outgoings with a concerted economy drive.
- Keep track of when bills have to be paid — especially credit card bills. Missing a

COMMON CAUSES OF FINANCIAL CHALLENGES

- getting married
- attending other people's weddings
- buying a house
- buying a car
- holidays
- maternity leave
- having a baby

- bringing up children
- childcare
- school fees
- critical illness
- looking after infirm or otherwise dependent relatives
- redundancy
- retirement

- accidents
- legal fees
- medical fees
- dental fees
- veterinary fees
- unexpected tax bills
- insurance excesses

payment or paying late attracts stiff financial penalties.

- Talk to the financial advisor at your bank to see what services are available and how much they cost — it often pays to take out a small overdraft or loan to pay off credit cards balances as the annual interest rate is usually much less.

- Set yourself a weekly or monthly budget, and stick to it. If the budget is tight, aim to balance income and outgoings — don't allow small deficits to start accumulating at the end of each month.

- Try to put aside a certain amount of money each month as savings — no matter how small — in a savings account where you can access it fairly quickly if necessary.

- Once you have sufficient cash built up in an account for emergencies, seek independent financial planning about how to build up further 'safe' nest eggs according to the amount of risk you are prepared to take.

- Seek independent advice on financial planning services such as insurance, pensions and planning for redundancy or critical illness. Think hard about taking on any new financial commitments, however — no matter how good the deal seems. Remember that nothing comes free — every deal is intended to make money, somewhere, for someone else.

MAKE A WILL

Everyone should ensure that they have made a will. Although there is no legal obligation to do so, the lack of one will result in major stress and possible money problems for surviving members of your family should you die. As many as seven out of ten people fail to make a will and die intestate because they feel making a will is tempting fate in some way, or they don't want to think about their own death. Look upon your will as your family's insurance for the future, however — and your right to ensure your wishes are carried out after your death. Although property and assets will be divided among the family according to legal regulations, this takes time and causes a lot of unnecessary suffering compared with when someone's wishes have been legally drawn up beforehand. Having made a will, it is equally important to keep it up-to-date, especially if financial circumstances change and this could have implications for inheritance tax.

Work-related stress

Most people spend the major part of their waking life at work, and more often than not you are identified with the type of work you do. People will say, for example, he is an architect, she is a professor of anthropology, he is an electrician, she is unemployed. Your work goes a long way towards denoting your status in life, and it is common practice for social introductions to include a statement or questions about what someone does for a living. As well has paying the bills, work should be a valuable source of satisfaction and of positive pressure. All too often, however, it becomes a source of negative stress.

What happens to you at work is important to your health and well-being. When you lose your job, it means far more than just losing a source of income; it can feel like a judgement on your lack of worth and lead to low self-image, a feeling of helplessness, increased fatalism and loss of essential contact with other people.

Job stress can undermine your sense of personal worth and dignity. Different administrative styles can stir up different kinds of unconscious conflicts within each member of a group. Different jobs are carried out by different types of worker — engineer, secretary, executive or printer — yet everyone expects to gain satisfaction from the particular job they perform. Nowadays, workers are demanding an increasing degree of fulfilment as human beings.

Stress and the working woman

The number of women working outside the home has more than doubled over the last twenty-five years. Many women work because of economic necessity, but increasing numbers work out of choice. Although the so-called glass barriers that make it difficult for women to advance in certain careers do still exist, women frequently now achieve senior posts as captains of industry, eminent scholars or capable politicians. Despite these achievements, women often pay an additional price for their success over and above that paid by male colleagues. For example, there is the familiar conflict between pursuing a career and rearing a family. Some studies suggest that men look on their home environment as a support system while women may see it more as a burden. As a result, women executives are far less likely to give their home life a high priority compared with their male peers and are twice as likely to be single or divorced. This is not surprising given that many women finish a full day's work at the office and are then still expected to do more than their fair share of cooking and household chores on arriving home.

Many women cope with the stress they feel due to the pressure of conflicting home and work demands through excessive eating, smoking, drinking and medication, all of which damage their health further and drain them of vitality. The nurturing role is not only burdensome in itself, but the conflict between playing the traditional role and developing an independent career outside the home is even more exhausting. Women are constantly at odds with themselves trying to perform both roles.

IS YOUR WORK A SOURCE OF STRESS?

A number of signs may indicate that your feelings of stress stem from your working conditions.

❑ Is your ability to concentrate on work affected?

❑ Does lack of confidence cause you to over-check your work?

❑ Has your productivity gone down?

❑ Has your absence rate increased?

❑ Are you irritable with colleagues?

❑ Are you starting to make irrational demands on juniors?

❑ Are you starting to make panic decisions?

❑ Do you feel dissatisfied with your job?

❑ Does the thought of going into work make you feel stressed?

In addition to carrying the dual load, women also have to put up with physiological disadvantages. Many women suffer from premenstrual syndrome which may affect the quality of their work and makes them more irritable and accident-prone, and more likely to make rash decisions. In addition, women reaching the end of their fertile life may also develop troublesome menopausal symptoms. This seems to be more likely in women who are stressed, in fact (see page 115).

What causes you stress at work?

Consider the following questions and see if any apply to your situation.

- Have you recently lost your job?
- Have you recently changed your job?
- Have you just taken on an additional new job?
- Have changes at work results in increased demands upon you?
- Have you recently been promoted?
- Have the immediate colleagues you work with changed?
- Have you recently had a new boss?
- Have you recently been placed in charge of new people yourself?
- Is your role and power base ambiguous?
- Are your skills underused?
- Do you feel overloaded with work?
- Are relationships at work a source of stress?
- Do you find using office technology a source of stress?

- Are you having to cope with study for work-related exams?
- Is the threat of redundancy hanging over your head?
- Do you find commuting and experiences of road rage stressful?

Unrealistic aims may be set, by yourself or your boss; work facilities may be inadequate; you may experience role conflicts with other people in the office. Just one of these major challenges in the work place will raise the pressure you are under, but small things can add up over time as well, such as:

- numerous deadlines
- lack of feedback or appreciation from the top for how well you are doing
- responsibility without adequate authority
- unclear goals
- boss with an abrasive or weak leadership style
- lack of communication about serious problems in the company
- lack of leadership in times of crisis
- feeling trapped in an unsatisfying job.

And that's not all. Physical and psychological environment stressors can also come into play to make your work life stressful:

- unsuitable chairs that cannot be individually ergonomically adjusted
- desk too high or too low
- lack of personal work space
- undue clutter or lack of storage/filing space
- noisy surroundings
- poor lighting
- VDU screen glare
- lack of access to natural light
- having to stand, walk or bend all day
- office politics — whether you are actively involved in them or not
- sarcastic remarks or put-downs from colleagues
- malicious office gossip
- bullying and racial, ageist or sexual harassment
- having to work in isolation
- having to work in an overcrowded environment
- having to work in an inhospitable physical environment (for example, having to wear bulky protective clothing or deep-sea diving equipment; having to work in sterile conditions or with toxins)
- having to work in shifts.

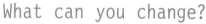

What can you change?

Having looked at the lists above and worked out some of the sources of your work-related stress, it will help to plan constructive ways round the major problems. Study the coping strategies right and put a tick next to those you believe you already practise effectively, and a cross by those where you need to improve your skills.

COPING STRATEGIES

- ☐ Time management.
- ☐ Setting sensible priorities.
- ☐ Planning skills.
- ☐ Delegation.
- ☐ Keeping to a sensible workload.
- ☐ Communication.
- ☐ Pacing yourself – taking time out for meals and tea-breaks will energize you.
- ☐ Sticking to your contracted hours more closely and leaving for home at a sensible hour.
- ☐ Improved communication within the company.

Premenstrual syndrome

Premenstrual Syndrome (PMS) is a common and distressing problem that affects at least three-quarters of menstruating women. Half have significant symptoms, and for one in twenty, these are incapacitating, necessitating regular days off work. PMS is associated with a variety of symptoms that come on in the fourteen days before a period is due and disappear soon after bleeding starts. Problems include headache, backache, bloating, cyclical breast pain, tiredness and food cravings.

QUICK FIXES TO HELP REDUCE THE EFFECTS OF PMS

- Eat little and often – be a grazer rather than a gorger.
- Eat a low-fat carbohydrate snack (for example, crispbreads, digestive biscuits, toast, rice cakes) every three hours, starting as soon as you wake. This helps maintain blood glucose levels – in one study it cured symptoms in 54% of cases and helped significantly in a further 20%.
- Eat oily fish three times a week (sardines, herrings, pilchards, salmon, mackerel, trout) for the hormone building-blocks (essential fatty acids) they contain.
- Eat at least five portions of fruit and vegetables per day, especially green leafy vegetables for their vitamin, mineral, fibre and antioxidant content
- Take evening primrose oil, which contains hormone building-blocks that can even out imbalances. You

will need to be take up to 3,000 mg a day for at least three months before an effect may be noticed.

- Follow a healthy, organic, wholefood diet with low intakes of salt, additives, table sugar, monosodium glutamate, caffeine and alcohol (see Chapter 3).
- Take a vitamin and mineral supplement especially designed for women with PMS, which includes B-group vitamins (100 mg per day) and magnesium (300–500 mg per day).
- If you smoke, try to stop as this has been shown to affect ovarian function and hormone balance to the extent that it can bring on the menopause two years earlier than normal.
- Take regular exercise – this helps to burn off excess adrenaline levels and is therefore helpful for reducing PMS symptoms in the long term (see Chapter 4).

Many emotional symptoms also occur such as anxiety, poor concentration, irritability, weepiness, mood swings, low sex drive and depression. In some cases, PMS is so bad the personality of the sufferer changes. Suicide attempts are more frequent and the incidence of accidents in the home and on the roads increases. Crimes such as shop-lifting and even murder may occur. PMS is therefore well recognized as a stressful event for many women and one that, unfortunately, can recur every few weeks. In extreme cases, it may affect a woman as long as two weeks out of every four.

The exact cause of PMS is unknown, but it is thought to be linked with an imbalance between the activity of two female hormones, oestrogen and progesterone. Some research shows that progesterone cannot work properly when adrenaline is present. As we have already seen, adrenaline is released during times of pressure and levels remain high when stress is prolonged. As a result, stress can make PMS worse, and as PMS itself is stressful, a vicious cycle is set up.

Low blood sugar levels can also increase adrenaline levels by triggering the fight-or-flight response in order to put blood glucose levels up again. Diet and in particular skipping meals (especially breakfast) because of lack of time are therefore contributing factors that make PMS worse during times of stress.

Could premenstrual syndrome be linked with your feelings of stress?

For a firm diagnosis of PMS, there must be a clear-cut relationship between symptoms and your menstrual cycle. Problems must start in the two weeks before a period and cease promptly when bleeding occurs. A symptom-free phase lasting at least seven days after menstruation to help distinguish PMS from 'menstrual distress' in which menstruation worsens pre-existing emotional or physical problems rather than causing them.

If you think you have PMS which is making your feelings of stress worse, select your three or four most troublesome symptoms (for example, anxiety, irritability, breast tenderness, bloating) and record when they occur in relation to your period using symbols on a menstrual chart such as that overleaf. Start the first month on the first day of your period (Day 1) and start a new line with each period. It can also help to record the days when you feel most stressed to see if there is a link with your hormone cycle.

SAMPLE MENSTRUAL CHART

DAYS OF CYCLE

	1 2 3 4 5 6 7......	14	15	16	17	18	19	20	21	22	23	24	25	26	27	28
Month 1	X X X X X								A	A	IB	IB	AIP	AIP	ASP	ASP
Month 2	X X X X X					A	A	A	AI	AI	SB	IB	ASP	ASP	ASP	ASP
Month 3	X X X X X		A	A	A	A	S	S	SI	AI	IB	IB	AIP	AIP	ASP	ASP

(X = bleeding S = really stressed A = anxiety I = irritability B = bloating P = breast pain and so on – use your own symbols depending on your worst symptoms.)

If you have PMS, most of your symptoms will occur between Day 15 and the start of each period. If this is a regular pattern, discuss the problem with your doctor.

Alternative therapies that can help PMS

Homoeopathy

Take one of the following remedies twice a day for three days, starting a day before symptoms are expected:

- PMS with tiredness and irritability: Sepia 30c
- PMS with fluid retention and breast pain: Calc. carb. 30c
- PMS with oversensitivity and tearfulness: Pulsatilla 30c

Homoeopathic hormones (oestrogen, progesterone, testosterone and/or thyroxine) are also prescribed by some practitioners.

Herbalism

- A gentle herbal diuretic (for example, containing dandelion and horse-tail) can help you maintain a normal fluid balance during this time of the month. Consult a herbalist to obtain extracts for making infusions, or to obtain tablets/capsules (usually taken three times a day). Fresh, young dandelion leaves can be eaten as salad greens, too.
- Valerian helps to relieve anxiety and to promote a good night's sleep.
- Agnus castus promotes the action of progesterone, and is invaluable in treating premenstrual syndrome. Studies show it is 90% effective in relieving physical symptoms such as headache, breast tenderness, bloating and fatigue as well as psychological changes such as increased appetite, sweet cravings, nervousness/restlessness, anxiety, depression, mood swings and lack of concentration. Agnus castus is usually taken as a single daily dose first thing in the morning, but it takes an average of twenty-five days for symptoms to start improving. The average length of treatment is six months. Agnus castus is not recommended during pregnancy, and

should not be taken at the same time as other hormone treatments, such as HRT or hormonal methods of contraception.

Aromatherapy

The aromatherapy essential oils of geranium and rosemary can relieve water retention. Add a few drops to a hankie for inhalation, or dilute with a carrier oil and use in the bath or for an abdominal massage. You may want to consider a course of lymphatic drainage massage by an experienced aromatherapist. A number of essential oils can help to reduce fluid retention (do not use during pregnancy), including: camomile, cedarwood, eucalyptus, fennel, geranium, juniper, lemon, peppermint and sandalwood.

Acupuncture

Stimulation of the bladder and kidney meridians is often successful in banishing excess fluid.

Floatation therapy

Floatation therapy seems to decrease production of anti-diuretic hormone and stimulates urine production — this effect is noticeable immediately after a float.

Reflexology

Manipulation of the feet at points corresponding to the kidneys, bladder and lymphatic areas may help.

Menopause

The menopause is often called the 'change of life', and as we have already seen, change is one of the commonest causes of stress. The word *menopause* literally means the time when your last period stops. This normally occurs between the ages of forty-five and fifty-five, the average being fifty-one. Some lifestyle factors can bring on your menopause earlier than otherwise expected. Heavy smokers reach the menopause an average of two years earlier than a non-smoker. This is because chemicals found in cigarette smoke affect the blood supply to the ovaries and cause oestrogen levels to fall. Excess alcohol also poisons egg-follicle cells to trigger an earlier menopause. High levels of stress also affect hormone balance and can trigger the menopause significantly earlier than expected — so the menopause can both result from excess stress and contribute to increased stress levels. Many women find that sex feels different after the menopause, and as oestrogen levels fall, one in five experience a profound loss of interest in sex. This is another powerful cause (and effect) of stress and is discussed on page 55.

Although the menopause is dated from the last period, it really starts five to ten years before – during a woman's early to mid forties – when the number of eggs remaining in the ovaries decreases and levels of the female hormone oestrogen naturally start to fall. When levels eventually become too low to control the monthly cycle, menstruation will stop. Some women quickly adapt to lower levels of oestrogen and notice few – if any – problems. Others find it harder to lose their oestrogen and experience unpleasant symptoms that last from one to five years – and occasionally longer.

Women who are experiencing a lot of stress seem more likely to suffer distressing symptoms around the time of the menopause than those with a less demanding lifestyle. Usually the adrenal glands help to smooth out the effects of falling oestrogen levels by producing extra amounts of other sex hormones that can be converted into oestrogen. If you have been under long-term stress, however, the adrenal glands are already working flat out making extra stress hormones such as adrenaline, noradrenaline and cortisol, and have no extra reserves to boost oestrogen levels to even out hormonal fluctuations at this time.

QUICK FIXES TO HELP REDUCE MENOPAUSAL SYMPTOMS

- Eat plants rich in natural oestrogen-like plant hormones, such as soya-bean products, celery, fennel, chinese leaves and other green or yellow vegetables.
- Cut back on sugar, salt, tea, coffee and caffeinated fizzy drinks.
- If suffering from hot flushes, avoid spicy foods and convenience foods.
- Avoid alcohol and smoking cigarettes, which lower oestrogen levels further.
- Try taking evening primrose oil (3,000 mg per day for at least three months) to see if it helps.
- If suffering from hot flushes, vaginal dryness, night sweats or anxiety, Siberian ginseng (Eleutherococcus) often helps.
- Homoeopathy: take achesis twice a day for a week.
- If vaginal dryness is a problem, try KY jelly or Replens.

Could menopausal symptoms be linked with your feelings of stress?

For some women, the first sign that they have reached the menopause is when their normal, regular periods suddenly stop. This is unusual, however. Most women notice their periods are changing and becoming irregular, lighter or heavier than usual. If you experience problems with your periods, it is important to consult your doctor for advice – especially if you experience heavy bleeding. Other early symptoms of the menopause can include:

- hot flushes and night sweats
- difficulty sleeping
- anxiety, irritability or mood swings that appear 'out of the blue'
- unusual tiredness
- vaginal dryness
- urinary symptoms
- headaches
- pins and needles
- poor concentration
- feelings of distance from those around you
- sudden difficulty coping with things you previously took in your stride.

IF YOU DEVELOP A HOT FLUSH

- Concentrate on breathing deeply and slowly.
- Cool down with a chilled drink, suck an ice cube or eat ice cream.
- Try to sit down near an open window or door so you can breathe fresh, cool air.
- Carry a small, battery-operated personal fan in your bag for emergencies.
- Carry a small packet of wet wipes to help you freshen up until you can wash or change.
- Carry a small wash bag around with you containing flannel, soap, towel and deodorant and crease-proof change of clothes, if necessary.

Some women enjoy their hot flushes, and find them useful – especially in winter when they have previously been sensitive to the cold.

If your doctor is unsure whether or not your symptoms are due to an approaching menopause, a blood test can help make the diagnosis by measuring the level of two hormones produced by your pituitary gland: follicle stimulating hormone (FSH) and leutinising hormone (LH). Falling levels of oestrogen cause FSH and LH levels to rise into what is known as the 'menopausal range'.

Preparing for the menopause

Every woman will eventually approach the menopause. To help make your passage through these changes easier there are a number of steps you can take before your first symptoms start:

- Follow a healthy diet that is low in fat and contains plenty of fresh fruit, vegetables, salad-stuff and unrefined, complex carbohydrates.
- Start increasing the amount of exercise you take to improve your fitness level.
- Try to lose any excess weight.
- If you smoke, make a major effort to stop.
- Keep your alcohol limit to within the recommended safe maximum for women of no more than two or three drinks a day and try to have at least one alcohol-free day per week.
- Don't let yourself be overburdened with tasks – learn to say 'no' and mean it so that people don't put upon you.

- Find time for relaxation and quiet, at least half an hour per day — soaking in an aromatherapy bath surrounded with flickering candlelight is a great way to end the day, for example.
- Keep your mind active and your spirits up with a new hobby such as learning a foreign language, taking painting lessons or joining a rambling club.

Alternative therapies that can help reduce menopausal symptoms

Homoeopathy

For hot flushes, take one of the following remedies until the flush recedes, for up to 10 doses:

- for hot face, sweaty skin and throbbing headache: Glonoin 6c (one dose every five minutes)
- for sudden flushing with headache and fainting: Lachesis 6c (one dose every hour)
- for sudden flushing of face with headache, heat and sweating: Amyl nitrosum 6c (one dose every ten minutes)
- for blood rushing to the head with throbbing in the whole body: Sanguinaria 6c (one dose every four hours).

For night sweats:

- for sweating with weakness and exhaustion: Sepia 6c (every hour as necessary, for up to ten doses)
- for sweating on face, scalp, back and thighs: Sulphur 6c (one dose twice a day).

Homoeopathic hormones (oestrogen, progesterone, testosterone and/or thyroxine) are available from some practitioners and are often prescribed according to the result of salivary hormone tests.

Aromatherapy

Aromatherapy essential oils have powerful effects on your moods. Many are also oestrogenic when absorbed from the skin into your circulation and can help to improve menopausal symptoms. Always use aromatherapy oils in a diluted form by adding a maximum of 5 drops to each 10 ml of carrier oil (almond or grapeseed, for example). This is because some neat oils can cause skin irritation. Diluted oils may be massaged into your skin, added to bath water or diffused into the air to scent your room. Do not use during pregnancy except under advice from a qualified aromatherapist.

Aromatherapy oils that help relieve oestrogen-withdrawal symptoms such as hot flushes, sweating and vaginal dryness include:

- camomile
- clary sage
- cypress
- fennel
- geranium

- grapefruit
- lemon
- lime
- rose
- sage

Herbal Supplements

Many plants contain hormones that have a weak effect in the body and are widely used to help relieve menopausal symptoms. (Do not take during pregnancy, breast-feeding or if you have had cancer of the womb, ovaries or breasts except under specialist advice.)

Black cohosh (*Cimicifuga racemosa*): some research suggests that standardized extracts of black cohosh are at least as effective in relieving hot flushes, vaginal dryness and mood swings as standard HRT.

Chaste berry (*Vitex agnus-castus*) contains substances that both increase the relative output of progesterone from the ovaries, and help to reduce hot flushes and night sweats. It is slow-acting, however, and it takes an average of twenty-five days for symptoms to improve.

Dandelion (*Taraxacum officinale*) is a natural diuretic that helps to reduce fluid retention and reduce the unpleasant effects of night sweats.

Dong quai (*Angelica sinensis*): Chinese angelica has a balancing effect on oestrogen levels, supporting normal ovarian function and relieving painful periods. One study found it was 1.7 times more effective than aspirin in relieving painful periods.

Ginseng (*Panax ginseng; P. quinquefolius*): Korean and American ginsengs are adaptogens that help the body adapt to physical or emotional stress and fatigue. American ginseng is more calming and relaxing, while Korean ginseng tends to be more stimulating. American ginseng is said to be best for fatigue caused by nervous conditions, anxiety and insomnia, while Korean ginseng is better for fatigue with general weakness and loss of energy. Ginseng is not advised if you have high blood pressure, glaucoma or an oestrogen dependent condition (for example, pregnancy, cancer of the breast, ovaries or uterus).

Hypericum (*Hypericum perforatum*): St John's wort is effective in lifting mild to moderate depression. One trial showed that *hypericum* plus black cohosh was effective in treating 78% of women with hot flushes and other menopausal problems within two to four weeks.

Red clover (*Trifolium pratense*): extracts have been shown to reduce menopausal symptoms of hot flushes and mood swings within three to four weeks.

Sage (*Salvia officinalis*) is a popular herbal remedy for treating menopausal hot flushes and night sweats. It should only be taken in small quantities (ideally as a tincture) and should be avoided by those with epilepsy.

Soy extracts: Soy extracts have been shown to help reduce menopausal symptoms such as hot flushes and night sweats.

Wild yam (*Dioscorea villosa*) is rich in hormone building-blocks from which progesterone can be synthesized in the laboratory. The body cannot carry out this conversion itself, but wild yam does seem to have some useful progestogenic actions that many women find helpful at the menopause.

Speaking in public

It is surprising how many people are filled with panic at the thought of speaking in public. Yet many people have to do this as part of their work and quickly come to realize there is no great mystery about the ability to do so, it just comes down to practice. Think about some of the presenters you have watched on TV, thinking, 'I could do better than that.' Well, you can. Public speaking is an art that is easily learned. Although some personality types such as the forceful and the extrovert will find it easier than others, practice will make perfect every time.

Tips on how to speak in public

- First of all, believe in yourself: you *can* do it.
- Prepare in advance by finding out:

   who your audience is

   what they want to hear from you

   why you need to speak to them

   how best to get your message across.

- Practise in advance: prepare notes on small index cards and use these to talk out loud in the privacy of your bedroom, bathroom, a field, your garden — wherever you won't be overheard. Learn to talk around your notes rather than reading them verbatim. Keep practising until you feel you have got it right. If using an overhead projector or slides, practise while using them so they won't fluster you on the day. Time how long your talk will last. Practice and preparation are the most important things you can do to boost your self-confidence.

- Use visualization exercises to imagine yourself giving the talk perfectly, exactly as you have practised (see page 194).

- Wear clothes that are appropriately smart and comfortable.

- Learn a breathing exercise to help calm you on the day. Also, for ten seconds before you start, take a deep, long, slow breath in through your nose, then slowly release it through your mouth. Use Rescue Remedy flower essence as necessary.

- Smile!

- Don't start until you feel ready. Take your time. Similarly, feel comfortable with pausing to collect your thoughts during your talk. If you make a mistake, don't panic. Pause, then start again.

- Greet the audience as a warm-up and to get the feel for your voice — don't forget to speak up.

- Make eye-contact with your audience while speaking, sweeping your gaze around to all corners so no one feels excluded.
- Don't fiddle, click a pen or jingle coins in your pocket.
- Smile while talking and animate your face — look interested in what you are saying.
- Use light humour to get the audience on your side, but be careful only to poke fun at yourself — not at others.
- Be brief and to the point. Try to stick to three main messages and get your most important point across first. It often helps to:
    1. Say what you are going to say.
    2. Say it.
    3. Then say what you have said.
- Get your audience to do some of the work: don't be afraid to ask questions.

RESPONDING TO DIFFICULT QUESTIONS FROM THE AUDIENCE

- Come clean: say, 'I don't know the answer to that, but I'll find out and let you know.' Then make sure that you do.
- Throw the question out to the audience. Say, 'That's a very interesting question. Does anyone know the answer?' If someone does, you've won. If no one does, say, 'We have a lot of experienced people here today and no one has come across the answer. Let's all take steps to find out.'
- Throw the question back to the asker: 'What do you think? You must have a feeling about that yourself.'
- If the question is one you feel obliged to refuse to answer, you can do so but give a reason, for example, 'I'm afraid I can't answer that as it is personal/ Would break a confidence/ Is something I have already discussed fully and do not have time to address again.'

Many people fear public speaking because they are afraid of looking silly if they are asked a question they don't known the answer to. There are a number of well-tried ways round this (see box above) — use whichever technique you feel the most comfortable with.

Holidays

Holidays feature surprisingly high on most people's list of major stresses. While poring over brochures and dreaming of exotic destinations can aid your visualization skills, it is easy to invest so much emotional energy in your holiday that it inevitably turns into an anticlimax. Try to keep a sense of realism on your side at all times. Many people would have a more pleasant and relaxing time if they stayed at home for a change. This is important if you are already feeling stressed and considering a holiday to recharge your batteries. Racing round trying to organize the perfect holiday will just put your stress level up even more. Consider the following list of common holiday-related stresses. How many have happened to you in the past?

Common causes of holiday stress

- Preparation.
- Packing — deciding what to take and fitting it into available space.
- Organizing passports, tickets, insurance, immunizations.
- Additional unexpected costs.
- Sorting out what to do with pets and dependent relatives.
- Travelling with small children.
- Motion sickness.
- Queues, delays and overbookings at the airport.
- Exhaustion from driving too far without a break.
- Destination not what was expected.
- Overcrowded resorts.
- Running round doing and seeing too much until you are exhausted.
- Culture shock.
- Excessive noise.
- Poor weather.
- Traveller's illnesses, especially vomiting and diarrhoea.
- Hangovers.
- Indigestion from foods you are not used to.
- Sunburn and insect bites/stings.
- Coming home to find a pipe has burst, you have been burgled or worse.
- Returning to work with an overflowing in-tray and everyone demanding large chunks of your time.
- Next month's credit card bill: you overspent or were caught out by credit-card fraud.

Why did you ever go away in the first place?

By staying at home on holiday, you can:

- Lie in and have a leisurely breakfast.
- Lounge around in your dressing gown until you feel ready to get dressed.
- Read the paper from cover to cover for a change.
- Read that book you keep meaning to get around to.
- Potter around the house and garden.
- Spend a little of the money you've saved in not going away on having a few good meals in a local restaurant, going to the cinema/theatre, arranging a local boat trip or coach tour, buying a barbecue for fun evenings on the patio.
- Spend time exploring local beauty spots and tourist attractions you would otherwise never get around to seeing.
- Invite friends around for a dinner or drinks party.
- Spend more quality time with your family.
- Save a significant amount of money.

QUESTIONNAIRE: ASSESSING STRESSFUL EVENTS

Look at the list below and tick all the stressful events you have experienced over the last two years. Add up the score next to each source of stress you ticked, then look at the interpretation below to see how your experience of life events is likely to affect your health.

MAJOR STRESS	SCORE
☐ Death of a spouse	10
☐ Divorce	7
☐ Marital break-up	6
☐ Jail term	6
☐ Death of a close family member	6
☐ Personal injury or illness	5
☐ Marriage	5
☐ Loss of job	5

HIGH STRESS	
☐ Marital reconciliation	4
☐ Change in health of family member	4
☐ Pregnancy	4
☐ Sexual difficulties	4
☐ Gain of new family member	4
☐ Change to a different line of work	4
☐ Business readjustment	4
☐ Change in financial status	4
☐ Death of close friend	4

MODERATE STRESS	
☐ Increased arguments with spouse	3
☐ Mortgage over £50,000	3
☐ Foreclosure of mortgage or loan	3
☐ Change in work responsibilities	3
☐ Son or daughter leaving home	3
☐ Trouble with in-laws	3
☐ Outstanding personal achievement	3
☐ Spouse begins or stops work	3
☐ Begin or end school/college	3
☐ Change in living conditions	3
☐ New year's resolutions	3
☐ Stopping smoking or drinking	3
☐ Trouble with boss	3

LOW STRESS	
☐ Change in work hours or conditions	2
☐ Change of residence	2
☐ Change in recreation	2
☐ Change in social activities	2
☐ Mortgage or loan less than £50,000	2
☐ Change in sleeping habits	1
☐ Change in eating habits	1
☐ Holiday	1
☐ Christmas	1
☐ Minor run-ins with the law	1
☐ Other (add score of nearest item in list)	

Over the last two years, I experienced _____ points.

SCORES

Less than 10: Life has been kind to you over the last two years and not dealt you too many blows. The stress you have experienced is unlikely to damage your health.

11–20: Your life events score is acceptable but you need to look after your health. You've had a reasonable amount to deal with over the last two years, so take regular time out to relax.

21–30: Your life events score is high and the stress you are under is in danger of affecting your health. Another stressful event may just tip the balance.

Over 30: Life has thrown so much at you over the last two years that your health is seriously at risk. Your reserves are running low and a minor event may prove to be the last straw. Stressed people who have been through one major life event after another are at increased risk of coronary heart disease, high blood pressure, stroke, mental illness and cancer. Consider seeking profession stress-counselling.

These figures are only intended to give you an idea of the amount of stress you are likely to be under. They are not meant to be exact, but help to remind you of all the events in your recent past that may have combined to affect your overall health.

Life events

As we have seen, causes of stress are found in all aspects of life — from your relationships with other people, your health and that of those you love to money worries, work, hormonal changes and even going away on holiday. A range of influences will affect your mood and susceptibility to stress, and these can accumulate until you reach your limit of being able to cope and start to feel undue pressure.

Research back in the 1960s by Holmes and Rahe found that an accumulation of 'life events' over a prolonged period of time can greatly increase your likelihood of stress-related health problems. The questionnaire on the previous page is a simplified version of their work and will help you consider your lifestyle and predict your risk of a serious stress-related illness in the near future.

Keeping a stress diary

Keeping a detailed diary will help you assess more immediate events in your life so that you can identify your main causes of stress and pinpoint any patterns. It will also help to show how effective your responses to stress are, and help you plan alternative strategies to avoid similar feelings of stress in the future.

Be honest with yourself and record the events from a dispassionate point of view. Keep the diary with you at all times, and try to fill it in after each event. Don't leave it until the end of the day — by then you will not be able to accurately record how you felt.

When you have completed a week check the material recorded in the diary. It will provide you with several useful pieces of information to help you plan the next steps in your stress-busting campaign.

- Which situations caused you most stress, and why?
- Are the main sources of your feelings of stress internal or external?
- Which feelings of stress were due to change or things imposed on you, and how much control are you able to exert over them?
- How do you perceive the situations that make you feel most stressed?
- What do you use as safety valves?
- Were your responses appropriate?
- Could you have reacted differently, in a more constructive way?

SAMPLE DIARY ENTRY

FRIDAY

TIME	SITUATION	FEELINGS	NEGATIVE RESPONSE	POSSIBLE CORRECTIVE ACTIONS
08.45	Stuck in traffic	Frustrated – afraid will be late for work again	Tried listening to Classic FM	Leave home earlier in future.
09.10	Late for work again – boss threatened a written warning	Dreadfully worried and afraid this will affect promotion prospects	Over-ate at break-time –a doughnut and a cream bun – yuk!	Apologize firmly to boss and promise it will not happen again. Don't go to canteen – take fruit to work instead
10.00	Unpleasant phone-call from an irate customer	Upset, angry. It wasn't my fault the wrong goods were sent.	Burst into tears – too much pressure	Attend a course on assertiveness and self-esteem for women
17.30	Shopped in crowded supermarket with long queues	Frustrated, hot and snappy with check-out girl for being so slow.	Cut shopping short – went home without several vital items	Go for a run to burn off effects of stress hormones. Shop when supermarket quieter. Look into having fruit and veg delivered by local organic farming co-op
19.00	Picked row with spouse for coming into house with dirty, muddy shoes	Even more upset – no one appreciates all I do for them	Phoned friend for a long moan. Cracked open a bottle of wine and drank most of it myself – husband stormed out to the pub.	Make up with spouse – explain we've both had a stressful day and are taking it out on our nearest and dearest. Drive to a quiet country pub for a relaxing evening and a quiet, candle-lit meal for two (forgot to buy the steaks for supper anyway!). Watch alcohol intake – stick to spritzers

WRITE DOWN TEN SITUATIONS THAT MAKE YOU FEEL STRESSED

1.

2.

3.

4.

5.

6.

7.

8.

9.

10.

EAT WISELY

A nutritious, well-balanced diet makes for a healthy body that is vibrant with energy. When you are under stress and juggling too many things in your life, it is easy to adopt an unhealthy diet and lifestyle. The old saying, 'you are what you eat' is increasingly known to be true. Every building-block in your body is ultimately derived from your food, which must provide all the vitamins, minerals, fibre, essential fatty acids, protein and energy needed for optimum health. Chinese medicine teaches that poor eating habits negatively affect physical, mental and spiritual health while a good diet increases feelings of well-being and energy by elevating the life-force, or *chi*.

Diet and stress

Some vitamins and minerals, for example vitamin C and the vitamin B complex, are quickly used up during stress reactions. Vitamin B is further depleted by the metabolism of alcohol and sugary foods, which are often resorted to in difficult times. As vitamin B deficiency in itself can lead to symptoms of anxiety and irritability, a vicious circle is set up that may make anxiety and irritability worse.

- Eat little and often to keep your blood sugar levels up – never skip a meal, especially breakfast.
- Eat a healthy, high fibre diet full of whole foods.
- Eat at least five servings of fresh fruit and vegetables every day.
- Cut back on sugar, salt, saturated fats and processed or convenience foods.
- Watch your alcohol intake and try to limit yourself to a maximum of one or two alcoholic drinks a day.

Caffeine

Caffeine has a chemical effect in your body that mimics the adrenaline stress response. A person weighing 11 stone (70 kg) who drinks more than six caffeine-containing drinks per day (for example, six cups of coffee) can easily develop caffeine poisoning, whose symptoms are restlessness, irritability, headache, insomnia and tiredness. It is therefore a good idea to make sure your intake does not go up at times of stress. Limit coffee and other caffeinated drinks to three cups a day or switch to decaffeinated brands. Herbal or fruit teas are an excellent soothing alternative. Although tea contains some caffeine, it is also rich in flavonoids — the chemicals known to give red wine its beneficial properties. Research suggests that drinking four cups of tea a day — 1,460 cups per year — may halve your risk of a heart attack. When under stress, it is therefore worth switching from drinking coffee to drinking tea. Green tea may be more beneficial than black, fermented tea.

Salt and stress

Table salt — sodium chloride — is commonly used to flavour food, and excess has been linked with an increased risk of high blood pressure. This sensitivity seems to be dependent on the genes you have inherited and affects around one in two people. The effects of stress will magnify this response, so if you are under excess pressure it is worth cutting back on your salt intake.

Ideally, you should take no more than 4–6 g salt a day. The average intake is 6 g, however, with some people eating as much as 12 g salt daily. Unfortunately, around three-quarters of dietary salt is hidden in processed foods such as tinned products, ready-prepared meals, biscuits, cakes, meat products and breakfast cereals.

Try to reduce your intake of salt by avoiding:

- adding salt to food during cooking or at the table
- obviously salty foods such as salted nuts, crisps, bacon
- tinned products, especially those preserved in brine
- cured, smoked or pickled fish/meats, meat pastes, pâtés
- ready-prepared meals
- packet soups, sauces, stock cubes and yeast extracts
- where salt·is essential, use mineral-rich rock salt rather than table salt, or use a low-sodium brand of salt sparingly.

Cut down on salt gradually and season your food with spices, black pepper and herbs instead — that way, you won't miss it.

When checking labels, those giving salt content as sodium need to be multiplied by 2.5 to give true salt content: for example, a serving of soup containing 0.4 g sodium contains 1 g salt.

The importance of breakfast

Eating a healthy breakfast gets you off to a good start for the day. Forget bacon and eggs, however — the best power breakfast contains cereal, fruit and skimmed or semi-skimmed milk. Not only can a low-fat, high-carbohydrate breakfast improve your physical performance during the day, but new research shows that a cereal breakfast acts as a stress-buster for adults. Those who regularly eat cereals first thing in the morning were found to be less depressed, less emotionally distressed and to have lower stress levels than those not eating breakfast. Eating a cereal breakfast has also been found to improve your mood and memory — especially for those over the age of sixty. It increases the speed at which new information can be recalled, and improves concentration and mental performance. As a result, it will help you work more effectively during the morning and encourage a positive mood so you cope better with situations that could otherwise lead to stress.

One of the main reasons why a cereal breakfast is important for fuelling the brain is because it boosts glucose levels at a crucial time of the day, after the long overnight fast. Glucose helps brain cells function properly, and is essential for coping with stress, for learning and for good memory. There is a complex link between what you eat for breakfast and your biorhythms, however, so the way carbohydrates affect your mood and stress levels only seems to be significant when they are eaten in the morning on waking — not if you eat them later in the day. When you are under pressure, therefore, you should always find time to fit in a good breakfast such as cereal, yoghurt and fruit. Even a muesli bar and a banana will be beneficial when you need to just grab something and go.

Vitamin B1

As well as providing the essential brain fuel, glucose, cereals are a rich source of vitamin B1 (thiamine), which has a beneficial effect on mood, so you feel more calm, agreeable, clear-headed, elated and energetic. People with low levels of thiamine are less likely to feel composed or self-confident and more likely to suffer from depression than those with higher levels.

Other foods rich in vitamin B1 that will help to produce a stress-busting effect are:

- brewer's yeast and yeast extracts
- brown rice
- wheatgerm and wheat bran
- wholegrain bread and cereals
- oatmeal and oatflakes
- soya flour
- pasta
- meat
- seafood
- pulses
- nuts.

SIMPLE HEALTHY-EATING MESSAGES

- Enjoy your food.
- Eat as wide a variety of foods as possible.
- Eat the right amount to maintain a healthy weight.
- Eat more fruit and vegetables to look after the vitamins and minerals in your diet.
- Eat plenty of foods rich in starch and fibre.
- Consider the overall balance of fats in your diet and don't eat too much of any.
- Eat at least two portions of fish, including one of oily fish per week.
- Switch to reduced-fat spreads and dairy products from full-fat ones.
- Eat more monounsaturated fats (for example, olive oil).
- Use salt and sugar in moderation.

Breakfast, stress and colds

When you are feeling stressed you are more likely to develop a cold because your immunity is depressed. Regularly eating a cereal breakfast can not only lower your stress levels, it has also been shown to help protect against the common cold. Researchers found that only around one in six of those eating a cereal breakfast every day developed a cold over the ten-week study, compared with one in three of those who ate a cereal breakfast less than once a week. In other words, those not eating cereal were twice as likely to develop a cold than those who did, even when other lifestyle factors were taken into account. Whether this is due to the cereal, the fortified vitamins and minerals it contains or even the milk that accompanies it is uncertain.

Do you eat breakfast?

Breakfast is the most important meal of the day, yet at least one in six people do not regularly indulge. They may have gone without food for fifteen hours or longer since eating their last meal the night before — yet they still expect their body and brain to carry on functioning as normal.

Some people skip breakfast because they don't feel hungry, others because they have not left enough time, or in the hope it will help them lose weight. It won't. Adults who regularly eat breakfast also tend to have lower blood cholesterol levels and to be slimmer than those who skip breakfast. This is because eating breakfast kick-starts your metabolism to help you burn up extra calories. In one study, overweight women who usually skipped breakfast lost more weight when eating three meals a day (including breakfast) than on a diet containing a similar number of calories spread over only two meals a day.

A healthy diet

A healthy, balanced diet should contain all the energy, protein, essential fatty acids, vitamins and minerals your body needs without providing any to excess. A number of experts have published healthy-eating guidelines to guide people towards an optimum healthy diet. These vary in complexity from general advice about your choice of food to more complex instructions including percentage energy intakes of different types of food.

The food pyramid

One of the most popular ways of depicting healthy eating is in the form of the food pyramid. At the base of the pyramid are the complex carbohydrates, of which you need to eat around 5–11 portions daily. Next up are the fruit and vegetable group, of which you need to eat 5–9 portions a day. Animal and dairy products should be limited to 2–3 portions a day, while at the top of the pyramid are the fats, oils, sugars and sweets that you should only eat infrequently.

Carbohydrate

Dietary carbohydrates provide your main source of energy and should ideally provide at least half your daily energy intake. This should mostly be in the form of complex, unrefined carbohydrates such as wholegrain cereals, brown rice, wholemeal bread, wholewheat pasta and jacket potatoes, since these contain additional valuable nutrients such as vitamins, trace elements and dietary fibre.

Some forms of carbohydrate cause large blood-sugar swings and are one of the internal triggers for the adrenaline stress response when blood-sugar levels rebound too low.

The way in which different foods make your blood-sugar levels rise is known as their glycaemic index (GI). For general health – and especially when you are under pressure – it is best to eat foods with a low to

MORE COMPLEX HEALTHY-EATING GUIDELINES

- Eat at least five portions of fruit or vegetables a day.
- Obtain 50–70% of your daily energy in the form of unrefined complex carbohydrates.
- Fats should make up no more than 30% of daily calories (around 75 g for men, 53 g for women).
- Saturated fats should make up no more than 10% of daily calories.
- Polyunsaturated fats should make up 3–7% of daily calories.
- Salt intake should be limited to a maximum of 6 g per day.
- No more than 10% of daily calories should come from simple sugars such as table and confectionary sugars.
- Aim to eat 300 g fish – preferably oily fish – a week.

moderate GI, and to combine foods with a high GI with those that have a lower GI to help even out fluctuations in blood-sugar levels.

Another benefit of eating complex carbohydrates is that they trigger the release of a brain chemical, serotonin, which helps to lift your mood and also controls your desire for food. By eating a high-carbohydrate diet, you will feel full quicker and eat less food overall. You are also less likely to suffer from low moods. Low levels of serotonin have been linked with overeating and carbohydrate cravings. Dietary carbohydrate also boosts your metabolic rate, speeds up the rate at which you burn excess energy, and makes you feel more energized.

GLYCAEMIC INDEX

The following chart shows the glycaemic index of a variety of foods compared with glucose (which has the highest glycaemic index, 100).

FOOD	GI	FOOD	GI
Glucose	100	Porridge oats	54
Baked potatoes	98	Crisps	51
Parsnips	97	Cake	50
Carrots	92	Grapes	44
Brown rice	82	Wholemeal pasta	42
Cornflakes	80	Baked beans	40
Weetabix	75	Oranges	40
Wholemeal bread	72	Apples	39
Chocolate bar	68	Ice cream	36
Shredded wheat	67	Milk	32
Raisins	64	Peaches	29
Bananas	62	Kidney beans	29
Chocolate biscuit	59	Grapefruit	26

Dietary fats

A certain amount of fat is important for health and is needed for healthy cell membranes and nerve function, and to provide building-blocks to maintain hormone balance. It is estimated that as many as one in three heart attacks are due to an unhealthy diet with too much fat and not enough starchy foods or fruit and vegetables. Fats are the richest dietary source of energy and most people eat too much. Ideally, fats should provide no more than 30% of your daily energy intake.

Essential fatty acids

There are many different sorts of fats in the diet and some, known as essential fatty acids (EFAs), are vital for health. These cannot be made in the body and must therefore come from your food. EFAs are found in nuts, seeds, green leafy vegetables, oily fish and wholegrains, or by taking supplements such as evening primrose and omega-3 fish oils. It is estimated that as many as eight out of ten people do not get enough EFAs from their diet. In addition, metabolic pathways involved in the metabolism of EFAs can be blocked by excess intakes of saturated fat, sugar and alcohol, lack of vitamins and minerals, smoking cigarettes or being under excess stress.

For a healthy fat intake, especially when you are under stress:
- concentrate on eating beneficial fats such as olive, rapeseed, walnut, fish and evening primrose oils
- avoid obviously fatty foods
- cut back on beefburgers, sausages, pies, pizza, crisps, chips, pastries, cakes, doughnuts, chocolate and cream
- trim excess fat from meat and only use lean cuts
- eat chicken in preference to fatty meats such as pork
- grill food rather than frying to help fat drain away
- soak up excess fat from cooked foods using kitchen paper
- eat baked potatoes rather than roasted or chipped
- have several vegetarian meals, which include pulses and beans for protein, each week
- switch to reduced-fat versions of mayonnaise, salad dressing, cheese, milk and yoghurt
- eat red meat only once or twice a week and have more vegetarian meals instead
- try to reduce your intake of margarines and processed foods.

Protein

Proteins are made up of building-blocks called amino acids. When you eat protein, it is digested down into individual amino acids which are then recombined to make the more than 50,000 different proteins that are needed to keep the body working properly. Twenty amino acids are important for human health. Of these, ten cannot

AMINO ACIDS

NUTRITIONALLY ESSENTIAL AMINO ACIDS
- arginine
- histidine
- isoleucine
- leucine
- lysine
- methionine
- phenylalanine
- threonine
- tryptophan
- valine
- tyrosine (synthesized from phenylalanine, which is essential)
- cysteine (synthesized from methionine, which is essential)

NON-ESSENTIAL AMINO ACIDS
- alanine
- asparagine
- aspartic acid
- glutamine
- glutamic acid
- glycine
- proline
- serine

be synthesized in the body in amounts needed by the metabolism and must therefore come from the diet. These are known as the nutritionally essential amino acids.

First and second-class proteins

Dietary protein can be divided into two groups:

- First-class proteins contain significant quantities of the essential amino acids, for example animal meat, fish, eggs, dairy products.
- Second-class proteins contain some of the essential amino acids but not all, for example vegetables, rice, beans, nuts.

Second-class proteins need to be mixed and matched by eating as wide a variety of foods as possible.

The average adult male needs to obtain around 56 g protein a day from his food. Protein deficiency is uncommon in the West, where most people obtain 80–90 g protein a day from their food, with around a third of this coming from meat or meat products.

Eat more fish

Oily fish contains essential fatty acids, that help to thin the blood, lower blood pressure and reduce the risk of a fatal heart attack by as much as a third. Ideally, you need to increase your consumption of oily fish (salmon, herrings, sardines, mackerel) to at least 300 g (2–3 servings) a week. If you don't like fish, consider taking an omega-3 fish oil supplement instead to help keep your circulation healthy during times of stress.

Fibre

Dietary fibre – or roughage – refers to the indigestible parts of plants. There are two main types of dietary fibre: soluble and insoluble. Soluble fibre is important in the stomach and upper intestines, where it slows digestion and absorption to ensure blood sugar and fat rise relatively slowly so that the metabolism can handle nutrient fluctuations more easily.

Insoluble fibre is most important in the large bowel. It bulks up the faeces, absorbs water and toxins and hastens stool excretion. As a result, every gram of fibre you eat adds around 5 g in weight to your stools. The additional weight comes from absorbed water and other substances plus the additional bulk of bacteria that multiply from the energy derived by fermenting insoluble fibre. In general, soluble fibre is totally broken down by bacterial fermentation in the large bowel, whilst insoluble fibre is excreted.

All plant foods contain both soluble and insoluble fibre, though some sources are richer in one type than another (see box below).

A high-fibre diet helps to keep your bowel function healthy during times of stress and can frequently help to reduce symptoms of irritable bowel syndrome, especially constipation. There is no consistent link between symptoms of IBS and fibre intake, however. Overall, following a high-fibre diet helps around one third of people with IBS. In up to a quarter of sufferers, changing to a high-fibre diet initially makes bloating and distension worse. This effect disappears after two or three weeks, so it's worth persevering, building up your fibre intake slowly so your bowel has time to get used to it. If you cannot tolerate bran, supplements containing other forms of fibre such as ispaghula, psyllium or sterculia are often effective.

It is important to eat as many different sources of fibre as possible. New research suggests that bowel bacteria quickly adapt to the types of roughage in your diet. If you mainly eat fibre of one type (for example, a bran supplement) your bowel bacteria will respond within a week or two by increasing their output of enzymes needed to ferment this. The fibre reaching your colon will then be broken down more quickly so that you lose much of the benefit gained.

Ideally, everyone needs to eat at least 30 g fibre per day. The easiest way to increase the amount of fibre in your diet is to eat more unrefined complex carbohydrates in foods such as wholemeal bread, cereals, nuts, grains, root vegetables and fruits. Bran-containing breakfast cereals provide one of the highest concentrations of dietary fibre.

GOOD SOURCES OF FIBRE

- Bran: 40 g fibre per 100 g.
- Dried apricots: 18.g per 100 g.
- Peas: 5 g per 100 g.
- Prunes: 13 g per 100 g.
- Cooked brown rice: 4 g per 100 g.
- Cooked wholemeal spaghetti: 4 g per 100 g.
- Brown bread: 6 g per 100 g.
- Walnuts: 6 g per 100 g.

DIETRY FIBRE

TYPE OF FIBRE	PLANT SOURCE	A FEW EXAMPLES
Soluble fibre	oats	porridge, muesli
	rye	rye bread, crispbread
	fruit	figs, dates, apricots, tomatoes, apples
	vegetables	carrots, potatoes, courgettes,
	pulses	baked beans, kidney beans
Insoluble fibre	wheat	wholemeal bread, cereals
	maize	sweetcorn, corn bread
	rice	brown rice
	pasta	wholemeal pasta
	fruit	rhubarb, blackberries, strawberries
	leafy vegetables	broccoli, spinach, lettuce
	pulses	peas, lentils, chick peas

Fruit and Veg

Fruit and vegetables — including nuts, seeds, pulses and wholegrains — are a rich source of water, carbohydrate, proteins, vitamins, minerals, fibre, essential fatty acids and at least twenty non-nutrient substances, known as phyto-chemicals, that help to protect our health and immunity. Many of these substances are powerful antioxidants (see opposite) that help to boost immune function and protect against a variety of conditions, including some cancers.

Protective, dietary phytochemicals have so far been identified in:

- apricots
- broccoli
- cherries
- chilies
- citrus fruits
- cranberry juice
- red peppers
- red wine
- soya products
- strawberries
- sweet potatoes
- tomatoes
- garlic and onions
- grapes
- green tea
- olive oil
- papaya
- parsley.

Aim to eat at least a pound (454 g) in weight of fruit, vegetables or salad-stuff per day, not counting potatoes. This works out at around five servings. This may seem like a lot but is fairly easy to do — for example, the following adds up to a healthy total of seven servings:

- fresh orange juice with breakfast
- banana mid-morning
- a large salad with lunch
- an apple mid-afternoon
- broccoli and sweetcorn with dinner
- fresh fruit salad for dessert.

Antioxidants

Antioxidants are protective substances that patrol the body, mopping up harmful by-products of metabolism, stress and disease known as free radicals. The most important dietary antioxidants are:

- vitamin A and betacarotene
- vitamin C
- vitamin E
- selenium
- riboflavin
- copper
- manganese.

A free radical is an unstable molecular fragment that carries a minute, negative electrical charge in the form of a spare electron. It tries to lose this charge by colliding with other molecules and cell structures in a process known as oxidation. Oxidation usually triggers a harmful chain reaction in which electrons are passed from one molecule to another with damaging results. Free radicals are produced by:

- metabolism in body cells, especially during times of stress
- muscles during exercise
- smoking cigarettes
- drinking excessive amounts of alcohol
- exposure to environmental pollutants
- exposure to x-rays
- exposure to UVA sunlight, especially if sunburned
- taking some drugs — especially antibiotics or paracetamol.

Body proteins, fats, cell membranes and genetic material (DNA) are constantly under attack from free radicals, with each cell undergoing an estimated 10,000 free radical oxidations per day. These collisions and chain reactions have been linked with:

- hardening and furring up of the arteries
- coronary heart disease
- cataracts
- premature ageing of the skin
- chronic inflammatory diseases such as arthritis
- impaired immunity
- cancerous changes in cells

- poor sperm count and poor sperm quality
- congenital birth defects.

Antioxidant vitamins and minerals are the body's main defence against free radical attack. They quickly neutralize the negative charge on a free radical before it can trigger a chain reaction.

Eat more plant-based hormones

One of the most helpful changes you can make is to eat more of the types of plant that contain weak, oestrogen-like chemicals. These mimic the effects of your own oestrogen hormones and can help to reduce symptoms linked with the menopause and possibly premenstrual syndrome. Plants containing oestrogen-like hormones include:

- legumes, especially soy beans chickpeas, lentils, alfalfa, mung beans
- vegetables: dark-green leafy vegetables (for example, broccoli, pak choi, spinach) and exotic members of the cruciferous family (for example, chinese leaves, kohl rabi); celery, fennel
- nuts: almonds, cashew nuts, hazelnuts, peanuts, walnuts and nut oils
- seeds, especially linseeds, pumpkin, sesame, sunflower and sprouted seeds
- wholegrains: almost all, especially corn, buckwheat, millet, oats, rye, wheat
- fresh fruits: apples, avocados, bananas, mangoes, papayas, rhubarb
- dried fruits, especially dates, figs, prunes, raisins
- culinary herbs: especially angelica, chervil, chives, garlic, ginger, horseradish, nutmeg, parsley, rosemary and sage.

An Australian bread (Burgen bread) fortified with soya and linseed to make it rich in natural plant oestrogens is now available in supermarkets. Eating at least four slices of this a day will help to boost your intake of plant hormones.

Vitamins

Vitamins are naturally occurring organic substances that are essential for life, although they are only needed in minute amounts. Vitamins cannot be synthesized in the body in enough quantity to meet your needs and must therefore come from your food. Most vitamins work by boosting the rate at which important metabolic reactions occur in your cells such as those involved in:

- digestion of foods
- converting fats and carbohydrates into energy
- cell growth and division
- repair of damaged tissues
- fighting infection
- overcoming stress reactions

DIETARY VITAMINS

VITAMIN RDA (recommended daily allowance)		WHY YOU NEED IT	SOME FOOD SOURCES
A	800 mcg	Regulates the way genes are read to make proteins. Controls normal growth and development. Maintains healthy skin, teeth, bones and mucous membranes. Is made into pigment, visual purple, needed for night vision.	Animal and fish liver, eggs, oily fish, milk, cheese, butter, margarine. Betacarotene (two vitamin A molecules joined together) is found in dark-green leafy vegetables and yellow-orange fruits.
B1	1.4 mg	B-group vitamins are needed for energy-yielding metabolic reactions involving proteins, carbohydrates and fats; healthy nerves and muscles; normal cell division; and immunity.	Brewer's yeast, yeast extracts, brown rice, wheatgerm and wheat bran, nuts, wholegrain cereals, meat, seafood, liver, dairy products, green leafy vegetables.
B2	1.6 mg		
B3	18 mg		
B5	6 mg		
B6	2 mg		
B12	1 mcg		
Biotin	0.15 mg	For healthy hair, skin and sweat glands. For the metabolism of fatty acids, amino acids, genetic material and the formation of energy storage molecules.	Liver, kidney, yeast extract, nuts, wholegrain cereals, egg yolk, oily fish, rice.
Folate	200 mcg	For cell division and to keep nerves healthy. In early pregnancy it helps to protect against some developmental abnormalities such as spina bifida.	Green leafy vegetables (for example, spinach, broccoli, Brussels sprouts), yeast extract, whole grains, nuts, liver, dairy products, citrus fruit, eggs.
C	60 mg	For making collagen, an important structural protein. For growth, repair and reproduction. For healthy skin, bones and teeth.	Citrus fruits, blackcurrants, kiwi fruit, mangoes, green peppers, green leafy vegetables (for example, broccoli, sprouts, parsley and other green herbs).
D	5 mcg	Needed for absorption of dietary calcium and phosphate in the small intestine. Essential for healthy bones and teeth.	Oily fish (for example, sardine, herring, mackerel, salmon, tuna), fish liver oils, margarine, liver, eggs, fortified milk.
E	10 mg	Protects body fats (for example, cell membranes, nerve sheaths, cholesterol molecules) from going rancid (oxidation). Strengthens muscle fibres. Boosts immunity and improves skin suppleness and healing.	Wheatgerm oil, avocado pear, nuts, seeds, margarine, eggs, butter, wholegrains, oily fish.

- mental function
- reproduction
- mopping up harmful by-products of metabolism such as free radicals.

Minerals

Minerals are inorganic elements, some of which are metals, that are also essential for healthy metabolism. Those needed in amounts of less than 100 mg are often referred to as trace elements. Minerals and trace elements can only come from your diet and depend on the quality of soil on which produce is grown or grazed. Minerals have a number of functions:

- structural, for example calcium, magnesium and phosphate which strengthen bones and teeth
- maintaining normal cell function, for example sodium, potassium, calcium.
- co-factor for important enzymes, for example copper, iron, magnesium, manganese, molybdenum, selenium, zinc
- involved in oxygen transport, for example iron
- hormone function, for example chromium, iodine
- antioxidant, for example selenium, manganese.

Some trace elements, such as nickel, tin and vanadium are known to be essential for normal growth in only tiny amounts, although their exact roles are not yet fully understood.

DIETARY MINERALS

MINERAL	RDA	WHY YOU NEED IT	FOOD SOURCES
Calcium	800 mg	For strong bones and teeth. Involved in nerve conduction, muscle contraction and energy production. Needed for blood clotting, some enzyme actions and immune functions.	Milk and dairy products such as cheese, yoghurt, fromage frais; green leafy vegetables, salmon, nuts and seeds, pulses, eggs.
Iodine	150 mcg	For production of two thyroid hormones, thyroxine and tri-iodothyronine, which control your metabolic rate.	Seafood, for example haddock, salmon, tuna, prawns, mussels, lobster, oysters; seaweed, iodized salt, milk.
Iron	14 mg	For production of haemoglobin, which transports oxygen around the body. Also found in myoglobin, which binds oxygen in muscle cells. Involved in energy-producing reactions and immunity.	Red meat, fish (especially sardines), brewer's yeast, offal, wheatgerm, wholemeal bread, egg yolk, green vegetables, parsley and other green herbs, prunes and other dried fruit.
Magnesium	300 mg	Maintains the electrical stability of cells and helps to regulate your heartbeat. Needed for most metabolic reactions – few enzymes can work without it.	Soya, nuts, brewer's yeast, wholegrains, brown rice, seafood, meat, eggs, dairy products, bananas, dark-green leafy vegetables and herbs, chocolate.
Phosphorus	800 mg	For healthy bones and teeth. For making energy-rich storage compounds.	Milk and dairy products, nuts, wholegrain cereals, poultry, eggs, meat, fish, legumes.
Zinc	15 mg	Essential for the proper function of over a hundred enzymes. Vital for growth, sexual maturity, wound healing and immunity.	red meat, seafood (especially oysters), offal, brewer's yeast, whole grains, pulses, eggs, cheese.

Supplements

During times of stress, your need for antioxidant vitamins and minerals (see page 137), and those involved in energy-producing reactions goes up. B-group vitamins in particular are depleted during times of stress and when drinking excess alcohol.

It is estimated that only one in ten people get all the vitamins, minerals and essential fatty acids they need from their foods. Although diet should always come first, it is important to ensure a good intake of vitamins and minerals when you are under excess pressure. It is therefore worth taking a good multi-nutrient supplement providing around 100% of the recommended daily amount (RDA) of as many vitamins and minerals as possible. Evening primrose oil (1,000 mg daily) will also help to ensure a good intake of essential fatty acids.

Coenzyme Q10 is a vitamin-like substance important for the release of energy in cells. It is also believed to keep blood-vessel walls healthy and to regulate blood pressure. Supplements containing coenzyme Q10 improve heart muscle function and can reduce a high blood pressure. If you are under stress, lacking in energy or have high blood pressure, coenzyme Q10 may be beneficial.

The yin-yang approach

The oriental concept of yin and yang can also be used to help construct a nutritionally balanced way of eating. This involves two balancing qualities that exist in every natural object and cycle.

- Yin is the 'dark side of the mountain': the cool, flexible, fluid side of nature with qualities of peacefulness, calm, creativity and relaxation. It is viewed as the female force.
- Yang is the 'bright side of the mountain' and represents the hot, strong and dynamic side of life whose qualities include activity, alertness, energy and precision. It is the male force.

Chinese philosophy holds that too much yin results in low moods, exhaustion and sleepiness, while too much yang can lead to feelings of stress, irritability, hyperventilation and insomnia. Most people who are stressed have a mixture of yin and yang symptoms.

The macrobiotic, wholefood way of eating revolves around the yin and yang properties of foods. A lifestyle that is too yang can be corrected by eating yin foods and vice versa. Yin foods are said to be calming while yang foods are strengthening. The aim of a macrobiotic diet is to eat in balance with your needs to offset the effects of stress and ill health.

Yin foods

These tend to grow above ground in hot climates, have a high water content, and to be more aromatic, soft and juicy. For example:

- fruit
- green leafy vegetables
- nuts
- seeds
- tofu
- tempeh
- natural juices.

Yang foods

These tend to consist of roots, stems and seeds and to grow in cold, wet climates. For example:

- wholegrain cereals
- root vegetables
- seafood
- cottage cheese
- beans, peas and lentils
- miso
- soy.

Herbal dietary supplements

Phytotherapy — the use of plant extracts for healing — is one of the most exciting and effective branches of alternative medicine. Different parts of different plants are used — roots, stems, flowers, leaves, bark, sap, fruit or seeds — depending on which has the highest concentration of active ingredient. In most cases, they are dried and ground to produce a powder which is made into a tea, or packed into capsules for easy swallowing.

Many herbal dietary supplements are helpful during times of stress, especially those that act as adaptogens. An adaptogen is a substance that strengthens, normalizes and regulates all the body's systems. It has wide-ranging beneficial actions and boosts immunity through several different actions to help you adapt to a wide variety of new or stressful situations.

Research suggests that adaptogens work by increasing the production of energy in body cells and by making the uptake of oxygen and processing of cell wastes more efficient. This encourages cell growth and increases cell survival. Many adaptogens have been shown to normalize blood-sugar levels, hormone imbalances, disrupted biorhythms and the physical and emotional effects of stress.

Adaptogens seem to work best as an energy stimulant if fatigue is not directly due to excess physical exertion but to an underlying problem such as poor or irregular diet, hormone imbalance, stress or excess consumption of coffee, nicotine or alcohol. Lifestyle changes to redress the balance (for example, stopping or cutting back on smoking) are also important to re-energize the body. When adaptogens are used together with vitamin C and the B-complex, results are often improved.

Ginseng

Ginseng – usually referred to as Chinese, Korean or Asian ginseng (*Panax ginseng; P. quinquefolius*)– is a perennial plant native to north-east China, North Korea and eastern Russia. White ginseng is produced from air-drying the root; red ginseng (which is more potent and stimulating) by steaming and then drying the root. The closely related American ginseng has a similar action and is generally preferred in Asia as it is sweeter tasting and thought to have more yin (heat-reducing capacity) than Chinese ginseng.

Ginseng has been used in the Orient as a revitalizing adaptogen for over 7,000 years. It is especially helpful during times of stress as it contains plant sub-stances that support the function of the adrenal glands when they are overworked. Clinical trials confirm that ginseng helps the body adapt to physical or emotional stress and fatigue. It is stimulating and restorative, improving physical and mental energy, stamina, strength, alertness and concentration. Those taking ginseng have faster reaction times than when not taking it, and it improves stamina while reducing muscle cramps and fatigue.

Make sure you buy a good quality product from a reputable company, or one standardized to contain at least 7% ginsenosides. This will generally be more expensive, but cheap versions may contain very little active ingredient.

Taking ginseng

The dose depends on the grade of root. Choose a standardized product, preferably with a content of at least 5% ginsenosides for American ginseng and 15% ginseno-sides for Korean ginseng. Start with a low dose and work up from 200 to 1,000 mg per day until you find a dose that suits you. 1,000 mg may be too stimulating, so

600mg is often ideal. The optimum dose is usually around 600 mg daily. Ginseng should not be taken for more than six weeks without a break. In the East, it is taken in a two weeks on, two weeks off cycle. Some practitioners recommend taking it in a six weeks on, eight weeks off cycle.

Ginseng is not advised if you have high blood pressure (it may make hypertension worse), glaucoma or have an oestrogen-dependent condition (for example, pregnancy, cancer of the breast, ovaries or uterus) as it contains oestrogenic compounds.

It is best to avoid taking other stimulants such as caffeine-containing products and drinks while taking ginseng. When taken in therapeutic doses in a two weeks on, two weeks off cycle, side effects should not be a problem. If you find Chinese ginseng too stimulating, however, you could try American ginseng which seems to have a more gentle action.

American ginseng is said to be best for fatigue caused by nervous conditions, anxiety and insomnia, while Korean ginseng is better for fatigue with general weakness and loss of energy.

Siberian ginseng

Siberian ginseng *(Eleutherococcus senticosus)* is a deciduous hardy shrub native to eastern Russia, China, Korea and Japan. Its root has similar actions to that of Korean and American *(Panax)* ginsengs, but it is not closely related.

Siberian ginseng is one of the most widely researched herbal adaptogens. It is used extensively to improve stamina and strength, particularly during or after illness and when suffering from other forms of stress and fatigue. Russian research suggests that as a result of boosting immunity, those taking it regularly have 40% less colds, flu and other infections compared with previous winters, and take a third less days off work due to health problems than those not taking it. Siberian ginseng is therefore taken by 20 million Russians every day to improve performance, general health and adaptation to stress or change.

Siberian ginseng is also used to counter jet lag, and has been shown to help normalize high blood pressure and raised blood-sugar levels. It is particularly popular with athletes as it can improve performance and reaction times by as much as a quarter.

Taking Siberian ginseng

Choose a brand that is standardized to contain more than 1% of eleutherosides and take 1,000–2,000 mg in capsule form per day. Occasionally up to 6,000 mg daily is recommended. It is traditionally taken for two to three weeks followed by a two-week break for those who are generally young, healthy and fit. Those who are older, weaker or unwell may take their doses continuously. Take on an empty stomach unless you find it too relaxing, in which case take it with meals.

As with Panax ginseng, Siberian ginseng is best taken cyclically. Take daily for two to three months, then have a month without. Most people begin to notice a difference after around five days, but continue to take it for at least one month for the full restorative effect.

No serious side effects have been reported. Do not use (except under medical advice) if you suffer from high blood pressure, a tendency to nose bleeds, heavy periods, insomnia, rapid heartbeat (tachycardia), high fever or congestive heart failure. Do not take during pregnancy or when breastfeeding except under specific medical advice.

Ginkgo

The *Ginkgo biloba*, or maidenhair tree, is one of the oldest known plant species on Earth and is often described as a living fossil. It is one of the most popular health supplements in Europe and can improve memory and concentration as well as increasing peripheral blood flow. It is also helpful for stress-induced anxiety, depression and migraine.

Taking ginkgo

Choose extracts standardized for at least 24% ginkolides and take 40–60 mg two or three times a day (take a minimum of 120 mg daily). Stimulating effects last from three to six hours but they may not be noticed until after ten days of treatment.

Gotu kola

Gotu kola *(Centella asiatica)* is an herbaceous perennial plant native to the Orient. It is known in India as *brahmi* and is one of the most important ayurvedic herbs, used to relieve anxiety and depression, improve memory, promote calm (in larger doses), relax muscle tension, boost adrenal function during times of stress and relieve pain. It is also said to increase physical and mental energy levels.

Taking gotu kola

Choose extracts standardized to contain 25 mg triterpenes, and take two to four capsules daily.

No serious side effects have been reported. High doses may cause headaches. Large doses are calming rather than energizing.

Garlic

Garlic *(Allium sativum)* is a popular culinary herb that has antibacterial and antiviral actions. Clinical trials using standardized tablets have shown that taking garlic regularly can reduce high blood pressure, lower levels of harmful blood fats (LDL-cholesterol and triglycerides), reduce blood stickiness and improve circulation to all parts of the body. Regular use reduces the risk of hardening and furring up of the arteries up to 25%, and garlic is therefore an important protective herb for those under stress who are at increased risk of high blood pressure and coronary heart disease.

Taking garlic
Take 600–900 mg standardized garlic-powder tablets per day.

Garlic products made by solvent extraction or by boiling garlic in oil are less effective than tablets made from garlic that has been freeze-dried and powdered.

St John's wort

St John's wort *(Hypericum perforatum)* has been used for over 2,000 years to improve emotional well-being. It is an effective and gentle antidepressant that can help to overcome many of the emotional effects of stress. It can lift low moods in at least 67% of those with mild to moderate depression. Studies involving over 5,000 patients shows that hypericum can lift mild depression within two weeks of starting the course — and the optimum effect is reached within six weeks. Eighty-two per cent also suffered less irritability, anxiety, low moods, hot flushes, sweating and disturbed sleep. Low sex drive — a common accompaniment to stress and depression — is improved in 60% of people within three months.

Taking St John's wort
Hypericum is best taken with food. Choose extracts standardized to 0.3% hypericin and take 300 mg three times a day.

Side effects are significantly less likely than with standard antidepressants. Those reported include indigestion, allergic reactions, restlessness and tiredness/fatigue, each in less than 1% of people. St John's wort should not be taken during pregnancy or when breastfeeding. Do not take together with other antidepressants except under medical supervision. It is best to avoid alcohol when taking hypericum. Those who are sun-sensitive should avoid exposing their skin directly to sunlight while taking it — especially if fair-skinned.

Valerian

Valerian *(Valeriana officinalis)* has been used since medieval times to calm the nerves and help induce a natural sleep. Modern research shows that it is one of the most relaxing natural herbs available and it is widely used as a sedative. Valerian has significant, positive effects on stress, and as well as relieving anxiety and tension induces sleep, eases smooth muscle spasm and promotes calmness. Trials involving people with mental symptoms due to stress showed that it helped to overcome low moods, loss of initiative, feeling unsociable, irritability, anxiety and difficulty sleeping. It is also used to relieve cramps, period pains, intestinal colic, migraine and rheumatic pains.

Taking valerian
Take 400–800 mg three times a day.
   Do not take if you are using prescribed sleeping tablets. It may cause mild drowsiness which will affect your ability to drive or operate machinery. Do not take if you are pregnant or breastfeeding.

Lemon balm

Lemon balm has been used since ancient times as a healing, soothing herb with calming properties. It was also known as the 'scholar's herb' as it was traditionally taken by students suffering from the stress of impending exams. It is widely used to ease a number of stress-related symptoms including digestive problems, nausea, flatulence, depression, nervous anxiety, headache and insomnia.
   When combined with valerian, the two herbs work in synergy to reduce symptoms of tension, stress and mild depression. They also have a gently lowering effect on the raised blood pressure that often accompanies stress.

Taking lemon balm
Take 650 mg three times a day.
   Do not take if you are using prescribed sleeping tablets. It may cause mild drowsiness which will affect your ability to drive or operate machinery. Do not take if you are pregnant or breastfeeding.

Eliminating toxins

The two main ways of eliminating dietary toxins are to go organic, or to fast temporarily.

Going organic

Non-organic fruit and vegetables tend to be bred for uniformity of colour and size, and the ability to keep their fresh appearance for longer. Often this is achieved at the expense of flavour and nutrients, and with the help of a range of agro-chemicals such as pesticides, weed killers, fungicides, fumigants, growth promoters, growth retardants and fertilizers. These chemicals are often applied regularly from the time the crop is still in its seed form, during germination and throughout its growing cycle. Each non-organic apple, for example, has been dosed around forty times with up to a hundred additives before you eat it. These chemicals do not just lie on the surface of the produce, but are found beneath the skin and sometimes throughout the flesh itself. Over 50% of all pesticides sprayed on fruit and vegetables are used simply to maintain its cosmetic appearance. While some of these chemicals are considered safe to use on crops, the full effects of many on our long-term health are still not completely understood. The Environment Protection Agency in the United States consider that 60% of all herbicides, 90% of all fungicides and 30% of all insecticides are potentially cancer-causing.

Going organic means eating foods produced using organic farming practices and which have received minimal processing. There are proven and sustainable methods of producing food in harmony with nature, without the use of pesticides, antibiotics, hormones, artificial fertilizers, genetic manipulation, irradiation or undue exposure to environmental pollution. Instead, farmers use traditional methods of pest control, crop rotation, growing green manure crops (for example, clover), careful timing of sowing and allowing land to lie fallow. This results in products that are full of flavour, vitamins and minerals, and which contain the lowest possible amounts of artificial chemicals.

The benefits of going organic

Non-organic crops are frequently grown in artificially fertilized soils boosted with nitrogen, phosphorus and potassium but depleted of other minerals and trace elements, which are not replenished regularly. In addition, many crops shipped from abroad are picked before they are ripe, so their nutrient content is

THE ORGANIC CHOICE

The range of organic foods available is vast and includes:

- fruit (for example, oranges, lemons, apples, clementines, tangerines, grapefruit, grapes, pears, bananas, mangoes)
- vegetables (for example, carrots, potatoes, onions, parsnip, courgettes, aubergines, beans, broccoli, spinach, garlic)
- salad-stuff (for example, lettuce, tomatoes, cucumbers, peppers, celery, spring onions, beetroot)
- bread, rice and pasta
- milk, cream, butter and eggs
- cheeses
- meats (for example, chicken, lamb, pork, beef, sausages, burgers, bacon, liver)
- game (for example, pigeon, guinea fowl, rabbit)
- fish (for example, lemon sole, monkfish, cod, plaice, turbot, haddock, mackerel, sardines, salmon, squid, mussels, oysters, lobster, crab) caught from some of the cleanest waters in the world
- fruit juices
- wines and beers
- olive and nut oils
- natural spring water
- cakes and biscuits
- preserves and condiments
- snacks and confectionery
- tea and coffee.

WHY GOING ORGANIC IS BETTER FOR HEALTH

Chemicals used in producing or rearing non-organic foodstuffs:

- are concentrated in the liver and may lead to liver problems
- have been linked with lowered fertility
- have been associated with intestinal problems such as irritable bowel syndrome, candida overgrowth and inflammatory bowel disease
- lower immunity and may increase the risk of allergies and some cancers
- are linked with the emergence of resistant bacteria that are difficult to treat.

naturally low. Organic foods contain, on average, twice the vitamins, minerals, trace elements, essential fatty acids, fibre and phytochemicals than commercially grown produce. This is partly because they contain less water and more solid matter, but also due to the rich soils in which they are grown. Fresh produce that is organically grown locally and has only recently been harvested will contain the most nutrients. Look for produce that is crisp and firm with a healthy colour. Reject any that look wilted, brown, faded or bruised.

Fasting

When an animal such as a cat is unwell or under stress, it will commonly stop eating until it is better again. Many holistic practitioners believe that controlled dietary restriction is of benefit to humans, too, as it is thought to help clear the body of toxins, which are released from body-fat stores as these are burned up as energy. As well as increasing spiritual awareness, fasting allows the body to break down and eliminate diseased cells in preference to healthy ones and may even delay the ageing process by increasing production of growth hormone.

COMMON SIDE EFFECTS OF FASTING

The side effects of a short fast are usually mild and short-lived (remedies are given in brackets):

- dizziness and light-headedness (rest; men should sit during urination to prevent fainting)
- palpitations (rest)
- headache (relieve with acupressure and relaxation, not drugs)
- insomnia (use relaxation, visualization and massage)
- nausea (relieve with acupressure)
- bad taste in the mouth and a coated tongue (scrape tongue and use a lemon-juice/water mouthwash to freshen mouth)
- increased body odour (take warm, not hot showers or baths daily)
- dry skin and scaly skin rashes (use a non-perfumed body lotion or dilute aromatherapy massage oils)
- aching, tired muscles (relieve with a gentle aromatherapy massage)
- runny nose, salivation, increased vaginal discharge (no treatment necessary)
- increased susceptibility to feeling the cold (wear an extra layer of clothes)
- lack of bowel motions (this is normal when not eating).

If more serious side effects develop, always seek medical advice.

There are several popular fasting regimes:

- Water only (two litres of mineral, spring or distilled water daily).
- Juice (for example, apple and carrot) only.
- Mono diet, in which a single food, for example apples or grapes, is eaten, and water drunk.
- Yoghurt and juice.

In a true, water-only fast, hunger usually disappears after the first day. When drinking juices or taking certain foods, hunger pangs tend to continue.

Some practitioners advise fasting for one day a week, while others recommend fasts lasting from four days to two weeks, and occasionally longer in a residential clinic under medical supervision. Fasting in itself can be stressful for the body, so if you are under extreme stress or if you suffer from a medical condition, always seek professional advice. You should only ever fast for periods of longer than two days while under the supervision of an experienced nutritional therapist (for example, a trained naturopath or a practitioner of ayurvedic medicine).

After fasting, your stomach will have shrunk and your production of intestinal juices will be much reduced. A fast should therefore be broken carefully by drinking diluted fruit or vegetables juices, and eating thin soups, watermelon and natural bio yogurt little and often for a day or two followed by a simple diet of oatmeal, rice and steamed vegetables plus cottage cheese. All foods should be organic if possible.

Never fast if you:
- are taking prescription medication that should not be stopped
- are underweight
- are pregnant
- are breastfeeding
- have anaemia
- have Type 1 (early-onset) diabetes
- have kidney failure
- have severe liver disease
- suffer from gout (except under specialist supervision).

Some practitioners also advise not fasting during menstruation.

During a fast, do not:
- take any drugs, including those bought over the counter
- smoke cigarettes
- drink caffeinated drinks
- drink alcohol
- take any supplements (except *Lactobacillus acidophilus* for a healthy bowel)
- take exercise (except for gentle stretching and strolling walks)
- take hot baths or showers (take warm ones only).

TAKE EXERCISE AND RELAX

Once you have taken your life and diet in hand, look towards increasing the amount of exercise you take each week. Start with some relaxation exercises, but don't forget to include other forms of activity to boost your heart rate.

Breathing

The way you breathe reflects the amount of stress you are under. When you feel relaxed, your breathing will be calm and regular (10–14 breaths per minute) and you will move your whole rib cage and diaphragm. When you feel anxious, however, your breathing rate speeds up to 15–20 breaths per minute and your breaths become shallow (involving the upper part of your rib cage only) and irregular, interspersed with deep sighs and gasps as you try to get more air.

Healthy breathing check

To help you recognize what normal, gentle breathing feels like:

1. Lie down and make yourself comfortable and relaxed.
2. Rest your hands on the upper part of your chest.
3. Breathe gently in and out for about a minute and feel the way your chest rises and falls.
4. Now place your hands on your rib cage so your fingertips almost touch when you breathe out.
5. Focusing your attention on when you breathe out rather than when you breathe in, breathe gently for another minute or so and feel your rib cage as it moves upwards and outwards each time.
6. Finally, place your hands on your abdomen with your fingertips just touching.

Breathe gently for another minute and feel your fingers part as your abdomen rises and falls.

7. Continue breathing gently and hold on to the calm feeling.

Repeat this breathing exercise daily until you recognize how slow, gentle breathing should feel.

When you are under long-term excess pressure, it is easy for bad breathing habits to build up. By consciously changing the way you breathe, you can help to switch off some of the effects of the stress response and reduce feelings of anxiety.

The following exercise is useful to help you control your breathing when you feel stressed, or to relax before meditation or visualization.

SIGNS OF A POOR BREATHING HABIT

- Rapid, shallow breathing involving the upper part of the chest only.
- Shoulders rise significantly towards the ears.
- No visible expansion of the abdomen.
- Irregular breathing pattern with lots of deep sighs.
- Air-gulping, which leads to abdominal wind and belching.
- Taking deep breaths and holding on to them without breathing out.

These are all signs of hyperventilation and can trigger a panic attack when anxiety is high (see page 42).

Breathing Exercise 1

1. Sit back comfortably, with your arms hanging loosely at your sides.
2. Breathe in slowly and deeply, concentrating on the rise and fall of your abdomen rather than your chest.
3. When you reach your limit of breathing in, immediately start to breathe out to empty your lungs as much as possible.
4. Get your rhythm right by slowly counting up to three when breathing in and slowly counting up to four when breathing out.
5. Repeat the exercise five times without holding your breath.

Breathing Exercise 2

1. Change your breathing rhythm if necessary to ensure that breathing out always takes longer than breathing in.
2. Gradually increase the length of exhalation until inhalation is short (2–3 seconds) and exhalation takes 7–8 seconds in a slow, continuous movement. Place your hands on your chest or abdomen, as described in the 'Healthy breathing check' above, if this helps you to feel your breathing movements.
3. Concentrate on emptying your lungs and on keeping the air movement continuous – don't breathe out all your air quickly and wait for the end of the count to breathe in. It will take practice to slow down to this rate of about six breaths per minute.

Once you have learned this technique and feel able to control your breathing, you will find it invaluable for calming rising panic.

When panic rises

Try this exercise to calm rising panic:

1. When the feeling of panic starts to rise, say 'Calm!' quietly to yourself.

2. Breathe out deeply, then breathe in slowly.

3. Hold this breath for a count of three and breathe out gently, letting the tension go.

4. Continue to breathe regularly, imagining a candle in front of your face. As you breathe the flame should flicker but not go out.

5. Continue breathing gently and consciously try to relax — let your tense muscles unwind and try to speak and move more slowly.

WHOLE BODY RELAXATION EXERCISE

The following exercise is excellent for helping you to achieve total body relaxation. It is useful when you want to relax at the end of a highly stressful day, when you can't sleep, or when you are preparing for meditation or visualization.

1. Pull the curtains to dim the light, and find a warm, quiet place to lie down flat on your back with head supported, arms and legs straight and slightly away from your body.

2. Loosen your clothing and relax.

3. Imagine you are ridding your body of stress and breathe in and out deeply for three breaths, then continue to breathe normally and close your eyes.

4. You are going to work on all the major muscle groups, starting with the lower limbs. As you work, you'll recognize the difference in feeling between tension and relaxation. Hold each constriction briefly and repeat each action twice with a short break between.

5. Pull your feet towards your body; hold the tension; release and feel the reduction in tension.

6. Point your toes firmly away from your body and feel the tension in your calf muscles; hold; and relax.

7. Next work on your thighs by drawing your legs tightly towards you or raising them into the air; hold; then drop them back to a relaxed position.

8. Tense your buttocks by squeezing them hard together; hold; and relax.

9. Tense your abdomen by first pushing it out as far as possible, then sucking it in; hold; and then relax.

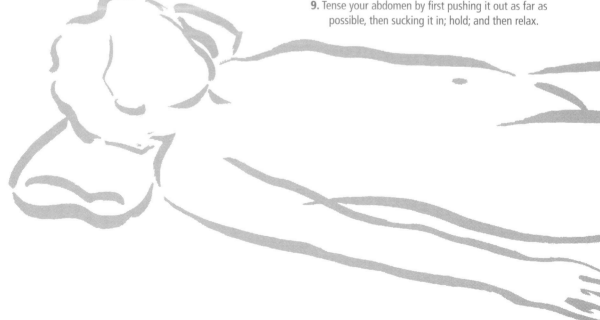

QUICK TIPS TO IMPROVE YOUR BREATHING

- Wear clothes that are loose rather than tight around your middle.
- Develop a slow, calm breathing rhythm with a slight pause after breathing out.
- Try dropping your shoulders slightly as you breathe out to help you relax.
- Be aware of your breathing on a day-to-day basis when you are doing different activities and monitor any changes.
- Try visualizing a stressful situation so that your breathing rate increases, then practise calming your breathing until you feel relaxed again. Do this several times until you feel confident that you are in control and can use this exercise to calm yourself when you start to feel stressed.

---

10. Check your lower body is relaxed – it should feel heavy, warm and without tension. **11.** Arch your spine away from the floor; hold; and let go. (Omit if you have a back problem.)

12. Move your shoulders backwards to expand your chest; hold; and release.

13. Tense your shoulders by raising your arms and pulling on your shoulders; hold; then relax.

14. Now work on your hands and lower arms by making a tight fist; hold; relax and let your fingers loosen. As you clench your fists for the second time, raise your arms slightly off the ground and notice the tension in your forearms; hold; and release.

15. Move to the upper arms by bringing your hands towards your body, close to your chest; hold; relax them down, palms upwards.

16. Relax your neck and throat by gently moving your head from side to side and then pulling your chin down to your chest; hold; and release.

17. Next clench your jaw by clamping your teeth together; hold; and let go so that your mouth is slightly open.

18. Now work on your facial muscles. Press your lips together; hold; and release. Push your tongue hard to the roof of your mouth; hold; and let it drop to the floor of your mouth.

19. Without opening your eyes, move them to the four quarters of a circle and then let your eyelids relax.

20. Finally, relax your forehead and scalp. Frown hard and pull your forehead down; hold; and let go so that your face droops.

Your whole body should now feel heavy and relaxed. Breathe calmly and slowly and feel all that tension drain away. Imagine you are lying in a warm, sunny meadow with a stream bubbling gently beside you. Relax for at least twenty minutes, occasionally checking your body for tension. In your own time, bring the session to a close.

Yoga

Yoga is a gentle and ancient form of oriental exercise that uses posture, breathing techniques and relaxation to increase suppleness and vitality, calm the body, improve sleep and relieve stress. Several different types of yoga exist and hatha yoga, which concentrates on posture and exercise, is the one most widely practised in the West. As with all therapies, it is best to receive training from a qualified teacher, who will help you achieve mental control and the right yoga positions for you. Yoga is based on the concept that physical exercises are linked to mental and spiritual development. Breathing is a major element since the breath embodies a person's *prana* or life-force, and plays an important role in helping problems associated with emotional and mental disharmony. Many yoga exercises and positions will help control the rapid breathing of hyperventilation, while the stretching and relaxing of muscles is a wonderful way to start or end the day, particularly for those experiencing stress, insomnia and anxiety.
Before starting there are a few points to make sure of.

- Check with your doctor if you have a back problem or high blood pressure.
- Do not use yoga within an hour of eating — wait three hours after a heavy meal.
- Empty your bladder and bowels.
- Don't mix yoga with smoking, drugs or alcohol.
- Wear comfortable, light clothing that stretches easily.

Breathing plays an important part in yoga. The exercise below is an example from the range of yoga positions that can help you achieve relaxation through posture and breathing.

The Triangle (*Trikonasana*)

This position alleviates anxiety and reduces mental stress.

1. Stand comfortably with your legs slightly more than a shoulder-width apart, with your feet facing forward.
2. Breathe in, and raise your right arm up alongside your left ear, stretching as high as possible. As part of the same movement, your right arm will follow over to the left, forming a graceful curve from your fingertips down to your right foot.
3. Breathe regularly and hold the position for thirty to sixty seconds
4. Make sure you keep looking forward, not down; that your knees and upper elbow are straight; and that your body and feet are not twisted.
5. Return to your original position as you inhale.
6. Repeat the exercise again, this time using your left arm and moving to the right.

T'ai chi ch'uan

T'ai chi ch'uan – often known as t'ai chi – means 'the supreme way of the fist'. It is a Chinese therapy that uses slow, graceful movements, meditation and breathing techniques to achieve total body control, improve the flow of the life-energy force, or *chi*, and to calm the mind. It is sometimes described as meditation in motion. It is a non-combative form of marital arts that stimulates the mind and body. One of the most popular versions, known as the short form, consists of twenty-four slow movements and postures that flow effortless one into another and can be performed in five to ten minutes. The long form consists of 108 different movements and takes twenty to forty minutes to complete.

Research confirms that t'ai chi can reduce stress and that, as a form of exercise, it can improve breathing efficiency.

It is important to learn t'ai chi from a teacher if possible, although training videos are available. Sessions start with a gentle warm-up exercise and are ideally performed every day.

Exercise and stress

Exercise burns off the effects of adrenaline and helps to neutralize the fight-or-flight response and return your systems to their rest/digest setting. Regular exercise can boost your immunity and even prolong your life. A study of more than 10,000 men found that exercise reduced the number of age-related deaths from all causes by almost a quarter – even if exercise was not started until middle age. Regular exercise is therefore essential for those experiencing high levels of stress.

Unfortunately, seven out of ten men and eight out of ten women do not take enough exercise to have a beneficial effect on their heart or to reduce their levels of stress. Ideally, you should exercise briskly for twenty or thirty minutes five

THE HEALTH BENEFITS OF EXERCISE

Exercise can:

- reduce anxiety and tension
- improve the quality of sleep
- improve strength, stamina and suppleness
- help maintain a healthy weight
- keep bowels regular
- protect against osteoporosis
- reduce high blood-cholesterol levels
- reduce high blood pressure
- reduce the risk of stroke by up to 50%
- reduce the risk of diabetes by up to 40%
- reduce the risk of intestinal haemorrhage
- reduce the risk of cancer of the colon, rectum or womb by up to a quarter.

times a week. Once you are fit, exercise every day.

Walking briskly (4.5 miles per hour) for thirty minutes burns up 200 calories — enough to lose one pound every two weeks if you do it every day.

Are you an apple or a pear?

Work out your waist:hip ratio by measuring your waist and hips in centimeters, then divide the waist measurement by the hip measurement to produce your ratio. For example, if your waist measures 99 cm and your hips 109 cm, your waist:hip ratio is 99 divided by 109, which is 0.9.

- If you are female, is your waist:hip ratio less than 0.85 ?
- If you are male, is your waist:hip ratio less than 0.95 ?

If it is, you're 'pear-shaped'; if not, you're 'apple-shaped'.

Why being apple-shaped is bad for your health

People who are apple-shaped have a higher risk of hardening and furring up of the arteries, high cholesterol levels, high blood pressure, coronary heart disease, stroke, and diabetes than those who are pear-shaped. The reason is not fully understood, but is probably linked with the way your body handles dietary fats. Lack of exercise and drinking excessive amounts of alcohol also seem to encourage fat gain around the waist. People who are under stress and also apple-shaped therefore need to take urgent steps to increase their level of activity. Luckily, people who are apple-shaped seem to lose weight more easily than those who are pear-shaped. This is because abdominal fat is mobilized and broken down more easily than fat stored elsewhere.

If you are overweight and also apple-shaped, you have a high risk of developing coronary heart disease — especially if this runs in your family. In fact, waist size alone may be a good indicator of health — or lack of it. New research suggests that men with a waist circumference larger than 102 cm and women with a waist circumference larger than 88 cm are more likely to have shortness of breath, high blood pressure, high cholesterol levels and diabetes than those with slimmer waistlines. Slight waist reductions of just 5–10 cm significantly reduced the risk of having a heart attack.

Are you in the healthy weight range for your height?

Using a calculator, work out your body mass index (BMI) — this is assessed by dividing your weight in kilograms by the square of your height in metres. For example, someone with a weight of 70 kg and a height of 1.7 m has a BMI of 70 ÷ 1.7 ÷ 1.7 = 24.22 kg/m2.

The calculation produces a number that can be interpreted by the table below.

BMI	Weight band
< 20	underweight
20-25	healthy
25-30	overweight
30-40	obese
> 40	morbidly obese

If your BMI is in the overweight range (25–30), you should try to lose a few pounds to bring you back into the healthy weight range for your height. Those who are overweight are one-and-a-half times more likely to have a heart attack than someone who maintains a healthy weight. Where excess weight is stored is also important. If you are overweight and also store fat round your middle (apple-

OPTIMUM HEALTHY WEIGHT RANGE

HEIGHT Metres/feet	MEN Kg	Stones	WOMEN Kg	Stones
1.47/4'10"			40–51	6st 4 – 8st
1.50/4'11"			42–54	6st 8 – 8st 7
1.52/5ft			43–55	6st 11 – 8st 9
1.55/5'1"			45–57	7st 1 – 8st 13
1.57/5'2"			46–59	7st 3 – 9st 4
1.60/5'3"			48–61	7st 8 – 9st 8
1.63/5'4"			50–63	7st 12 – 9st 13
1.65/5'5"			51–65	8st – 10st 3
1.68/5'6"	56–70	8st 12 – 11 st	53–67	8st 5 – 10st 7
1.70/5'7"	58–72	9st 1 – 11st 4	54 – 69	8st 7 – 10st 12
1.73/5'8"	60–75	9st 6 – 11st 10	56 – 71	8st 11 – 11st 2
1.75/5'9"	61–76	9st 9 – 12 st	57–73	8st 13 – 11st 7
1.78/5'10"	63– 79	9st 1 – 12st 6	59–75	9st 4 – 11st 11
1.80/5'11"	65–81	10st 3 – 12st 9	61–77	9st 8 – 12st 1
1.83/6 ft	67–83	10st 7 – 13st 1	63–80	9st 13 – 12st 8
1.85/6'1"	69–85	10st 11 – 13st 5		
1.88/6'2"	71–88	11st 2 – 13st 12		
1.90/6'3"	72–90	11st 5 – 14st 2		
1.93/6'4"	75–93	11st 10 – 14st 8		

shaped), you are twice as likely to develop coronary heart disease — especially if this runs in your family. Getting down to the healthy weight range for your height can reduce your risk of a heart attack by as much as 35–55%.

The chart on the previous page shows the optimum healthy weight range that you should aim for, for your height. The figures for women are slightly stricter than for men (a BMI of 18.7–23.8 for women, and 20–25 for men) to take account of their different muscle:fat ratio.

As well as helping to reduce an apple shape and helping you lose weight, exercise increases your strength (by building up muscle bulk), your stamina (by increasing muscle energy stores), and your suppleness (by improving the range of movement of joints and making ligaments and tendons more flexible). Increased stamina is particularly important when you are under stress.

How to start an exercise regime

If you are relatively unfit, don't launch straight into a jogging programme. To achieve fitness, start off slowly and take regular exercise lasting for twenty or thirty minutes, for a minimum of five times per week (for example, two days' exercise, one day's rest). Once you have achieved a reasonable level of fitness, you should do more.

Your level of exercise should be strenuous enough to work up a slight sweat, and to make you slightly breathless. Always warm up first with a few simple bends and stretches, and cool down afterwards by walking slowly for a few minutes. If you have problems with your joints (for example, arthritis) or find it difficult to manage a brisk walk, try a non-weight-bearing form of exercise such as cycling or swimming.

The golden rule is, if it hurts — stop. If at any time you become so breathless that you can't speak, develop chest tightness or pain, or feel dizzy or unwell, stop immediately and seek medical advice. If you have a heart problem, you should seek medical advice before embarking on a physical exercise programme.

Tips to help you exercise more

- Take up an active hobby such as ballroom dancing, bowls, swimming, golf, walking or cycling.
- If you dislike exercise, try to put more effort into DIY or gardening.
- Spend less time watching TV and more time pottering in the garden or around the house — listen to music or the radio if you like background noise.
- Borrow a dog and take it for regular walks.

- Walk up stairs rather than using the lift or escalator.
- Walk or cycle reasonable distances rather than taking the car.
- Walk around the block in your lunch hour.
- If you can't go out, try walking up and down stairs a few times a day.
- Reintroduce the traditional habit of a family walk after Sunday lunch.
- Get off the bus or tube one stop earlier than usual and walk the rest of the way.
- Start getting up an hour earlier than usual and go for a walk, cycle, do some gardening, fetch the daily paper, or visit the gym.
- Buy a home exercise machine and use it while watching the evening news.

Stretch exercises to perform at your desk in your lunch hour

Try to enrol others in your office to take part in these lunch-hour exercises and make it a regular stress-busting session.

Relaxing your neck (two exercises)

1. Stand comfortably with feet apart and shoulders relaxed.
2. Slowly drop your left ear towards your left shoulder and hold the stretch for a count of five.
3. Repeat with the right ear.

1. Imagine you are carrying a heavy briefcase in each hand so that your shoulders are pulled towards the floor.
2. Now imagine dropping the briefcase weight and feeling the tension release.
3. Repeat several times and feel your neck become less tense.

Shoulders (two exercises)

1. Stand comfortably, with feet apart.
2. Bend your arms up and clasp your hands behind your head.
3. Pull your elbows forward so they almost touch in front of your chin, then swing them out so they are as wide apart as possible.
4. Repeat several times until your shoulders have loosened up.

1. Circle your left shoulder in a backward direction five times. Repeat with right shoulder.
2. Circle your left shoulder in a forward direction five times. Repeat with right shoulder.
3. Repeat, circling both shoulders together.

Arms

1. Stand up and take a few deep breaths.
2. Raise your arms above your head, keeping them straight, and stretch as high as you can.
3. Now stretch both arms out in front of you at shoulder height.
4. Let you arms relax and drop to your sides, swinging, until they come to a stand-still. Repeat several times.
5. Finally, raise your arms above your shoulders again and swing energetically.

Hand-shaking

1. Shake each hand and arm in turn for a minute or two: when you stop your muscles will feel soft and relaxed.
2. Repeat using your legs and feet if you wish.

Wrists

1. Bend both wrists up and down, side to side and round and round as far as possible.

Fingers

1. Squeeze a soft foam ball in the palm of your hand by clenching your fingers as tightly as possible.
2. Hold for a count of five, then relax your fingers.

Hips

1. Stand comfortably with your feet apart and your hands on your hips.
2. Without moving your lower body, rotate your upper body and hips to the right, to the back, to the left and to the front again.
3. Repeat five times in one direction, then five times in the other.

Legs (two exercises)

1. Stand comfortably with your back and head straight, your abdomen and pelvis tucked in and your feet apart.
2. Rest your left hand on a desk for support. Bend your left knee slightly, and raise your right leg to grasp your right ankle with your right hand. Keep your knees facing forward.
3. Gently ease your foot in towards your bottom until you feel a mild stretch.
4. Hold for a count of five. Repeat with the other side.

1. Stand comfortably with your feet apart, knees bent and hands on your knees.
2. Flex your knees up and down, keeping them bent throughout. Don't let your bottom go lower than the level of your knees.

3. Repeat five times and slowly increase the number you can do.

Ankles (two exercises)

1. Stand comfortably, resting one hand on a desk for support.
2. Lift one foot and rotate the ankle in ten complete circles, first clockwise then anticlockwise.
3. Repeat with the other foot.

1. Stand comfortably, feet slightly apart, with one hand resting on a table for support.
2. Lift both heels up so you are stand on the balls of your feet, then relax down again.

Regular exercise such as swimming, walking, cycling, or other non-competitive sports will help you to overcome stress and make you fitter to cope with life's challenges. Adrenaline has primed you for activity and by exercising you will help to reverse its effects, burn off the stress hormones and reset your stress responses to a lower level. Spend at least thirty minutes exercising, two or three times a week – and put in enough effort to feel glowing and slightly out of breath. Even if you don't have time for regular exercise sessions, try to make activity part of your everyday routine.

- Walk part or all of the way to work, for example get off the bus/tube one stop earlier.
- Use the stairs rather than the lift wherever possible.
- Walk briskly around the office corridors.
- Use the vacuum cleaner vigorously.
- Swap watching television for a family bike ride or walk.

THE EFFECT OF VARIOUS SPORTS ON STRENGTH, STAMINA AND SUPPLENESS

Activity	Stamina	Suppleness	Strength
Aerobics	★★★	★★★	★★
Athletics	★★★	★★	★★★
Badminton	★★	★★★	★★
Circuit training	★★★	★★★	★★★
Cricket	★	★★	★
Cycling	★★★★	★★	★★★
Football	★★★	★★★	★★★
Golf	★	★★	★
Jogging	★★★★	★★	★★
Karate/judo	★	★★	★
Rounders	★★	★	★★
Rowing	★★★	★	★★
Skiing (downhill)	★★	★★	★★
Skipping	★★★	★★	★★
Squash	★★★	★★★	★★
Swimming (hard)	★★★★	★★★★	★★★★
Tennis	★★	★★★	★★
Walking (ramble)	★★	★	★
(brisk/hill)	★★★	★	★★
Weight training	★	★★	★★★★
Yoga	★	★★★	★

★ = slight effect ★★★ = very good effect

★★ = beneficial effect ★★★★ = excellent effect

Swimming

Swimming is an excellent cardiovascular exercise as it involves just about every muscle in your body and rapidly builds stamina, strength and suppleness. To get the most benefit from swimming, try to develop a variety of different strokes and indulge at least two or three times a week, and preferably every day. Swimming is a non-weight-bearing form of exercise that is excellent for those with joint problems. The fact that you are exercising against the weight of water means it is also good for building up muscle strength.

Aqua aerobics

Aqua aerobics is a fun form of exercise that makes use of the 'weight' of water to exercise your muscles more than on dry land. It is excellent for those who do not enjoy swimming lengths. Most swimming pools hold regular classes, and it is a good way to make new friends.

Walking

Brisk walking is an excellent form of exercise, especially when carried out in bracing country air. Walking boosts your stamina and can help to burn of the effects of stress. A beginner should aim to walk a mile in around twenty minutes, increasing to three miles in about fifty minutes after about three months.

Invest in a good pair of walking shoes with cushioned soles and some ankle support to protect your feet and lower joints. Always warm up first with a few simple bends and stretches. Cool down afterwards by walking slowly for a few minutes.

To maintain your new fitness level, try to take at least thirty minutes' exercise three times a week.

SUGGESTED REGIME TO WALK-YOURSELF FIT OVER THREE MONTHS

WEEK	TUESDAY	THURSDAY	SATURDAY	SUNDAY
1	10 mins	10 mins	10 mins	
2	10 mins	10 mins	10 mins	
3	10 mins	15 mins	10 mins	15 mins
4	15 mins	15 mins	15 mins	15 mins
5	15 mins	15 mins	15 mins	15 mins
6	15 mins	20 mins	15 mins	20 mins
7	20 mins	20 mins	20 mins	20 mins
8	20 mins	20 mins	20 mins	20 mins
9	20 mins	25 mins	20 mins	25 mins
10	25 mins	25 mins	25 mins	25 mins
11	25 mins	30 mins	25 mins	30 mins
12	30 mins	30 mins	30 mins	30 mins

Cycling

Cycling is efficient at improving strength, stamina and suppleness. It is a low-impact, non-weight-bearing aerobic activity which, like swimming, doesn't put your muscles, ligaments or joints under excessive strain. This makes cycling particularly good for the overweight or those with joint problems. Cycling can be performed at home with a machine, in the gym or outdoors. Studies have shown that people who exercise in the fresh air derive greater benefits and get fitter quicker. Start off with a low gear ratio to keep resistance low and concentrate on pedalling technique and speed. As your stamina increases, introduce more intense bursts of exercise to increase your fitness.

Suggested cycling regimes

In the gym

The average non-fit person should start off on an exercise bike using a simpleregime such as Hill Profile programme. A trainer will help you to tailor a cycling regime to suit your fitness goals. A typical one is shown in the box right.

Out and about

If you own your own bike, it is important to be aware of cycling safety:

- use lights at dusk
- fit a red reflector to the rear mudguard and amber reflectors to your pedals
- maintain and oil your bike regularly
- wear reflective clothing at night
- avoid roads where there is fast or heavy traffic
- consider taking a cycling proficiency test
- always wear a safety helmet that complies with BSI 6863 (not for speed cycling or racing) or to American Snell or ANSI standards.

BEGINNER'S INDOOR CYCLING ROUTINE

WEEK	DIFFICULTY LEVEL	VISIT 1	VISIT 2	VISIT 3
1	two	6 mins	6 mins	6 mins
2	two	6 mins	6 mins	6 mins
3	three	6 mins	6 mins	6 mins
4	three	12 mins	12 mins	12 mins
5	three	12 mins	12 mins	18 mins
6	three	18 mins	18 mins	18 mins
7	four	18 mins	18 mins	18 mins
8	four	18 mins	18 mins	24 mins

If at any time you feel you have reached your comfortable exercise level and do not fancy increasing the difficulty level or time spent on your cycle, then stick at that level. After a while, when that level becomes easier and you feel like increasing the resistance of the bike or the time you spend on the cycle, you can slowly build up your work-out at your own pace.

Initially, cycle during the day on a route you know well where there are plenty of other people about and little traffic. Keep to level ground for the first few weeks, then slowly introduce gentle hills. When you feel up to it, try cycling up steeper inclines.

To maintain your new fitness level, continue cycling three or four times per week. Try to average at least three hours of brisk exercise spread out over each seven-day period.

BEGINNER'S OUTDOOR CYCLING REGIME

WEEK	TUESDAY	THURSDAY	SATURDAY	SUNDAY
1	15 mins	15 mins	15 mins	
2	15 mins	15 mins	15 mins	
3	20 mins	20 mins	20 mins	
4	20 mins	20 mins	20 mins	20 mins
5	20 mins	20 mins	20 mins	20 mins
6	20 mins	25 mins	20 mins	25 mins
7	25 mins	25 mins	25 mins	25 mins
8	30 mins	30 mins	30 mins	30 mins
9	30 mins	30 mins	30 mins	35 mins
10	35 mins	35 mins	35 mins	35 mins
11	35 mins	35 mins	35 mins	40 mins
12	40 mins	40 mins	45 mins	60 mins

If at any time you feel you have reached your comfortable exercise level and do not fancy cycling further or for longer, stick at that level. After a while, when that level becomes easier and you feel like cycling further or trying a gentle hill, slowly build up your work-out at your own pace.

EXPLORE ALTERNATIVE THERAPIES

Alternative therapies are becoming increasingly popular and accepted as a viable alternative to conventional medicine. They use an holistic approach that treats the mind, body and spirit rather than isolated symptoms, and this can be especially helpful in overcoming stress. More and more people now realize that a healthy body stems from healthy emotions, and by encouraging a more positive frame of mind, complementary techniques offer a gentler form of healing.

The following alternative therapies have helped many people with stress, but just as with orthodox medicine, not every treatment will suit every individual. Some therapies can be used for self-help, while others will involve consulting a therapist.

When choosing an alternative practitioner, bear in mind that standards of training and experience vary widely. Where possible:

- Select a therapist on the basis of personal recommendation from a satisfied client whom you know and whose opinion you trust.
- Check what qualifications the therapist has, and check their standing with the relevant umbrella organization for that therapy. The organization will be able to tell you what training their members have undertaken, what their code of ethics is, and refer you to qualified practitioners in your area.
- Find out how long your course of treatment will last and how much it is likely to cost.
- Ask how much experience the practitioner has had in treating stress and what their success rate is.

Acupuncture

Acupuncture is based on the belief that life energy (*qi* or *chi* — pronounced 'chee') flows through the body along different channels known as meridians. This flow of energy depends on the balance of two opposing forces: yin and yang — a balance which is easily disrupted through factors such as stress, anger, poor diet, spiritual neglect and even the weather. There are twelve main meridians — six of which have a yang polarity and are related to hollow organs (for example, the stomach), and six are ying and relate mainly to solid organs (for example, the liver). Two further meridians, the 'conception' and 'governing' vessels control the other twelve.

Each meridian ha a number of acupuncture points (acupoints) overlying it where chi energy is concentrated and can enter or leave the body. Traditionally, 365 acupoints were described, but more have been discovered in modern times and now around 2,000 acupoints are illustrated on charts. When the flow of chi energy becomes blocked or imbalanced, symptoms of illness or emotional disturbances are triggered. By inserting fine needles into acupuncture points overlying these meridians, the flow of chi energy can be stimulated or suppressed to overcome blockages or imbalances associated with various symptoms. A therapist will select which acupoints to access depending on your individual symptoms, the appearance of your tongue, and on the quality, rhythm and strength of twelve pulses (six in each wrist). These represent the twelve main organs and functions in acupuncture, and help to identify areas where the flow of chi is blocked.

Fine, disposable stainless-steel needles are inserted which cause little if any discomfort. You may notice a slight pricking sensation, or an odd tingling buzz as the needle is inserted a few millimetres into the skin. The needles are usually left in place from a few minutes to half an hour, and may be periodically flicked to enhance the quality of *chi*, or vigorously rotated to stir up a

STRESS SYMPTOMS THAT ACUPUNCTURE CAN BE GOOD FOR

Acupuncture can help treat a number of stress-related conditions including:

- headache and migraine
- hyperventilation
- asthma
- high blood pressure
- palpitations
- indigestion
- nausea
- diarrhoea
- irritable bowel syndrome
- anxiety
- depression
- obsessive-compulsive disorders
- addictions
- insomnia
- panic attacks
- premenstrual syndrome
- menopausal problems
- eczema
- psoriasis
- sexual problems.

Make sure you only consult a qualified practitioner.

stagnant *chi* and draw or disperse energy from the point. Sometimes, a small cone of dried herb (moxa – usually mugwort, *Artemesia vulgaris*) is ignited and burned near the active acupoint (or attached to a copper-handled needle) to warm the skin. This is known as moxibustion. It is believed that the warmth stimulates energy in areas that are cold or painful because *chi* is weak.

Cupping may be used to stimulate the flow of blood over certain points, and involves burning cotton wool soaked in surgical spirits inside a glass cup which is then held against the skin. This creates a vacuum that sucks the flesh into the mouth of the cup. Ear needles or ear 'seeds' can also be pressed on to the ear and retained between sessions. Altogether there are 120 auricular points on each ear, which are very close together.

Most patients start to notice a benefit after four to six treatments. Sometimes you may feel worse at first, which suggests your energies have been over-stimulated. Let the therapist know, as they will need to use fewer needles for a shorter length of time during your next treatment.

Research suggests that acupuncture causes the release of natural, heroin-like chemicals that act as painkillers and stress-busters. Acupuncture has gained increasing acceptance since the introduction of a simple, hand-held machine that measures electrical potentials across the skin. It can identify acupuncture points with great accuracy as they have a lower electrical resistance than the surrounding skin. This has helped to demonstrate that the ancient Chinese acupuncturists were more than 2,000 years ahead of their time.

Acupressure

Acupressure is an ancient skill that has been practised in China and Japan for over 3,000 years. It is similar to acupuncture, but instead of inserting needles at points along the meridians, these are stimulated using firm thumb pressure or fingertip massage. Sometimes the therapist will use their palms, elbows, knees and feet to massage and balance the flow of *chi* energy throughout your body. The best known example of acupressure is Japanese shiatsu – meaning 'finger pressure'.

You can use acupressure on yourself to help relieve minor stress-related conditions but more specialist treatments should be performed by a trained therapist. Only a specialist should use acupressure on someone who is pregnant.

When energy flow becomes abnormal, acupoints on the surrounding skin become tender and painful to touch. These are known as tsubos and are important areas to apply acupressure or acupuncture treatments to.

To relieve a tension headache

Various points may be massaged to help relieve a tension headache. Try treating both left and right sides of the body (if appropriate) to see which helps best.

Hand acupressure: reduction of hegu

1. Identify the point on the back of your hand just in front of the place where the bone at the base of your thumb meets the bone at the base of your index finger. This point is nestled deep in the web of flesh between your thumb and index finger. When you have found the right spot it will often feel tender.
2. Massage by applying firm pressure and making small rotations both clockwise and anticlockwise over the point. This will help to reduce an excess of stagnant *chi*. Pressure needs to be firm enough to cause some initial discomfort.
3. Treat the point for three minutes and repeat as necessary.

Forehead acupressure: reduction of yintang

1. Identify a point between your eyebrows in the middle of your forehead.
2. Massage by applying firm pressure and making small rotations both clockwise and anticlockwise over this point. This will help to reduce an excess of stagnant *chi*.
3. Treat the point for three minutes to help clear the mind and lift the headache.

Ear acupressure: reduction of the yifeng

1. Identify a point just to the rear of the exact middle of your ear lobe. When you have found the right spot it will often feel tender.
2. Massage this point firmly with thumb pressure.

Scalp acupressure

1. Feel the scalp overlying the main site of your headache and try to identify tender spots.
2. Massage any tender spots firmly.

Aromatherapy

Aromatherapy harnesses the beneficial properties of aromatic essential oils produced by special glands in the leaves, flowers, fruit and seeds of medicinal plants. These essential oils can help to treat a variety of conditions but are particularly effective for stress or emotional problems since they can produce a powerful effect on your moods. Aromatherapy oils directly stimulate the sense of smell which is connected with a part of the brain (the limbic system) closely involved in regulating the emotions. Oils are also absorbed from the skin into

the circulation and can have powerful effects on the body. Too much of them can
be harmful and it is important that oils are chosen with care and used according
to the instructions.

Aromatherapy oils are extracted by:
- simple pressing (for example, bergamot, lemon, orange)
- distillation (for example, cardamom, basil)
- *enfleurage* (pressing petals between glass sheets coated with animal fat) followed by
  solvent extraction (for example, rose, jasmine)

Where possible, use natural rather than synthetic essential oils: they have a
fuller, sweeter aroma that is of greater therapeutic benefit. Similarly, 100% pure
essential oils are preferable — although they are usually more expensive — since
they are not mixed with alcohol or other additives.

Aromatherapy essential oils may be inhaled, massaged into the skin, added to
bath water, or heated in a variety of ways to perfume the atmosphere. Oils that
come into contact with skin should always be diluted with a carrier oil (for
example, almond, avocado, jojoba, sunflower or wheatgerm oil). Dilution is
important as oils that are too concentrated may have an adverse effect or cause
skin irritation. Add a maximum total of one drop of essential oil to each 2 ml
(24 drops) of carrier oil. Two teaspoons (10 ml) of carrier oil should therefore
contain no more than 5 drops of essential oil blend, while two tablespoons (30
ml) should contain no more than 15 drops of essential oil blend. Oils that are
twice as dilute as this often suffice (i.e., only 5 drops of essential oil blend
per 20 ml of carrier oil). A 5 ml medicinal teaspoon measure (or a 5 ml syringe
if you prefer) can be bought cheaply from a chemist to ensure accuracy; kitchen
teaspoons tend to hold slightly less than 5 ml.

The chemistry of essential oils is complex, with hundreds of components, which
is why a single essence can help a range of disorders. Different oils have
different healing properties and can be blended to treat specific problems and to
dampen or stimulate stress-related symptoms.

When making up a blend, choose oils whose aromas you like and experiment with
different quantities of each to produce a perfume you like. If a blend isn't
quite to your liking, add more drops of one or more of the oils — or introduce
another that you feel is missing. Keep a note of the total number of drops used
so that you can ensure it is correctly diluted by adding extra carrier oil.
Altogether, every 5 drops of essential oil should be balanced with 10 ml of
carrier oil.

CHOOSING ESSENTIAL OILS

	PHYSICAL TIREDNESS OR MENTAL EXHAUSTION	LOW MOODS OR MOOD SWINGS	STRESS OR OVER-WORK	RELAXING AND CALMING	HELP TO LOWER HIGH BLOOD PRESSURE	HELP TO RELIEVE TENSION HEADACHES	INSOMNIA
Angelica	●	●				●	
Basil	●	●	●				
Benzoin	●	●	●	●			
Bergamot		●	●				
Black pepper	●						
Cardamom	●					●	
Camomile		●	●	●		●	●
Cedarwood			●	●			
Clary sage		●	●	●	●		
Coriander	●	●	●				
Geranium		●	●		●	●	
Ginger		●					
Grapefruit	●	●	●				
Jasmine		●	●	●			
Juniper berry			●	●			●
Lavender		●	●	●	●	●	●
Lemon	●	●	●		●		●
Marjoram			●	●	●		●
Neroli		●	●	●			●
Nutmeg				●	●		
Orange	●	●	●	●			
Patchouli		●	●				
Pettigrain		●	●	●			●
Peppermint	●					●	
Pine	●	●					
Rose		●	●	●		●	●
Rosemary	●				●	●	●
Rosewood	●	●	●				
Sandalwood	●		●	●			●
Vanilla		●	●	●			
Vetiver		●	●	●			
Ylang-ylang		●	●	●	●		●

How to use essential oils

To make a relaxing massage oil (see page 189 for instructions on how to give a massage): Add a maximum total of one drop of essential oil to each 2 ml (24 drops) of carrier oil (almond, avocado, jojoba, sunflower or wheatgerm).

To add to your bath: Add 5 drops of essential oils to a tablespoon of carrier oil (for example, almond or avocado) and mix. Draw your bath so that it is comfortably hot, then add the aromatic oil mix after the taps are turned off. Close the bathroom door to keep in the vapours and soak yourself for 15–20 minutes, preferably by candlelight.

In the shower: Add 8 drops of essential oil to a tablespoon (15 ml) of carrier oil. After cleansing your body with soap or gel, rinse well then dip a wet sponge in the oil mix and use it to gently massage your whole body while under a warm jet spray.

In a sauna: Add 2 drops of essential oil to 300 ml (half a pint) of water and throw over the coals to evaporate.

To scent pot pourri: Add a few drops of essential oils to a pot pourri mix. Refresh the scent regularly as it starts to fade.

To help you sleep: Add 2 or 3 drops of a relaxing oil blend to a tissue and allow to dry before tucking under your pillow.

As a room spray: Fill a small sprayer with 100 ml water and add 10 drops of de-stressing essential oils. Shake the sprayer well before using to perfume your bedroom. This mix can also be placed in special porous holders that will sit over a radiator.

With a ring burner designed to sit over a light bulb so the oils it contains are gently diffused by the heat energy of the bulb.

With a candlelit diffuser: Add 2 or 3 drops of essential oil to a little warm water over a candle burner to diffuse relaxing oils into a room.

With an electric ionizer/diffuser: To fill the room with beneficial negative ions plus a relaxing scent, buy an ionizer/diffuser that has a hot plate on to which you add oils or oils mixed with water.

Cautions

- Do not take essential oils internally.
- Before using an essential oil blend on your skin, do a patch test (put a small amount on a patch of skin and leave it for at least an hour) to make sure you are not sensitive to it.
- Do not use essential oils if you are pregnant, or likely to be, except under specialist advice from a qualified aromatherapist.

- Do not use essential oils if you suffer from epilepsy, except under specialist advice from a qualified aromatherapist.
- Avoid using aromatherapy oils that are known to be capable of putting blood pressure up. These include thyme, clove and cinnamon.
- Keep essential oils away from the eyes.
- If you are taking homoeopathic remedies, do not use peppermint, rosemary or lavender essential oils as these may neutralize the homoeopathic effect.
- Essential oils are flammable, so do not put them near an open flame.

Ayurveda

Indian medicine, known as ayurveda or 'the science of life', is one of the oldest forms of holistic medicine, and can be dated back to almost 5,000 years ago. The body, like the universe, is said to be made up of five elements: earth, ether (space), fire, water and air, which make up three internal forces or *doshas*, known as *pitta* (the metabolic force centred in the stomach), *kapha* (the fluid force centred in the lungs) and *vata* (the driving force, seated in the colon). Each person has one (and occasionally two) dominant *doshas* which determine their constitution and the type of illnesses to which they are susceptible. The level of each *dosha* is said to rise and fall according to the time of day, the season, the type of diet you eat, the stresses you are under, and the extent of repressed emotions. When the *doshas* become unbalanced, they are thought to block the flow of the life-force, *prana* which is comparable with the Chinese life-force, *chi*. During times of stress, the three *doshas* become unbalanced enough to lead to disease. *Vata* imbalance, for example, can result from irregular meals and working long hours, which leads to anger and exhaustion; *pitta* imbalance can cause indigestion; and *kapha* imbalance can occur as a result of lack of exercise.

Ayurveda may use a variety of techniques to help relieve stress and bring internal balance in the doshas. These include diet, meditation, posture control, breathing exercises, yoga, hydrotherapy and herbal medicines. One of ayurveda's main doctrines is that prevention is better than cure, so changes will be suggested in your diet and lifestyle to help stop levels of stress from rising. Points on the head known as marma, which are similar to acupoints, may be massaged to stimulate the flow of life-energy, *prana*. Another relaxation techniques, shirodhara, may also be used: this involves pouring warm sesame oil over the forehead continuously for up to an hour. Purging with enemas, emetics and fasting may be recommended, plus dietary changes such as eating oats for breakfast, meat and spices for lunch (to raise energy levels), and mashed bananas and cooked vegetables for supper. Dairy foods are used to lower excess energy, while insomnia is treated using spices such as ginger, cinnamon or cardamom in warm milk.

By balancing your internal systems, ayurveda can help you achieve emotional and physical health and can treat the symptoms of stress, as well as maintaining good health in those who are unstressed.

Colour therapy

Natural sunlight contains all colours of the spectrum: red, orange, yellow, green, blue, indigo and violet. It bathes us in a sea of colour, although this is only obvious when light is split with a prism or atmospheric water to create a dazzling rainbow.

Every colour vibrates at its own frequency, as does every living thing — including all the cells in your body. Colour therapy use colour vibrations to correct imbalances in the energy vibrations of your cells to restore wellness during times of stress or ill health.

Each colour can have a profound effect on your emotions, stress levels and well-being. Colour therapy uses exposure to different wavelengths of light to produce powerful effects on your mind, body and spirit.

Red, orange and yellow come from the warm end of the spectrum and have a stimulating effect, while blue, indigo and violet come from the cool end and have a calming effect. Green is in between and is the calming yet vibrant colour of nature and harmony that can reduce anxiety and tension. It contains a balance of vibrational energies that can aid recovery from stressful situations and ill health. This is widely recognized in hospitals, where natural green settings full of plants are used to reduce anxiety in waiting rooms and to speed recovery on the wards.

Colour therapy is especially useful in reducing stress-related problems to restore balance and health. Restful shades of blue will help you feel more calm as well as

YOUR AURA

Everyone is surrounded by an aura of energy that is revealed by Kirlian photography as a halo of different colours. Some clairvoyants and healers are also able to see the aura and to use it to diagnose unhealthy emotions, physical stress and ill health. The aura is made up of seven influences or chakras, each of which is associated with a particular colour:

- the root chakra at the base of the spine is red
- the sacral chakra in the pelvis is orange
- the solar plexus chakra below the sternum is yellow
- the heart chakra is green
- the throat chakra is blue/turquoise
- the brow chakra is indigo
- the crown chakra at the top of the skull is violet.

lowering your blood pressure and increasing your pain threshold. Exposure to red light can have the opposite effect, however, and make you feel more stressed as well as putting your blood pressure up, since it triggers the release of adrenaline. You only have to imaging the discordant effect of vibrant reds and oranges together to appreciate how much this can put you on edge. Red does have a role to play, however, as magenta red is also the colour of 'letting go', and used in small amounts can help to free you from some harmful emotions.

While vibrant fuchsia pinks can be stressful, passive, bubble-gum or pastel pinks are calming and have been used to help soothe overactive children and to reduce stress and violence in prisons. Those suffering from migraine have fewer attacks when wearing rose-tinted spectacles.

Most colour therapists use a colour together with its complement (the colour that is opposite and balancing in its qualities and effects). You may be asked, for example, to choose three coloured cards out of eight you are shown to reveal your emotional and physical state. These colours may be used along with their complementary colours to help balance your vibrational health.

Colour therapy is often combined with other holistic therapies such as reflexology, aromatherapy and acupuncture.

How you see colour

Light energy stimulates two types of light-sensitive cells in the retina at the back of the eye called rods and cones. Rods detect dim light but only see in black and white. Cones give colour vision and can only work in bright light. Rods and cones contain photosensitive pigments. The pigment responsible for night vision is rhodopsin (visual purple), which is derived from vitamin A. The first sign of vitamin A deficiency is loss of sensitivity to green light, followed by difficulty adapting to dim light. Betacarotene – which can be converted into vitamin A in the body – is found in yellow-orange fruits and vegetables. Carrots really can help you see in the dark if your vitamin A levels are low.

Seeing complementary colours

You can identify a colour's complement simply by staring at a particular colour for a while, then closing your eyes and seeing the complementary colour in the after-image on the inside of your lids:

- blue complements red
- yellow complements violet
- orange complements indigo
- green is neutral.

Using colour therapy to reduce your stress levels

Listen to your intuition which will often let you 'see' the rightness of certain colours to use for healing your own vibrational imbalances.

- Use red to uplift, energize, give confidence and overcome anxiety, depression or inertia.
- Use orange to stimulate you mentally and physically, increase a low sex drive, free blocked energy and lift your spirits
- Use yellow to improve clear thinking and self-control, to encourage optimism, boost inner strength, and to help resolve unaddressed emotions and feelings
- Use green for freshness, regeneration and growth. It is especially helpful for neutralizing stress, relieving nervous tension and freeing repressed emotions and fears.
- Use blue to lower high blood pressure or to boost self-expression and communication, and to calm over-excitability or stressful feelings that tend towards hysteria. Also useful for insomnia.
- Use turquoise to increase your emotional resistance, boost immunity and to protect you from the influences and demands of others.
- Use indigo to calm anger and rage, lower stress-related high blood pressure, and to help you overcome obsessions, compulsions and addictions.
- Use violet to calm anxiety, highly strung nerves and phobias.
- The colour magenta is also used to help overcome compulsive behaviours.

Tips on how to use colour therapy

- Paint your bedroom with restful blues and greens to induce sleep.
- Colour your living areas with warm sunshine tones for invigoration.
- Surround yourself with plants to reduce stress levels.
- When feeling especially stressed, wear green as often as possible.
- When you feel the need to boost your inner strength, wear yellow.
- Eat blue, green and yellow foods when you are under excess pressure.
- Use healing lights fitted with transparent films to expose yourself to particular light frequencies. As a rough guide, expose yourself to a healing colour for ten to fifteen minutes, then use the complementary colour for half that time. NB Red is not normally used for more than seven minutes.
- Relax and visualize a healing colour at times of stress – imagine being totally immersed in that colour and breathing it into your body.
- Drink solarized water that has been treated by exposure to sunlight through stained glass of a particular colour, for example solarized 'blue' water may be drunk to help insomnia.

Craniosacral therapy

Craniosacral therapy is a modern version of cranial osteopathy which involves the gentle laying on of hands, mainly over the skull and lower spine. Experienced therapists assess the flow of cerebrospinal fluid (known as the cranial rhythmic impulse) and 'listen' to the inner movements and tensions inside the patient. Due to the continuity of fluids and tissues in the body, the laying on of hands releases inner energy and tensions to produce relaxation and healing. Craniosacral therapy is able to help headaches, migraines, TMJ (temporo-mandibular joint) syndrome and other stress-related aches and pains using a holistic rather than a symptom-orientated approach. Most people experiencing craniosacral therapy feel deeply relaxed during the treatment and experience a spontaneous unwinding of tension due to the release of physical and emotional imbalances. It is not a technique you can perform on yourself.

Homoeopathy

Homoeopathy is based on the belief that natural substances can boost the body's own healing powers to relieve symptoms and signs of illness. Substances are selected which, if used full-strength, would produce symptoms in a healthy person similar to those it is designed to treat. This is the first principle of homoeopathy, that 'like cures like'.

The second major principle of homoeopathy is that increasing the dilution of a solution has the opposite effect of increasing its potency: 'less cures more'. By diluting noxious and even poisonous substances many millions of times, their healing properties are enhanced while their undesirable side effects are lost.

On the centesimal scale, dilutions of 100^{-6} are described as potencies of 6c, dilutions of 100^{-30} are written as a potency of 30c, and so on. At these levels of dilution, the homoeopathic remedies are no longer dilutions but biophysically altered solutions. To illustrate just how diluted these substances are, a dilution of 12c (100^{-12}) is comparable to a pinch of salt dissolved in the same amount of water as is found in the Atlantic Ocean.

Nearly all the homoeopathic remedies are derived from whole, natural substances, vegetable, animal or mineral — no attempt is made to isolate an active ingredient. Source materials may include:

● plant substances, for example pulsatilla, belladonna

- animal substances, for example snake venom (lachesis), spider venom (latrodectus), bee venom (apis)
- minerals or metals, for example arsenic, calcium carbonate, platinum
- allergens, for example house dust mite, pollen grains.

Homoeopathy is thought to work in a dynamic way, boosting your body's own healing powers. The most popular theory to explain how homoeopathy works is that the original noxious substance added to the water somehow left a footprint in the solution that the body can recognize and respond to.

Homoeopathic treatments are prescribed according to your symptoms rather than any particular disease, so two patients with different stress-related symptoms will need different homoeopathic treatments.

Homoeopathic remedies may be prescribed by a medically-trained homoeopathic doctor on the normal NHS prescription form and dispensed by homoeopathic pharmacists for the usual prescription charge or exemptions. Alternatively, you can consult a private homoeopathic practitioner or buy remedies direct from a pharmacist.

Over 2,000 homoeopathic remedies are available. It is best to see a trained homoeopath who can assess your constitutional type, personality, lifestyle, family background, likes and dislikes as well as your symptoms before deciding which treatment is right for you. Some homoeopathic treatments are selected according to emotional traits such as anger, timidity, anxiety or depression. These so-called 'mentals' are of particular importance in treating stress-related problems.

Homoeopathic remedies should ideally be taken on their own, without eating or drinking for at least thirty minutes before or after. Tablets should also be taken without handling — tip them into the lid of the container, or on to a teaspoon to transfer them into your mouth. Then suck or chew them, don't swallow them whole.

If there is no obvious improvement after taking the remedies for the time stated, consult a practitioner. Don't be surprised if your symptoms initially get worse before they get better — persevere through this common reaction to treatment; it is a good sign which shows the remedy is working. After completing a course of homoeopathy, you will usually feel much better in yourself, with a greatly improved sense of well-being that lets you cope with any remaining symptoms in a much more positive way.

Homoeopathic remedies for stress

Physical exhaustion

- For exhaustion due to overwork: Calc. carb. (calcarea carbonic) 30c (take twice a day for up to two weeks).
- For exhaustion due to anxiety: Arsen. alb. (arsenicum album) 30c (take twice a day for up to two weeks).
- For exhaustion linked with stress, overwork and insomnia: Nux vomica 30c (take twice a day for up to two weeks).

Headache

- For tension headache that comes on suddenly and feels like a tight band: Aconite 30c (take every ten minutes for up to ten doses).
- For tension headache brought on by emotional stress — a sharp severe pain in the side of the head accompanies the tight band sensation: Ignatia 30c (take every ten minutes for up to ten doses).
- For a tension headache that feels bursting and crushing, with sharp pain brought on by the slightest eye movement: Byronia 30c (take every ten minutes for up to ten doses).
- For tension headache with muscular spasm and stiffness in the neck: Cimic. (cimi-cifuga) 6c (take every hour for up to five doses).

Intestinal symptoms

- For indigestion, nausea or weepiness due to emotional stress: Pulsatilla 6c (take every ten minutes for up to five doses).
- For nausea due to stress or embarrassment: Ipecac 6c (take every hour for up to ten doses).
- For nervous diarrhoea: Argent. nit. (argentum nitricum) 6c (take every thirty minutes for up to ten doses).
- For bloating and loss of appetite due to nerves: Lycopodium 6c (take every thirty minutes for up to ten doses).

Anxiety

- For eczema made worse by stress: Petroleum 6c (take four times a day for up to ten days).
- For anxiety with lack of confidence and high standards: Lycopodium 6c (take every two hours for up to ten doses).
- For anxiety with restlessness and deep underlying insecurity: Arsen. alb. (arsenicum album) 6c (take every two hours for up to ten doses).
- For anxiety linked with overwork: Phos. (phosphorus) 6c (take every two hours for up to ten doses).

- For anxiety and fear of making a fool of oneself: Calc. carb. (calcarea carbonica) 6c (take every two hours for up to ten doses).

Fear
- For fear of failure: Argent. nit. (argentum nitricum) 6c (take every thirty minutes for up to ten doses, then four times a day for up to ten days).
- For stress following bereavement: Arnica 30c (take every hour for up to ten doses, then four times a day for up to ten days).

Irritability
- For irritability and over-criticism linked with overwork, exhaustion or excesses: Nux vomica 6c (take every thirty minutes for up to ten doses).
- For irritability and anger linked with insecurity: Lycopodium 6c(take every thirty minutes for up to ten doses).

Insomnia
Take the appropriate remedy half an hour before going to bed and repeat every thirty minutes if necessary. Use for ten nights then stop and see if your normal sleep pattern has returned.
- For insomnia with an inability to relax: Coffea 30c.
- For insomnia with irritability, exhaustion and stress: Nux vomica 30c.
- For insomnia linked with fear or panic: Aconitum 30c.

Severe stress
- For sudden physical or emotional stress: Aconite 30c (take every thirty minutes for up to ten doses).
- For severe stress following a shock or major ordeal: Gelsemium 30c (take every thirty minutes for up to ten doses).

Bach Flower Remedies

Flower Remedies were devised earlier this century when Dr Edward Bach noticed that patients suffering from the same emotional problems benefited from the same homoeopathic treatment, irrespective of the physical symptoms they were suffering. He came to believe that physical disease was due to underlying emotional stresses that would inevitably lead to more serious illness in the future. Using his medical skills, he classified emotional problems into seven major groups, which were further subdivided into a total of thirty-eight negative or harmful states of mind. Using his homoeopathic skills, he then formulated a series of plant-based remedies to treat these emotional conditions, correcting the harmful states of mind and restoring emotional balance before the adverse effects of stress led to physical disease.

Bach Flower Remedies are prepared either by infusion or boiling. In the infusion method, flower heads are placed on the surface of a small glass bowl filled with pure spring water. This is left to infuse in direct sunlight for three hours, then the flowers are discarded and the infused spring water preserved in grape alcohol (brandy). This resultant solution is called the mother tincture and is further diluted five times to create the individual stock remedies.

In the boiling method, short lengths of twig bearing flowers or catkins are boiled in pure spring water for thirty minutes. The plant material is then discarded and the water allowed to cool before being preserved in grape alcohol to produce a mother tincture.

To use a flower remedy, add two drops of it to any-sized glass of mineral or spring water, or fruit juice. Sip and hold each mouthful in the mouth for a few seconds before swallowing.

For emergency situations (for example, panic attacks, just before public speaking) use Rescue Remedy, which is a composite of five remedies: rock rose, impatiens, clematis, star-of-Bethlehem and cherry plum. Add four drops to a glass of liquid and sip slowly every few minutes until symptoms subside. Hold each sip in your mouth for a moment before swallowing.

If no fluid is available, remedies may also be dropped directly on to the tongue or rubbed on to the lips, behind the ears or elsewhere on the body.

Flower Remedies for stress

Fear

- Rock Rose (*Helianthemum nummularium*) for extreme terror, panic, hysteria, fright and nightmares.
- Mimulus (*Mimulus guttatus*) for known fears (for example, phobias), timidity and shyness.
- Cherry plum (*Prunus cerasifera*) for fear of losing control, uncontrollable rages, tempers, impulses, fear of causing harm to oneself or others.
- Aspen (*Populus tremula*) for vague fears and anxieties of unknown origin, sense of foreboding, apprehension or impending doom.
- Red chestnut (*Aesculus carnea*) for excessive fear or over-concern for others.

Uncertainty and indecision

- Cerato *(Ceratostigma willmottianum)* for those who doubt their own ability to judge situations or make decisions.
- Scleranthus *(Scleranthus annus)* for the indecisive and those subject to energy or mood swings.
- Gentian *(Gentianella amarella)* for the easily discouraged, those who hesitate, are despondent or self-doubting.
- Gorse *(Ulex europaeus)* for feelings of despair, hopelessness and futility.
- Hornbeam *(Carpinus betulus)* for 'Monday morning' feelings of not being able to face the day, tiredness, procrastination, and those needing inner strength.
- Wild oat *(Bromus ramosus)* for those dissatisfied in their current lifestyle or career, and who cannot decide which alternative path to follow.

Insufficient interest in present circumstances

- Clematis *(Clematis vitalba)* for those who live more in the future than the present (escapism), lack of concentration, daydreaming, lack of interest in present circumstances, out-of-body sensations.
- Honeysuckle *(Lonicera caprifolium)* for those living too much in the past, nostalgia, homesickness.
- Wild rose *(Rosa canina)* for apathy, resignation to circumstances, making little effort to improve situations or find happiness.
- Olive *(Olea europaea)* for total exhaustion, mental or physical; weariness, sapped vitality especially during convalescence.
- White chestnut *(Aesculus hippocastanum)* for persistent, unwanted thoughts, mental arguments, preoccupation with worry.
- Mustard *(Sinapis arvensis)* for deep gloom descending for no apparent reason, melancholy and heavy sadness.
- Chestnut bud *(Aesculus hippocastanum)* for those who fail to learn from their mistakes.

Loneliness

- Water violet *(Hottonia palustris)* for those who prefer to be alone, or are superior, aloof, proud and reserved in attitude; for those who will advise but do not get personally involved in others' problems.
- Impatiens *(Impatiens glandulifera)* for those who are quick in thought and action but irritable or impatient, especially with those who are slower.
- Heather *(Calluna vulgaris)* for excessive talkativeness and those constantly seeking companionship and an ear to listen. For the self-absorbed who find difficulty in being alone.

Oversensitivity to influences and ideas

- Agrimony *(Agrimonia eupatoria)* for those not wishing to burden others, covering problems up with a cheerful façade; for those seeking solace in drugs or alcohol.

- Centaury *(Centaurium umbellatum)* for those who cannot say no; for the subservient, those who are anxious to please and easily exploited.

- Walnut *(Juglans regia)* for stabilizing the emotions during periods of transition; for example puberty, menopause; for adjusting to new beginnings or relationships.

- Holly *(Ilex aquifolium)* for negative feelings, for example, envy, suspicion, revenge, hatred; for those needing more love.

Despondency or despair

- Larch *(Larix decidua)* for those lacking in self-confidence, who anticipate failure and make little effort to succeed.

- Pine *(Pinus sylvestris)* for self-reproach, guilt and those who are not satisfied with their own actions; for those who blame themselves for the misfortunes of others.

- Elm *(Ulmus procera)* for those who overextend themselves, who are overwhelmed or burdened with responsibilities.

- Sweet chestnut *(Castanea sativa)* for those who have reached the limits of their endurance, for deep despair or unbearable anguish.

- Star-of-Bethlehem *(Ornithogalum umbellatum)* for mental and emotional stress following traumatic experiences, for example, grief.

- Willow *(Salix vitellina)* for those suffering unjust misfortune, and for resentfulness and bitterness.

- Oak *(Quercus robur)* for the brave and determined, who never usually give up despite adversity or illness, but who are losing their strength to fight.

- Crab apple *(Malus pumila)* for feelings of shame, unworthiness, uncleanliness, poor self-image or fear of contamination. Helps to detoxify and cleanse.

Overcare for the welfare of others

- Chicory *(Cichorium intybus)* for those who are obsessive or overly concerned with others; those who are demanding or full of self-pity; those who need others to conform to their own standards and ideals

- Vervain *(Verbena officinalis)* for those with strong opinions, those incensed by injustice, the over-enthusiastic, argumentative and over-bearing.

- Vine *(Vitis vinifera)* for the strong-willed with a tendency to be ruthless, domineering, dictatorial or inflexible.

- Beech *(Fagus sylvatica)* for the critical and intolerant, those who seek perfection and are continually finding fault.

- Rock water *(Aqua petra)* for those who are overly strict with themselves, hard taskmasters with a severely disciplined lifestyle.

Hydrotherapy

Hydrotherapy — or the use of water in healing — is a popular technique that takes a wide variety of forms. Bathing in essential oils, mineral solutions, seaweed extracts, mud, peat, hot spas and sea water have been used for medicinal purposes since ancient times.

Temperature plays an important role, with cold baths used to stimulate metabolism and boost immunity, warm water used for flotation therapy, and hot water to treat muscle aches and joint pains as well as to generally soothe, relax and heal. The ancient Greeks believed in the use of a sitz bath in which the bottom was immersed in a hip bath of one temperature, and the feet in a bowl of water at a different temperature.

Thalassotherapy is a form of hydrotherapy based on the healing properties of sea water and seaweed. Seaweed extracts are added to baths or used as body wraps and poultices to encourage sweating and to draw impurities out of the skin. Seaweed is rich in trace elements and minerals, some of which can be absorbed by the skin — people who are allergic to iodine should therefore avoid this therapy.

While everyone uses the bath and shower at home for cleansing, a daily immersion ritual also has a therapeutic effect and — especially if combined with candlelight and aromatherapy oils at the end of a stressful day — can be immensely relaxing.

How to use your bath to relax you at the end of a stressful day

When using any of the following treatments, don't get up too quickly from the bath as your blood pressure may temporarily drop low enough to make you feel faint. Do not use the following treatments if you are pregnant, within two hours of a heavy meal, or if you have been drinking alcohol.

- Add a sachet (around 450 g) of Dead Sea salts to a warm bath and relax for twenty minutes. Then wrap yourself in a warm towel and lie on a bed in a warm room for a deeply relaxing experience. (NB Do not allow the salts to get in your eyes. Cover cuts or grazes with Vaseline or they will sting.)
- Add 450 g Epsom salts to a warm to medium hot bath and relax for ten minutes then rinse or wash off the salt water. (NB Do not allow the salts to get in your eyes. Cover cuts or grazes with Vaseline or they will sting.)
- Add diluted camomile, lavender, jasmine, sandalwood or ylang-ylang oils to a bath of warm water and relax for fifteen minutes to help reduce anxiety.
- Add diluted basil, bergamot, camomile, lavender, jasmine, rose, sandalwood or ylang-ylang

oils to a bath of warm water and relax for fifteen minutes to help reduce low moods.

- Add diluted camomile, lavender or rose oils to a bath of warm water and relax for fifteen minutes to help overcome insomnia.
- Add diluted camomile, lavender or ylang-ylang to help defuse anger.
- If you have access to a jacuzzi bath, use it whenever you feel stressed; or you could buy a mat that fits inside your bath and circulates air to give a jacuzzi feel.

Flotation therapy

Flotation therapy is one of the most successful forms of hydrotherapy for neutralizing the effects of stress. Paradoxically, it evolved from original studies in the fifties designed to induce stress in humans. Few people could endure more than eight hours of water immersion and isolation (Restricted Environment Stimulation Therapy — also known as REST), and it was not until researchers experimented with flotation on salt solutions rather than complete water immersion that the beneficial effects of flotation therapy were discovered.

Flotation therapy involves floating in a light- and sound-proof tank containing a shallow, ten-inch-deep pool of warm saline solution in which 700 lbs of Epsom salts (magnesium sulphate) are dissolved. This forms a super-saturated solution that is more buoyant than the Dead Sea. The floater is suspended on this bed of minerals which are kept at a constant skin temperature of 93.5° F (34.5°C). The tank is specially designed to screen out light and sound so the brain is cut off from virtually all external sources of stimulation — even the effects of gravity are minimized. This is probably important as it has been suggested that 90% of all brain activity is concerned with the effects of gravitational pull on the body (correcting posture, maintaining balance, and so on). Reducing the sensory inputs to your brain allows you to rest, focus in on yourself and effortlessly achieve a meditative state. Your blood pressure and stress levels will go down, levels of your brain's natural painkillers will rise and sleep improves.

When brainwaves are recorded during relaxation, two patterns are clearly seen. During deep meditation, another, more elusive pattern of theta waves usually occurs. Theta waves are accompanied by vivid memories, creative thought and feelings of serenity, but are difficult to maintain without falling asleep. During flotation therapy, however, your brain quickly starts generating theta waves while you remain awake — and what's more, you continue to make large amounts of creativity-promoting theta waves for up to three weeks after each float.

Many of the beneficial effects of floating are due to a significant fall in the levels of stress hormones in your blood — a fall which is maintained for up

to five days after treatment has stopped. Interestingly, because sensory depriva-
tion in a float tank allows the brain to focus in on body functions, many people
also learn how to slow their heartbeat and blood pressure at will while floating
and this can help them relax at other times when they feel under stress.

For best stress-busting results, try a course of five weekly floats. Most
larger towns have a float centre or oasis. You can obtain a similar deep relaxation in your own bathroom using mineral salts from the Dead Sea (available from
larger health food stores and chemists). After soaking in your bath for twenty
minutes, lie down in a warm, darkened, quiet room to fall asleep.

Hypnotherapy

Hypnotherapy is a technique in which suggestion is used to help someone in a profoundly relaxed or trance-like state to heal themselves. Hypnotherapy helps to
strengthen your resolve and is most commonly used to help people overcome
addictive or obsessive behaviour patterns and phobias. The therapist will implant
the suggestion that you are no longer afraid of spiders, for example, or that you
no longer wish to smoke cigarettes, and this will effectively change your pattern
of learned responses or behaviours. A common suggestion imprinted during hypnotherapy is that a particular source of stress, fear or panic has been packaged
up in a parcel, attached to a balloon and allowed to float away. Although this
may seem simplistic, it is surprisingly effective.

Hypnotherapy can also be used to help you gain control over your life by
achieving relaxation in times of anxiety and stress. To help you achieve a
relaxed state for self-hypnosis, you can:

- use meditation (see page 190)
- use breathing exercises (see page 153)
- sit quietly and imagine your hands and arms becoming heavier and heavier until you
  are unable to lift them.

Self-hypnosis for stress

1. Relax in a warm, quiet, dimly lit room where you will not be disturbed. Sit or lie
   comfortably with your hands and feet apart.
2. Roll your eyes up until you feel them straining and fix your eyes on an imagined
   (or real) spot on the ceiling.
3. While still fixating on the ceiling, breathe in deeply as far as you can. Hold the
   breath to a slow count of ten, then exhale as fully as possible while saying

quietly to yourself, 'Relax!'. Repeat twice more, holding your breath for as long as possible after breathing in.

4. Breathe in once more then, as you breathe out and tell yourself to relax, let your eyes close.

5. Imagine your body has become weightless and is slowly floating upwards as you feel more and more relaxed.

6. Imagine you have floated to the top of a hill which has ten terraces leading down on to a plain.

7. Let yourself float down to the first terrace while counting backwards from the number five. Again, use your imagination so you really feel yourself there.

8. Keep floating down until you reach the plain at the bottom. Once there, focus on the change you want to make in yourself, for example, 'I am calm and relaxed', 'I am no longer smoking', 'I am coping well' or 'I am self-confident'. Always use the present tense as this is what your subconscious mind responds to best.

9. Use your imagination to feel yourself in your new, stronger role, repeating the positive phrase over and over again.

10. After ten to twenty minutes of visualizing the new empowered you, tell yourself that on the count of five you will slowly float back up the hill, open your eyes and feel refreshed. 'One…two…three…four…five…'

Try to practise this self-hypnosis every day as it is an excellent technique for promoting relaxation, releasing tension and increasing self-confidence. You will soon be able to achieve a state of relaxation wherever and whenever you want, to find your secret inner place of calm and strength to help you overcome stressful situations.

Your positive thoughts can also be taped and replayed when you go to bed.

Massage

Massage is one of the oldest alternative therapies and is based on the healing power of touch. It is especially helpful for easing muscle tension, anxiety, high blood pressure, insomnia, low moods and other stress-related symptoms.

There are several different types of massage, which use a variety of touches — stroking, rubbing, pummelling, kneading, wringing and pressure. All are very relaxing and produce physical effects in the blood and lymphatic circulation at the site of treatment. Many therapists believe that unexpressed emotions such as anger and grief build up in the body to cause muscle tensions, and that these unhealthy emotions can be dissipated through the process of physical massage since mind and body are closely linked. Massage also seems to stimulate release of the body's natural painkillers which ease aches and can lift your mood. Many people have found that the psychological, emotional, physical and behavioural symptoms of stress can be largely neutralized simply by receiving a weekly therapeutic massage. Massage forms the basis of many other therapies including acupressure, aromatherapy and shiatsu.

How to give an aromatherapy massage

Giving and receiving an aromatherapy massage is a relaxing, pleasurable experience. Massage your partner for thirty minutes, then relax while the touch experience is returned. Choose appropriate stress-relieving oils from the chart on page 172. Do not massage someone within two hours of a heavy meal. Only a qualified masseuse should work on a woman who is pregnant.

1. Choose a firm surface: try lying on several towels spread on the floor (beds, with the exception of a futon, are usually too soft).

2. Remove jewellery and check your fingernails are short enough not to cause scratches.

3. Make sure the room is warm and quiet. Soft candlelight and slow, relaxing background music will help to set the right ambience.

4. Ask your partner to lie on their front, and cover them with a large bath towel. Make sure they are comfortable.

5. Warm the massage oil or lotion by placing the bottle in a bowl of comfortably hot water. Alternatively, rub some oil in your hands to warm it before using. If adding extra oil during the massage, warm it before it comes into contact with your partner's skin.

6. Expose each area as you start to work on it, then re-cover it before moving on to the next area.

7. Begin with long, flowing, simple strokes that follow the body contours, to warm the skin. As a general rule, stroke towards the heart from whichever part of the body you are working on. The areas around the upper trunk are most prone to tension: shoulders, arms, neck, and forehead.

8. When you feel confident, start to vary the pressure and length of stroke you use, keeping movements flowing and rhythmic, with one hand in contact with their body at all times. Try alternating firm movements with feathery ones. If you find a muscle that seems knotted or tense, concentrate on that area with gentle kneading movements. Avoid heavy pressure directly over the spine.

SHIATSU

Shiatsu is a Japanese form of massage based on traditional Chinese medicine. Shiatsu practitioners use their fingers, thumbs, palms, forearms, elbows, and sometimes even their knees or feet to stimulate pressure points on the skin. These points – known as *tsubos* – overlie the energy lines, or meridians, through which the life-force (*chi* in Chinese, *ki* in Japanese) is believed to flow. Stimulating the *tsubos* reduces excess *chi* where the flow is blocked or overactive. Energy centres (*hara*) in the abdomen may be gently assessed and stimulated to diagnose and correct energy-flow imbalances. There is a form of shiatsu which is self-administered, known as *do-in*. Self-treatments include massaging the base of the skull, at the back of your neck, to relieve a tension headache.

9. Communicate with each other — say what feels good and whether the pressure and timing are right.

10. When you have finished massaging the back, ask your partner to turn over so you can work on their front. Stroke towards the heart and finish by holding your partner's feet for a few seconds since this helps to 'ground' them.

Meditation

Meditation is a discipline in which the power of concentration is used to control thoughts, calm the body and achieve a state of heightened mental or spiritual awareness. By focusing your mind on a particular object or vision, you can screen out distractions and induce a state of profound relaxation and serenity which can reverse the fight-or-flight response and trigger the rest/digest state of calm. Those experienced in meditation can enter a trance-like state in which the brain generates theta waves, which are associated with creativity, visions and profound relaxation. At the same time, muscle tension is reduced and some adepts can also lower their pulse and blood pressure at will. Meditation is an excellent way to help you sleep at the end of a stressful day.

There are several types of meditation, each of which favours different techniques such as concentrating on your breathing rhythm, a universal sound (for example, om), a word or phrase with personal meaning (a mantra), or a physical object (for example, a flickering candle or a vase of fresh flowers) or an image such as a picture of a loved one. Some techniques, such as t'ai chi ch'uan, involve repetitive movements or feeling objects such as pebbles or worry beads — as each object is moved it is felt and counted in a rhythmic and repetitive manner. The distracting object or thought is not important: it's purpose is to help you shut out other intrusions rather than to form the focus of intensive study. Joss sticks are frequently used to help create a relaxed atmosphere.

Posture

It is important to adopt a comfortable, neutral posture when meditating since tension in your muscles or joints will send distracting, stressful messages to your brain and interfere with meditation. Traditional meditative poses include the lotus position from yoga; kneeling as in prayer; sitting erect; or standing — they all have one thing in common: they keep your spine straight. Maintaining total immobility helps to enhance self-control and discipline.

Before starting to meditate it helps to have learned how to relax by more orthodox methods such as breathing exercises (see page 153) so you can more easily achieve a tranquil state.

Meditation through concentration

Sit comfortably in a neutral position with your eyes closed. Breathe slowly and rhythmically while concentrating your mind on an imagined object. If you wish, you can also repeat a silent sound in your mind such as a low-pitched hum. Passively concentrate on the image and sound, pushing away intrusive thoughts so your mind stays focused on the image or sound you have created. At first you will find that external thoughts keep creeping in every few seconds as your mind wanders. Simply acknowledge that this has happened and return to your focus of meditation. With time you will learn to concentrate on your central focus for ten to twenty minutes. Try to keep as still as possible, and resist the urge to move or scratch. This technique is especially helpful when you are feeling stressed and need to switch off — just a few moments spent in your quiet inner realm can reset your stress button and help you relax when all around is in chaos. When you come to the end of your meditation period, take a minute to 'come to' before slowly opening your eyes and greeting the outer world. Stretch and stand up slowly while enjoying your sense of inner peace and relaxation.

Try imagining one of the following objects when meditating to free stress — choose whichever appeals to you most:

- a slowly rotating green sphere
- a glistening, dew-coated yellow flower slowly moving in the breeze
- bubbles rising in water
- rivers of colour bathing you in light — start with red, orange and yellow then imagine the cooler colours of the spectrum — green, blue, indigo and violet
- a white cloud floating in an azure-blue sky.

OM

Sacred sounds or words, known as mantras, are believed in oriental philosophies to encapsulate cosmic energies that bind the atoms of the world together. *Om* is the highest mantra, believed to be the sound of vibration from which the Gods and universe were created. By reciting *om*, you are experiencing the power of creation and vibrating in harmony with nature.

Meditation through contemplation

Meditation through contemplation is similar to the method above, but instead of concentrating on a image or sound, you focus on an abstract thought such as peace or love. This induces a deep feeling of inner relaxation.

The value of meditation increases the more you practise. Make it a daily activity, for example while lying in bed before drifting off to sleep. You can even integrate meditation into everyday actions by focusing your senses when carrying out simple tasks such as washing your hands.

Reflexology

Reflexology is a relaxing therapy that relies on the healing power of touch to balance the body's energy. It is based on the principle that points (reflexes) in the hands or, more commonly, the feet are indirectly related to distant parts of the body. The technique originated in ancient China over 5,000 years ago and involves stimulating the reflexes through massage and tiny pressure movements to relieve fatigue and stress-related symptoms such as tension, migraine, breathing disorders, premenstrual syndrome and digestive problems. The presence of tenderness and subtle textural changes in the feet can also help the practitioner to diagnose more distant problems.

At the end of each session you will usually feel warm, contented, relaxed and much less stressed. You can buy a variety of mats, rollers, shoes and brushes that stimulate the reflexes for self-help, but if you are unable to visit a therapist, you and a friend or partner can easily learn to give each other a relaxing foot massage. Use a little aromatherapy oil to make the experience more therapeutic.

How to give a foot massage

1. Hold your partner's foot in both hands for a few moments to allow your auras to interact. Then start stroking the top and bottom of the foot by moving both hands from the toes towards the ankles and back again. Use a light, firm motion and repeat several times to warm the skin.

2. Holding the foot firmly, gently rotate and rock it from side to side and round and round to explore the range of movement at the ankle.

3. Holding the foot still, use your thumbs to apply gentle but firm pressure over the sole of the foot. Cover the whole sole with small circular movements of your thumbs.

4. Repeat the circular thumb massage on the top of the foot and the base of the toes.

5. Holding the foot under the heel with one hand, use the other to gently grasp all the toes and flex the end of the foot up and down.

6. Gently squeeze and massage each toe one at a time, starting with the big toe.

7. Finish by stroking the foot a few times as before, finally letting your fingers slide towards the ends of the toes. Hold the toes for a few moments then gently place the foot on the ground and cover with a towel while you massage the other foot.

Visualization therapy

Visualization is a technique which harnesses the power of the imagination and helps you learn how to boost self-confidence and ease the symptoms of stress. It relies on the power of suggestion and positive thought to visualize a desired outcome. This imagined role-acting then makes it easier to achieve the desired outcome in real life through improved self-awareness and self-confidence. It literally helps you to picture your way out of a stressful situation to achieve relaxation, calm and an elevated mood.

Visualization is similar to meditation but is less structured and easier to perform. It involves entering a relaxed state and allowing your own inner thoughts (or someone else's voice) to guide you on a self-improvement quest or to take you to a quiet place of peace and pleasure. By creating a feeling of contentment and pleasure, the stress fight-or-flight response is switched off and the rest/digest response activated.

Guided visualization

Guided visualization most commonly involves the use of a relaxation tape in which you are instructed on how to relax before imagining yourself somewhere pleasant such as in a leafy glade, by a brook or lying on a beach.

Unguided visualization

Unguided visualization uses the same elements as the exercise above, except the journey is replaced by your own wandering thoughts. Imagine looking through a window, for example, and describe what you can see. Then allow your imagination to take you closer so you can see, hear, feel, touch and smell what is happening there. Explore the shapes, sizes and colours of different objects to heighten your senses. Stay in this state for about ten minutes and then bring yourself slowly back to everyday feelings.

A JOURNEY TO LET GO OF STRESS

Close your eyes and imagine you are lying on a deserted tropical beach. Feel the sun warming your skin while a light salt-tanged breeze keeps you cool and refreshed. Hear the gentle waves lapping against the sand near your feet and the distant sound of birds singing in the palm trees.

Get up and walk through the silver sand, feeling the warm grains trickling through your toes. You see boats bobbing on the distant blue horizon and hear the dull plop of a coconut falling on to the sand. Sweet-smelling tropical flowers scent the air as you walk down to the water's edge. You feel the cool water close over your toes as you bend down to pick up a smooth pebble. Turn it between your fingers, feeling its smooth, cold contours, then gently toss it into the water. Your time is your own and no one wants you for anything. Now turn around and retrace your steps back along the beach to lie down on the warm sand again.

It is time to bring the journey to an end, so in your own time, open your eyes, stretch your limbs and start to think about the present.

Symptomatic visualization

If a particular stress-related symptom is troublesome, picture an image in your mind that represents that symptom, and imagine it away. For example, if you are troubled by tension headaches, visualize the headache as an iron band around your head which gets progressively looser and looser until it falls away.

Affirmations and visualization

One of the most successful visualization techniques is performed just before you go to sleep. This allows your subconscious mind to dwell on what it has learned and improves the chance of a successful outcome. This exercise should involve a visualization that is pertinent to your life, for example if you have an upcoming interview, visualize that going well.

1. Choose an appropriate positive affirmation, such as 'I am an interesting and confident candidate for the job.'

2. Every night when you go to bed, imagine yourself greeting the interview panel calmly, dealing logically and confidently with their questions and impressing the board with your knowledge, experience and capabilities.

3. Feel the confidence growing inside you as you answer all their questions and make insightful comments on the qualities and benefits you can add to the team.

4. Repeat your positive thought slowly and carefully to yourself.

5. Now touch the bed with the little finger of your left hand. Repeat the thought and touch the bed with the ring finger of your left hand while concentrating on the warm, self-confident feeling of having achieved an excellent interview.

6. Keep repeating Step 5, using each finger (and thumb) of your left hand, and then your right. Then reverse the process, touching the bed starting with the little finger of the right hand. By the time you have finished, you will have repeated the thought twenty times.

USING A MANDALA

A mandala is an intricate diagram used to represent the universe in Hindu and Buddhist traditions. This can be used to assist your visualization or meditation. A mandala usually consists of a series of concentric circles surrounded by an outer enclosure. The circles in turn may surround other geometric shapes containing the symbols or images of Gods. Eastern mandalas are basically of two types, representing different aspects of the universe: the *garbha-dhatu,* in which the movement of the eye across the mandala is from the one to the many; and the *vajra-dhatu* in which the eye moves from the many into one. Concentrating on the images on a mandala can help you enter a guided visualization or a meditative state.

Repeat this procedure every night for a week, staying awake throughout the entire process. The following week, repeat the process but let yourself fall asleep when you are ready. The statement should now have become part of your normal thinking patterns.

6

DEVELOP SELF-ESTEEM

To help you take control of your life and develop healthy self-esteem, it helps to learn how to assert yourself, how to think rationally and how to communicate better; and to develop a variety of hobbies and interests outside your work and home life.

Assertiveness

Assertiveness training is based on the underlying belief that everyone is equal and has the same basic rights. Your goal is to learn to say 'no' in a calm, responsible manner without violating the rights of others. Being assertive is the desirable mid-path between being passive and being aggressive.

Being too passive usually leads to loss of self-esteem and resentment. Learning how to effectively challenge the demands made on you by others is important if you are to deal with situations in a pleasant, relaxed manner, avoid misunderstandings, and prevent yourself being persuaded to do things against your better judgement.

YOUR RIGHTS

You have the right to:
- be yourself
- express your own opinions and beliefs
- be listened to and respected
- consider your own needs
- set your own priorities
- take responsibility for your own actions
- get things wrong
- not to understand
- say yes and no
- disagree
- be assertive without feeling guilty
- not to be assertive when you choose.

PASSIVITY, ASSERTION AND AGGRESSION

BEING PASSIVE	BEING ASSERTIVE	BEING AGGRESSIVE
Keeping quiet about your thoughts, feelings and needs, and letting others walk all over you.	Expressing your thoughts, feelings and needs clearly and openly while recognizing those of others, and taking steps to identify and solve potential conflicts.	Insisting on your own rights and needs at the expense of others.
Having no control over events.	Maintaining control over your own rights while respecting those of others.	Controlling events and getting your own way through verbal attacks and put-downs.
Letting others make decisions for you.	Playing an equal role in reaching decisions with others.	Insisting on making decisions for others.
Giving in to avoid conflict at all costs.	Upholding your rights calmly and pleasantly while looking for compromises that suit everyone.	Winning and dominating others at all costs.
Accepting the role of victim.	Not allowing others to take advantage of you just as you wouldn't dream of taking advantage of others.	Insisting on being top dog.
Avoiding eye contact.	Maintaining firm eye contact without staring.	Glaring, staring down and trying to intimidate.
Wringing your hands, hunching your shoulders, hiding your mouth with your hand; trying to disappear.	Maintaining an open, relaxed posture.	Clenching your fists, making stabbing finger movements, pointing, banging the table, leaning forward, crossing your arms.

How assertive are you?

Consider the following situations and decide which response is the one you are most likely to make. Try to be honest in answering the questions – don't give what you think is the correct answer, but the one that is most likely to be the way you would behave.

1. **You order a meal in a restaurant but three-quarters of an hour later have still not received any food.**

   A: You continue to wait quietly as you don't want to make a fuss or cause a scene.

   B: You call the waiter over and ask if there is a problem as you would have expected to receive your food by now. The waiter explains the food will be another fifteen minutes. You politely request a round of drinks on the house to make up for the inconvenience, to which the waiter agrees.

   C: You call the waiter over and loudly demand your food immediately, otherwise you will leave. The waiter explains the food will be another fifteen minutes. You say this simply isn't good enough and start demanding a large discount on your final bill.

2. Your boss criticizes a report you have handed in because it is incomplete. You apologize and say you were unable to complete the figures due to lack of time. When he asks you to stay behind that night to complete it:

A: You meekly agree, even though you had arranged to go out after work with friends.

B: You say you are unable to do so. When he insists, you repeat that you are unable to do so, but offer to complete it first thing in the morning.

C: You say that is totally out of the question. You then blame him for setting you too much work — what does he think you are, a slave?

3. You belong to a babysitting rota and hope to swap your regular night with another mum. When you ask her, she hesitates. You reply:

A: Don't worry, I'll do it myself. It's not really important.

B: 'I'd really appreciate it if you could help me out — just like I did for you a couple of weeks ago. You did say you owed me one.'

C: 'You have to swap — I did the same for you a while ago. You owe me one and now it's pay day.'

4. You buy a shirt and when you get home, realize it has a black mark on it.

A: You shrug and decide to wash it. It's bound to come out. Anyway, you're too embarrassed to go back to the shop.

B: You take the shirt back to the shop, point out the mark and politely ask them to change it.

C: You go back to the shop and start having a go at the assistant for selling shoddy goods, before demanding to see the manager.

5. Your friend has a habit of clicking her pen, which really annoys you when you are trying to concentrate.

A: You say nothing and put your hands over your ears to help block out the sound.

B: You say 'Julie, I know you're working hard and don't realize you're doing it, but I'd appreciate it if you would stop clicking that pen. It makes it hard for me to think straight. Perhaps you wouldn't mind putting it down?'

C: You say 'For heaven's sake, Julie. Some of us are trying to work round here. Stop clicking that pen, or I'll take it off you and chuck it out the window.'

6. You are asked out to the cinema by someone you find boring. You don't really want to go, and say:

A: 'Yes, of course. That would be nice.'

B: 'I'm sorry, I'm really busy at the moment. Why not ask Susan — I know she's been wanting to see that film.'

C: 'You must be joking. I've got far better things to do with my time.'

7. You are sitting on a bus and the old lady next to you starts prying and asking you personal questions about your life and family.

A: You answer her stiffly, not really wanting to upset her, then say, 'Oh look, here's my stop', and get off early so you have further to walk home.

B: You say politely, 'I prefer not to discuss these things with strangers. Would you excuse me if I just read my book?'

C: You say, 'Mind your own business', get up and pointedly move to another seat two rows in front.'

8. **You overhear a colleague telling someone you are always untidy.**

A: You sneak away to the toilets, upset, and don't let them know you heard them. It's not true, but you make a point of being extra tidy anyway, just to scotch the rumours.

B: You walk up to them and say, 'Why do you say that? I am occasionally untidy but no more than anyone else.'

C: You barge in and say 'Excuse me? How dare you! I'm never untidy and even if I were, it's no business of yours. You've no right to criticize me like that.'

9. **You are asked a question to which you don't know the answer.**

A: You mumble that you don't know the answer and feel you must be stupid.

B: You say, 'That's a good question. I haven't a clue. Let's ring the library and find out.'

C: You say, 'Don't ask me. I've far more important things to worry about. Find out yourself. Honestly, you're always expecting me to do your work for you.'

10. **You lent a book to a friend over a month ago and now need it back. You say:**

A: 'I wonder, if you've finished with it, could you possibly let me have that book back sometime? No hurry.'

B: 'I really need that book back now. Perhaps you would bring it in tomorrow morning?'

C: 'I need that book back now. If you don't return it tomorrow, I'll never lend you anything ever again.'

How did you score?

Mainly As: You are too passive and need to learn some assertiveness skills. These will help to build your self-esteem and allow you stand up for yourself better than you are at present.

Mainly Bs: You are already skilled at being assertive but it is important to continue expressing yourself in a pleasant but forceful way to ensure you don't get put upon.

Mainly Cs: You handle problems too aggressively, and need to learn the difference between assertion and aggression so you can defend your rights without putting other people's backs up.

Learning to be assertive

Assertiveness skills are based on a few tried-and-tested techniques that give you the verbal tools to say 'no' politely and firmly. This helps you express your rights and can deal with many of the sources of stress in your life.

Basic assertion

This involves making a straightforward statement in which you calmly insist on your rights. Use a short statement that clearly sums up your needs, feelings or opinions. If, for example, your boss wants you to work on a Saturday, when you have made other plans, just say: 'I'm unable to work on Saturday.' When the person reinforces their argument, you do the same. 'I'm still unable to work on Saturday.' Never feel you have to explain – don't, for example, start telling your boss exactly what plans you have arranged for the weekend. This is irrelevant. Equally, don't feel you have to apologize – you have done nothing wrong!

The cracked record

This is a simple skill which is sometimes necessary when you need to be persistent in order to resist someone who is very persuasive. It merely depends on selecting a phrase and repeating it as often as necessary until the other person gives up trying to manipulate you. For example, just keep saying calmly, 'I am unable to work on Saturday at such short notice.' Keep repeating your statement each time the other person comes back with another demand or suggestion. If they don't respond after you have repeated your point, stay quiet – being comfortable with maintaining silence is vital since you need to state your case one more time than the other person makes their point.

Negotiation

It will usually help to reduce the tension if you can offer an acceptable compromise. 'No, I am unable to work this Saturday. However, I can work next Saturday and am willing to swap with anyone who can work this Saturday instead. Is that OK?' Keep calm and in control, and breathe slowly. Compromise makes everyone feel better as no one really loses. You have asserted your right not to change your plans at short notice, and have also offered your boss a possible solution to the dilemma.

Dealing with recurrent irritations

If someone repeatedly does something that upsets you, you need to deal with it calmly without causing resentment. It helps to work out a statement in advance that simply describes:

1. The nature of the problem.

ASSERTIVE WORDS

People who are assertive rather than aggressive choose phrases such as:

- I think...
- I would like...
- I would prefer...
- We could...
- Why don't we...
- Let's...
- What do you think?
- Is that OK?
- How do you feel about that?

LEARNING HOW TO SAY NO

You may find it surprising how often you have agreed to do something you would really rather not do simply because you did not know how to say no. Even more annoying are the times you say no but are then, somehow, persuaded to change your mind and say yes instead. Being assertive means knowing how to say no and mean it.

The secrets of successfully saying no are to:

- Not use the word 'No' or 'I can't' at all. Instead say, 'I am unable to...' or, 'I am unwilling to...'
- Remember that by declining you are rejecting the request, not the person.
- Accept that sometimes you may have to upset someone if you cannot comply with their request – their upset is their problem, however. Don't make it yours by giving in and saying yes when you really are unable to do something.
- Pause before answering a request if you are not sure about it – it is permissible to say, 'Can I get back to you on this?' or, 'Can I let you know later?'
- Practise saying, 'I am unable to...' out loud in private, using a variety of phrases until you find one or two you are comfortable with.

- Acknowledge their need without giving in: 'I understand you need someone to help, but I am unable to do that right now.'
- Be brief. Don't give a long speech about why you have to say no. A non-committal phrase such as 'other priorities I have to attend to' is more than enough explanation. If you are interrogated about why you cannot do something, reply, 'I prefer not to say'. Keep repeating your statements like a broken record if necessary to deflect their insistence.
- Be calm and pleasant. Don't snap. If necessary, thank the person for asking you but still say no. 'No, I'm afraid I can't make that, but thank you for asking me.' 'I understand the importance of this assignment, but without extra resources, I cannot take it on.'
- If they persist and you are finding it difficult to resist, then say so. 'I'm afraid I can't do that, and you are making it difficult for me by trying to insist. Please don't.'
- It usually helps to end the conversation quickly. 'I'm afraid I can't do that, but thank you for asking me. I don't want to sound abrupt, but I really do have to go now.' This reduces further opportunities to change your mind.

2. How it affects you.

3. How it makes you feel.

4. How you would like it resolved.

If, for example, your boss keeps expecting you to work overtime on Saturdays, you could try to deal with it by saying: 'You keep expecting me to work overtime on Saturdays. This means I have little quality time with my family, which upsets me. I don't mind being flexible occasionally in an emergency, but I feel it is unreasonable to keep expecting me to work at the weekend. I would like to stick to my contracted hours more closely in future.

Owning up

Asserting your rights also means taking responsibility for your own actions. If you make a mistake, it is important to acknowledge the fact. Say sorry, give your personal commitment that it will not happen again, and learn from the experience. This allows you to retain your self-respect and shows that you have sufficient confidence and maturity to take full responsibility for your behaviour. For example, if you agreed to do something by a certain time but failed, say, 'I apologize. I fully intended to complete this task by the agreed date, but it has taken longer than I expected. It is my fault and I will stay late tonight to ensure it is ready first thing tomorrow morning. This will not happen again.'

How to accept criticism

Being assertive and having more self-esteem means being able to accept constructive criticism but defending yourself against unearned criticism. For example, if someone says you are late, and you know this is true, agree by saying, 'Yes, I am sometimes late but I am trying to be more punctual.' If they unjustly say, 'You are always late,' and you are not, reply calmly: 'No, I am not always late. I have been late on only two occasions in the last three months.' Or you could ask for clarification. 'No, I am not always late at all. Why do you say that I am?'

Rational thinking

Rational thinking means overcoming common irrational ways of thinking, challenging upsetting thoughts, and thinking more positively. These skills will help you plan your thoughts rationally in a way that can help to lower your stress levels

Psychologists have identified a number of common errors in the way people think when they are under pressure. These ways of thinking are essentially irrational and can significantly increase your stress levels. Try to avoid:

Fixing labels such as 'I'm stupid', 'He's a loser', 'She's a complete idiot', 'I'm not good enough'.

Jumping to conclusions by mind-reading, such as, 'He must think I'm useless', 'They must think me stupid', 'She must be fed up with me by now'; or by fortune-telling, such as, 'I'm going to fail, I know I will', 'I know she won't like my work', 'There's no point in asking him, he's bound to refuse'.

Concentrating on negatives and ignoring positives: 'Nothing's going right', 'Everyone hates me', 'I always mess up'.

Downplaying positives: 'I only got invited

THINKING MORE RATIONALLY	
INSTEAD OF:	TRY USING:
terrible	inconvenient
dreadful	annoying
catastrophe	nuisance
awful	unfortunate
I ought to	I would prefer to
I have to	I would like to
I must	I intend to

because they needed someone to make up the numbers', 'I only got that right through sheer luck', 'I only won that promotion because they need to keep me sweet'.

Thinking in all-or-nothing terms: 'There's no point in trying as I'll never get it right', 'I have no option but to complain', 'I hate this, there's nothing good about it at all'.

Exaggerating: 'That would be the worst thing ever to happen to me', 'If I don't do that, he'll kill me', 'If she ever finds out what happened, I'll die', 'I can't stand it any more'.

Accepting inappropriate blame: 'The meeting went badly, it's all my fault', 'She didn't get that job — it's my fault for not coaching her properly', 'We failed to win that account — I'm to blame for giving a lousy presentation'.

Blaming others: 'It's all his fault — he should have warned me it was coming', 'It's all their fault for not thinking things through properly', 'I've mislaid my pen — who's nicked it?'.

Generalizing: 'I always get it wrong', 'She's always late', 'Everyone's against me'.

Minimizing events: 'I managed to pass, but it wasn't exactly with flying colours', 'OK, so I got a promotion. So what?', 'He gave me a grade A, but I could have achieved an A-plus if I'd put more effort in'.

Letting your emotions rule: 'I feel stupid, so I must be', 'He made me feel upset, so he must be really horrible', 'I don't feel like doing that now, so I'll think about doing it later'.

Thinking in shoulds: 'I should have done that', 'He should have said so', 'I should try harder'.

Thinking in oughts: 'I ought to say yes', 'I ought to do that', 'I ought to try harder'.

Thinking in musts: 'I must do this', 'I must give in', 'I must say yes'.

Thinking in have-tos: 'I have to agree', 'I have to go ahead', 'I have to believe that'.

When you are under excess pressure, it helps to write down your thoughts and analyse them to see what errors you are making in the way you think. If you can eliminate these irrational thoughts, you will be able to deal with your stress more easily.

- If, for example, you are looking at a situation in black-and-white, all–or-nothing terms, or are exaggerating things, try to find some middle ground that helps you keep things in better perspective.
- If you find you are putting a label on someone as a result of their actions, is that label really justified?
- If you believe your own performance is poor, are you being too harsh on yourself? Where is the evidence? Try asking other people for their opinion and use their feedback in a positive, constructive manner to improve your performance where necessary, and to accept you've done well when you have.
- Don't make mountains out of molehills. It is common to use words that greatly exaggerate events. You may do this almost without thinking, and it can greatly increase the level of stress you feel in a particular situation. Look at the list of words below for suggestions on more realistic vocabulary.

Thinking more positively

It is common to compare yourself unfavourably with others, and this is a powerful source of internal stress. Write down ten qualities you like about yourself (for example, sense of humour, good with children, patient, good cook, strong will-power, musical, interesting to talk to, caring, loyal, flexible):

1 _____

2 _____

3 _____

4 _____

5 _____

6 _____

7 _____

8 _____

9 _____

10 _____

These are your ten aces – the things you like best about yourself which no one can take away from you. Write this list of affirmations down again on a small piece of card, in order of their importance to you. Put this card in your wallet/purse and next time your self-esteem feels low or you feel you are not good enough, take that list out and read it. These are the top ten qualities which you like about yourself – and which others will appreciate and like, too. Feel free to add to the list until you have twenty or more qualities that make you feel good about yourself as a person. Read these as often as you need to boost your self-esteem.

Now write down ten qualities in yourself that you often feel negative about:

1 _____

2 _____

3 _____

4 _____

5 _____

6 _____

7 _____

8 _____

9 _____

10 _____

SELF-ESTEEM ESSENTIALS

Remember:

● No one can make you feel inferior without your permission – they can only invite you to. How you respond is up to you. Believe in yourself.

● Everyone has a right to be wrong sometimes, including you.

You only feel bad about these qualities because you have somehow convinced yourself they are true. Isn't it surprising how easy it is to believe these negative thoughts, and how difficult it is to believe the positive ones you wrote down in the previous exercise?

The best thing to do with these negative thoughts is to turn them into positives. Go through the list of negatives, turn them into positives, and write these new positives down on another piece of card. For example:

- 'I am not good enough' becomes 'I am good enough'
- 'I am not important' becomes 'I am as important as everyone else'
- 'I'm not very bright' becomes 'I am an intelligent human being'
- 'I'm not very interesting' becomes 'I am an interesting person'
- 'I'm not very lovable' becomes 'I am lovable'
- 'I don't really like myself' becomes 'I really like myself'
- 'I'm not very special' becomes 'I am special'
- 'I'm a nobody' becomes 'I am unique'
- 'I'm going nowhere' becomes 'I am capable of great things'
- 'It's too difficult' becomes 'I can do difficult things'
- 'I can't cope with change' becomes 'I can cope with change; changes are challenges and challenges are opportunities to learn'.

Again, keep this list of adopted positive affirmations in your wallet/purse along with your other ten affirmations and refer to them whenever you start thinking negative thoughts about yourself. The more you read these affirmations, the more quickly they will become imprinted on your belief systems and the sooner they will start to improve your positive mental health.

Accepting criticism

Constructive criticism can be useful, but destructive criticism is something you want to offer up and forget about. It is not always easy to work out which is which at the time the criticism is made, however. You may need to go away and analyse what was said; whether the person was in a good mood or feeling vindictive; and whether or not they had your best interests at heart.

In the meantime, you need to know how to accept criticism so that you can see clearly whether it is constructive or destructive, and disarm the critic if necessary. It is important to stay relaxed, and to breathe slowly, deeply and calmly. Smile, lean slightly towards the person rather than drawing back, and don't respond until you've had time to think about what you want to say. The following techniques can help:

- First, pause and decide whether the criticism is valid: Yes? No? Maybe?
- If the criticism is valid:
    1. Agree with them :'You're right, I can be untidy, but I'm working on it'.
    2. Thank them :'Thank you for letting me know', or, 'That's a useful comment, I'll think about it / I'll take it on board', or, 'I'm glad you told me'.
    3. If necessary, apologize: 'I'm sorry. I'll take steps to put that right'.
    4. Learn from the criticism.

- If the criticism is invalid:
  1. Challenge them: 'Why are you saying that?'; 'Why do you feel the need to say that'?
  2. Ask for specifics: 'Would you mind telling me exactly what I did to make you say that?'
  3. Tell them you disagree with their assessment: 'I'm always willing to hear what you have to say. However, on this occasion I disagree for the following reasons...' If they continue to assert their criticism, say something along the lines of, 'Clearly we disagree. I still don't feel your criticism is valid.'
- If the criticism may be valid:
  1. Ask for clarification: 'Could you be more specific?' or, 'What exactly do you mean?'
  2. Ask their advice:'How would you have done that differently?'
- If they were unkind enough to make the criticism in front of someone else, you could draw the other person in if you are sure you are on firm ground: 'What do you think?' or, 'Do you agree?' or, 'Do you believe that's the case?'

Consider criticism a gift — an opportunity to improve if the criticism is valid, and an opportunity to re-affirm your self-esteem if the criticism is invalid. Put-downs can only really hurt you if you believe there is a nugget of truth in what is being said. If, for example, someone criticized you by saying, 'You have green hair', this would not hurt at all and you would easily laugh it off. If, however, they said, 'You're lazy', this would hurt if you secretly thought it might be true. If you know you are not lazy, but the criticism has still hurt, add 'I am not lazy' to the list of affirmations in your wallet/purse.

Improving relationships

Good communication is important in all relationships, whether they involve your parents, children, friends, work colleagues, boss, acquaintances or anyone else you need to deal with. Good communication means:
1. Expressing yourself clearly and assertively: say what you mean, and mean what you say. Don't use veiled hints and comments.
2. Listening carefully to others: both to hear what they are saying, and to check how well you have been understood.
3. Reaching an agreed endpoint where you both know what is happening and how things will progress, if necessary.
4. Becoming more aware of other people's needs and wants.

Expressing yourself

Expressing yourself properly means exploring your feelings in order to understand exactly how you feel about a particular situation; recognizing that certain issues need to be dealt with rather than passively endured; and acting assertively to protect your rights.

1. To express yourself well, you need to choose the right time and place for making your statement. Some issues need to be dealt with immediately, as soon as the situation has arisen. Other, more long-term problems should be addressed in private when you and the other person have time to deal with the problem fully.

2. Choose a phrase that succinctly sums up what you want to say. Use 'I' language: 'I feel…I would prefer…I would like…' Rather than 'you' language: 'You must…You should…' and so on.

3. Stick to the point without nagging or getting sidetracked.

4. If you are dealing with a problem that annoys or upsets you, use a formula that states what the problem is (for example, 'You were late again this morning'); how this affects you (for example, 'I was left hanging around for half an hour'); how this makes you feel (for example, 'I felt annoyed and upset'); how you would like the issue resolved (for example, 'Please make sure you do not leave me waiting again') — this is the desirable endpoint that you are requesting.

5. Listen to their response to ensure they have understood what you have said, have taken it on board, and agree. If they do not agree, then you may have to agree to differ.

If the tables are turned, and you are the one being criticized, tips on the best way to deal with this are given on page 205.

Learning to listen

Being a good listener is a skill that others will quickly appreciate. It involves:

1. Facing the person who is speaking to you, giving them your full attention, and making eye contact without staring.

2. Giving verbal encouragement: use words or sounds such as 'Uh-huh?', 'Really?', 'Yes'.

3. Giving non-verbal encouragement: nod your head, or animate your face to reflect what you are hearing — look sad, happy, interested, amused or concerned as appropriate.

4. Not interrupting until the person has had their say. Don't be tempted to finish their sentence for them. Be patient and give them all the time they need to express themselves fully.

5. Reply appropriately with a phrase that sums up what you have just heard: for example, 'That was quite an experience you've just had. You obviously feel shaken and upset.' Or, 'So you're saying you are upset with me because I was late…'

6. Make a suitable closing statement: 'Let's go and have a cup of tea while you try to relax and calm down.' Or, 'That was a great story, but we'd better get back to work

now.' Or, 'I'm sorry I've upset you, I'll do my best to ensure it doesn't happen again.' This is the desirable endpoint you are suggesting, or that the other person is requesting.

Helping your relationship grow rather than stagnate

It is important to become more aware of other people's needs and wants, especially in a close relationship. It is easy for couples to start taking each other for granted or at least to appear as if they are. It is important to:

- make time to do things together
- find time for fun and joking around
- look at each other when speaking: put the newspaper/magazine down; switch off the TV
- tell your partner you love them regularly
- give shows of affection in private – a hug, peck on the cheek, card or small present goes a long way
- give shows of affection in public – an arm round the shoulder or holding hands means a lot
- share household chores
- enquire after each other's day
- share successes with them
- discuss worries with them
- ask their opinion on things that matter to you
- avoid criticizing them in public
- be faithful
- respect each other's independence
- respect each other's privacy
- provide unflagging loyalty and support.

Dealing with jealousy

Jealousy is one of the most destructive emotions and can increase your levels of stress as well as destroying your self-esteem. This is because jealousy is based on deep-seated fears, misplaced beliefs and insecurities such as:

- she is better than me (i.e., I am not good enough)
- why her and not me? (i.e., I am not good enough)
- I am going to lose him (i.e., I am not good enough)
- everything's going to change (i.e., I can't cope)
- I am going to be alone (i.e., no one loves me).

When you experience feelings of jealousy, get the cards containing your two lists of affirmations from your wallet or purse (see page 203) and read them several times. If necessary, add a few extra affirmations because you are good enough, you can cope, you are loveable and you do deserve success.

You are responsible for your feelings of jealousy. No one else can make you feel jealous without your permission. By reinforcing your self-esteem, there is less for you to feel jealous about. You are equally as capable and deserving as the next person. The fact that they are lucky today does not mean that you cannot be lucky tomorrow.

- Allow yourself to congratulate other people on their success. Really let yourself feel happy for them just as you would want them to be happy for you if things were the other way round. You are the master of your own emotions and jealousy is an emotion you do not wish to hold on to for it is both stressful and destructive.

- Make sure you are not over-exaggerating a situation and making a mountain out of a molehill. Remember that even when someone is chosen over you for a promotion it does not mean that you were not good enough. It means that for some reason they were more suited to the job at that particular time. Their success does not detract from your skills and abilities.

- If someone passes an exam that you have failed, then equally their success does not deserve your jealousy but your praise. You tried and failed this time, but this provides you with an opportunity to keep trying until you achieve a pass, too. Failure is acceptable as long as you don't give in. Keep aiming for your goal.

- Don't allow jealousy and mistrust to ruin a close relationship. If your partner wants to go out alone with their friends, let them do so. Show them that you love and respect them, and that you trust them not to let you down.

- Convert feelings of jealousy into an opportunity to examine where you want to be in relation to where you are now, and if necessary redouble your own efforts to help you achieve your life goals.

Remember that jealousy can become a self-fulfilling prophesy: it can make you suspicious, distrustful and emotionally cold. You can waste so much energy looking for signs of betrayal or doling out punishment for perceived transgressions that you push people away until they do leave you, avoid you or stop returning your phone calls.

Developing hobbies and interests

A well-rounded, self-confident person is aware of the world around them, keeps up-to-date with current affairs and develops a number of hobbies and areas of special interest. These interests are what help to define you as an individual and what helps to make your conversation stimulating and educational. Hobbies that involve joining groups or taking classes are also an excellent way of meeting like-minded people with whom you are likely to have a lot in common.

It is important to have at least one hobby or interest outside your work and family life. Hobbies can help you keep fit (for example, gardening, DIY, playing team sports, swimming, golf, bowling, tennis, rambling, jogging, dancing, going to the gym); they can exercise your mind (for example, doing crosswords, studying for an exam in a subject that interests you, teaching yourself chess or Egyptian hieroglyphics); and can even provide extra income (for example, creative writing, buying and selling antiques or stamps). Hobbies can also be spiritually rewarding (for example, bird-watching, voluntary work, visiting the elderly and lonely).

While many couples share similar interests and hobbies, it is important to have at least one activity that you can call your own, and which helps you maintain an identity outside your relationship.

List below the hobbies that you currently indulge in:

1 _____

2 _____

3 _____

4 _____

5 _____

List below the activities you have often thought about doing but never got around to:

1 _____

2 _____

3 _____

4 _____

5 _____

Promise yourself that you will start at least one of these activities within the next two weeks.

STREAMLINE YOUR LIFE

And finally, to help ensure that high stress levels remain a thing of the past, the last step in this seven-point plan looks at practical ways to keep life running as smoothly as possible.

At home

Whether you work at home, away from home, or in the home it is helpful to stream-line certain aspects of your domestic life to help free up more time for rest and relaxation.

Organizational skills are as useful in the home as they are at work. Delegate jobs to others where appropriate and ensure that you are not put upon to do more than your fair share of chores.

It will help to set a routine as much as possible. This is especially important if there are times of the day when you tend to function less effi-ciently, such as early morning or late evening. Before going to bed, for example, do whatever you can to minimize tomorrow's morning rush, such as laying the breakfast table and getting out the clothes you intend to wear. Always eat breakfast, even if up until now you haven't made time. Breakfast is the most important meal of the day when you are under pressure (see Chapter 3).

An excellent tip to help save time is to get up when you wake up rather than lying in bed. You could even set your alarm clock an hour earlier than usual and get up to go for a gentle jog or even a swim to get you off to a good start to the day. It is often more pleasant to exercise when you are feeling fresh rather than at the end of a long, tiring day.

Being organized means doing jobs when they need doing rather than putting them off until they have to be done. Rather than transferring dirty clothes from the bedroom laundry basket into the 'waiting-to-be-washed' basket in the utility room, put them straight into the washing machine and set the machine going.

TAKING TIME OUT

When you have created more time for yourself at home, it is important to use it for rest and relaxation, otherwise the benefits will be lost. Try setting yourself incentive rewards to help you use your time more constructively. For example, promise yourself: 'If I complete the ironing this morning, I will read a novel this afternoon'.

Tips to help you get more organized at home

- Keep pen and paper (or if you prefer, a dictaphone) by your bed so you can write down important thoughts that come into your head while going to sleep.

- Write Post-It notes to yourself to remind yourself to do things and stick them somewhere obvious where you will see them, such as on the fridge door, or on the kitchen table. Discard them when they have fulfilled their purpose.

- Assign a usual place for important items (for example, keys) and do your best to ensure they are always returned there after use

- Communicate with the family via a message board if you are all coming and going at different times.

- Limit your wardrobe of clothes, and their colours, so you spend less time thinking about what to wear. This is especially easy for clothes you wear around the house (for example, leggings, T-shirt, cardigan).

- Invest in sheets of labels containing your name, address and phone number so you don't have to keep writing out your personal details on forms, envelopes, etc.

- Eliminate jobs around the house that aren't essential — it isn't usually necessary to vacuum every day, for example.

- Delegate as many jobs to others as you can afford (for example, invest in a domestic help to vacuum, dust and iron; a gardener to mow your lawn; a friendly teenager to wash your car).

- Assign chores (for example, putting out the bins, loading the dishwasher) to other family members — use a rota if necessary.

- Buy supplies of essential items in bulk so you are less likely to run out (this will also help save money).

- Keep a selection of greetings cards at home so you always have a suitable last-minute card available for a birthday or celebration.

- Whenever you buy something new, try to get rid of something old.

- Keep financial papers, bills, insurance, mortgage details, birth certificates, wills, etc. all together in one lockable desk or file box so you always know where everything is.

- Use direct debit facilities to pay as many bills as possible.

- Make a list of things that really matter to you and spend more time doing these — and less time on everything else.
- Spend at least twenty minutes relaxing in the evening before going to bed. Indulge in an aromatherapy bath and review your day in your mind as well as thinking about things you would like to do tomorrow.

At work

Goal planning is important in all aspects of your life, for you can only achieve your goals if you know exactly what they are. Spend a little time thinking realistically about where you would like to be in:

- 1 year's time
- 5 years' time
- 10 years' time.

Your goals should encompass all areas of your life, including your personal life, career, financial standing, work-related skills, qualifications, experiences, abilities and qualities. Set realistic short- and long-term goals which do not conflict with one another. If you want to spend more time studying, for example, it may be difficult to spend more quality time with your partner, too. Don't pile too much pressure on yourself, as unrealistic goals can be a source of stress in themselves, and multiple failures to achieve those goals will also erode your self-esteem. For example, within the next five years you may like to have:

- passed a work-related examination
- achieved a promotion
- moved to a larger house
- become more fit
- started to learn a foreign language
- travelled to Australia
- read more widely
- learned more about the opera
- got married
- had a baby.

Once you have written down your lists, keep them somewhere safe such as in your wallet or purse, where you can refer to them regularly to keep them firmly fixed in your mind.

Now consider where you are now in relation to where you want to be. You then need to draw up a plan that will help you to achieve your goals. In the example quoted, you will need to enrol on appropriate courses and study to help achieve the necessary qualification. This will, in turn, help your bid for promotion and a larger salary, which will help you move to a larger house. When your study is under way, you can allocate more of your quality time towards pursuing reading and listening to operas and invest in a home-study foreign language course. You can listen to the foreign language course tapes while stuck in traffic, and listen to opera cassettes while concentrating on driving. At the same time, you will need to start putting aside regular savings to help fund your planned trip to Australia. If you are not already in a permanent relationship, then joining a foreign language evening class and organizing trips to the opera with friends and colleagues will help to widen your circle of friends — as will taking up a regular physical activity (for example, joining a gym, joining a tennis club, going swimming) in order to get fit. You are in control of 80% of the activities on your long-term goal list — getting married and having a baby will rely on fate — but a non-stressed, interesting individual with long-term goals and lots of outside interests is more likely to achieve the final two items on this list than an over-stressed, over-worked, irritable, unfit person who spends all their time working and too little time relaxing and having fun.

Having started to put you goal plan to work, you will need to hold regular self-audit sessions to see how far along the road you are. Only by honestly assessing your progress and by reformulating or reinforcing your goals are you likely get to where you want to be.

Finally, it is important to remember that you are not alone, even if it feels that way. There are millions of people out there striving to be successful and to reach their individual life goals, too. Some will be better at achieving their goals than others, some worse. Use other people as a resource and try learning from each other. Share what you feel you are doing well. Ask about areas of uncertainty. Curiosity, despite the proverbial cat, usually pays off!

Controlling perfectionism

No one is perfect, yet many people waste a lot of time trying to be so. Perfectionism involves getting everything exactly right, down to the last detail. This is usually a waste of precious time, however, because, according to the Law of Diminishing Returns, the more time you spend on the minutiae of a particular task, the less you will achieve per unit of time. Even worse than wasting time is the very real risk that not getting something right will be deemed as a failure by your hardest task-master — you. Even if they get something 99% right, a perfectionist will focus only on the 1% of the task that was wrong.

Getting something wrong can be an advantage, however, as it means you then have an opportunity to learn from your mistakes. Everyone is allowed to make mistakes and you should be comfortable with that. Otherwise, you may subconsciously start to fear making mistakes and avoid undertaking new challenges because of your fear of failure.

- Set yourself a time-limit for a particular task.
- If at the end of this time, the task is still not completed to your satisfaction, allow yourself an additional short deadline (for example, fifteen minutes) and no more.
- Adopt the saying, 'It is better to have tried and failed, than not to have tried at all' as your rationale when you experience fear of taking a particular task on because it seems too daunting.
- Make sure that all the resources you need are available before starting a task — and warn others if necessary that you may well fail at a particular task but you are still willing to give it your best shot.
- Don't necessarily play to win — play for the glory of taking part in the game.

Time management

Time is a finite commodity — a fact that it is easy to forget when you are stressed and working long hours. The best way to remember the importance of time management is to consider this equation:

Quality Time (leisure, family, sport)

+ Work Time (getting to and from the workplace, paper-pushing, telephoning, planning, finances, feeling stressed)

= Total Time (i.e., the sum total of your adult life)

The more time you spend on work and feeling stressed, the less time is available for rest, relaxation, recuperation and fun. Your battle cry should be that you work to live, not that you live to work, and it is important to make work time as efficient as possible to prevent it eating into quality time.

Manage time firmly or it will happily manage you. The most important skills of time management are prioritizing tasks and delegation.

Prioritizing

When managing time, it is vital to do the most important and pressing jobs first before turning your attention to those that can wait a little longer.

Making a 'To Do' list

A 'To Do' list will help you improve your organizational skills and prioritize tasks so that the most important get done first. You can buy printed tear-off booklets designed for such lists or you can draw up your own.

1. Make a list of all the tasks you need to do during the next few days.

2. Put them in order of importance using an A, B, C coding, for example, A1, A2, A3. Jobs labelled A are urgent, Bs are less immediate but should not be left too long. Cs are non-urgent but still represent important tasks.

3. Add to the list during the day as new tasks appear, and tick off items as they are completed.

4. At the end of each day, rewrite your list, re-prioritizing the coding as necessary.

As you review your list you will notice that some items follow a regular pattern – they stay static, appear often or move up and down.

- If they remain static, can you justify having them on your list? *Do* them, or remove them as unimportant.

- If an item appears regularly, consider whether you can remove it by delegating the task to someone else.

- If the item moves up and down but doesn't get done, consider why. Are you dithering or avoiding the issue?

TAKE REGULAR BREAKS

A refreshed person is a more efficient person. Make sure you build in time for regular breaks during your day. Use these for brisk exercise, for light meals and refreshments, to meditate for twenty minutes, to do a visualization exercise, or to practise breathing control.

USEFUL TIME MANAGEMENT TIPS

- Use enforced activities like washing the car, walking the dog or mowing the lawn as important thinking and planning time.

- Set goals that are realistic and achievable.

- Don't agree to do more work than you know you are able to manage in the time available.

- Spend time at the start/end of the day planning your workload and making a 'To Do' list to focus your mind.

- Don't waste time dithering – decide what you need to do and do it.

- Pace yourself – work at a steady rate, and build in a little extra time to cope with traffic or meetings that overrun if necessary.

- Learn to speed-read.

- Prepare in advance for meetings so you stick to the agenda.

- Reserve blocks of time for different activities and don't jump from job to job.

- Group essential telephone calls together and set a time limit to complete them all.

- Deal swiftly with interruptions.

- Delegate as much as possible – you can still retain responsibility for the final result.

- Use a team approach so that everyone plays a reasonable part.

- Make the best use of available technology.

- Analyse your use of time by doing a time-and-motion study of an average week (see right) to find out where you are managing time and where it is managing you.

TIME MANAGEMENT EXERCISE

Try keeping an accurate time-and-motion log for a week. This is less onerous than you might think. Simply write down the normal waking hours of your days (for example, 07.00–24.00) down one side of a sheet of A4 paper and after every task, jot down on the appropriate time line:

1. What you have done.

2. Approximately how long you spent doing it.

Analyse the result critically after a week. Did you spend more time on tasks than intended? Identify where:

1. You were in control of your time.

2. You had lost control of your time.

- Were you wasting time performing tasks that could have been delegated to others?

- Were you shifting aimlessly from hour to hour, responding only to other people's demands on your time rather than shaping your own day?

- How often should you have said no and meant it? An unreasonable request for your time does not become more reasonable by you squandering time to fulfil it. For tips on how to say no and mean it, see Chapter 6.

Delegating

Delegation is the art of freeing up your own time and resources by donating a task previously under your control to someone else who is equally capable of performing it. Some people find delegation easy, while others find it hard. In some cases, giving up a job may mean shedding a boring or onerous task, but it also means giving up some control and admitting to yourself that you are not indispensable for this particular task. People with good self-esteem are usually good delegators, while those with poor self-esteem may find it difficult to hand over responsibilities to others.

A job cannot be done properly if no one knows what the job entails, however, so communication is important when delegating important tasks. Those who know what is expected of them and who are given incentives to achieve it tend to be the most loyal and hard-working. It may help to:

- Write down exactly what is expected of the person to whom you are delegating a complex task.
- Hold a regular forum for communication. Allow feedback. Give praise when it's due. Reprimand fairly and *not* in public.
- Give an incentive for peole to meet an important goal.
- Learn to give authority yet at the same time retain responsibility.

RESOURCES

Please send a large, stamped, self-addressed envelope when writing to the following addresses.

Alcohol
Alcohol Concern
Waterbridge House
32-36 Loman St
London SE1 0EE
(0171 928 7377)
Information service.
Drinkline
(0171 332 0202, London only; 0345 320202,
nationwide. All calls charged at local rates.
Or dial and listen on 0500 801802 — free call.)
National alcohol helpline.

Alternative therapies
British Herbal Medicine Association
Sun House
Church St
Stroud GL5 1JL
(01453 751389)
Information leaflets, booklets, compendium,
telephone advice.
British Homoeopathic Association
27A Devonshire Street
London W1N 1RJ
(0171 935 2163)
Send SAE for list of medically qualified homoeo-
pathic doctors.
British Reflexology Association
Monks Orchard
Whitbourne
Worcester WR6 5RB
(01886 821 207)
General Council and Register of Naturopaths
Frazer House
6 Netherall Gardens
London NW3 5RR
(0171 435 8728)

International Association for Colour Therapy
PO Box 3688
London SW13 0NX
(0181 878 5276)
Massage Therapy Institute of Great Britain
PO Box 26/27
London NW2 4NR
(0181 208 1607)
The Register of Chinese Herbal Medicine
PO Box 400
Wembley
Middlesex HA9 9NE
(0181-904-1357)
Send an SAE and £1.50 for the register.

Anxiety/stress
International Stress Management Association
The Priory Hospital
Priory Lane
London SW15 5JJ
(0181 876 8261)
Information on stress management and control.
Leaflets, booklets, counselling.
No Panic
Randlay
Telford TF3 2JQ
(Helpline: 01952 590545, 10 a.m. — 10 p.m. every
day of the year)
Aims to help people suffering from phobias,
obsessive-compulsive disorders and other related
anxiety disorders, including tranquillizer with-
drawal.

Bereavement
CRUSE – Bereavement Care
Cruse House
126 Sheen Road
Richmond
Surrey TW9 1UR
(0181 940 4818)
Offers counselling, advice and social contacts
for all bereaved people.

Counselling
British Association of Art Therapists
11a Richmond Road
Brighton
Sussex BN2 3RL
**British Association for Behavioural
Psychotherapy**
Social Services Department
7 Whittaker Street
Radcliffe
Manchester M26 9TD
British Association for Counselling
1 Regent Place
Rugby Warwickshire CV21 2PJ
(01788 578328)
Send an SAE for a register of local accredited
counsellors and a publication list.
British Confederation of Psychotherapists
37 Mapesbury Road
London NW2 4HJ
(0181 830 5173)
Provides a register of psychotherapists and a
free brochure, 'Finding a Therapist'.

Depression
Depression Alliance
PO Box 1022
London SE1 7QB
(0171 721 7672)
Samaritans
(0345 909090)
Seasonal Affective Disorder Association
PO Box 989
London SW7 2PZ
(0181 969 7028)
Help and support for sufferers of SAD. Light-box
hire scheme.

Hair Loss
Attention X
316 King Street
Hammersmith
London W6 0RR
(0181 741 8224)
Medical hair design to disguise trichotillomania
and alopecia, etc.

Herbal suppliers
The Nutri-Centre
The Hale Clinic
7 Park Crescent
London
W1N 3HE
(0171 436 5122)
Supplies many of the aromatherapy, herbal and
homoeopathic supplements mentioned in this book
by mail order.

Catuaba is only available from:
Rio Trading
2 Centenary Estate,
Hughes Rd
Brighton
BN2 4AW
(01273 570987)

Impotence
Impotence Association
PO Box 10296
London SW17 9WH
(confidential helpline: 0181 767 7791, 9 a.m. –
5 p.m.)
Please send a large stamped SAE for the leaflet
'Impotence Explained – A Couples' Guide to
Erectile Dysfunction'.

ME
ME Association
Stanhope house
High Street
Stamford-le-Hope
Essex SS17 0HA
(01375 361013)
Information and support for sufferers of ME.

Migraine
Migraine Action
178a High Road
Byfleet
Surrey KT14 7ED
(01932 352468)

The Migraine Trust
45 Great Ormond Street
London WC1N 3HD
(0171 278 2676)

Organic food
Baby Organix Infants Cereals (01202 479701).
Craig Farm, Wales: Award-winning organic meat
(for example, Welsh black beef) and fish (for
example, cold smoked tuna) by mail order (01597
851655.).
Mericks Organic Farm: Award-winning organic box
scheme (01458 252901).
Organic Health
139–141 Ilkeston Road
Marlpool
Heaner
Derbyshire DE75 7LX
(01773 717718)
Organic dry goods by mail order.
The Fresh Food Company
326 Portobello Road
London W10 5RU
(0181 969 0351)
Prize-winning mail-order suppliers of a wide
range of organic foods.
The Soil Association
86 Colston Street
Bristol BS1 5BB
(0117 929 0661)
Provides a directory of local organic box
schemes and home delivery services for a small
cost.

Premenstrual syndrome
**National Association for Premenstrual
Syndrome**
PO Box 72
Sevenoaks
Kent TN13 1QX
(01732 741709, 10 a.m. – 10 p.m.)
PMS Help
PO Box 83
Hereford HR4 8YQ

Premenstrual Society
PO Box 429
Addlestone
Surrey KT15 1DZ

Relationship problems
Relate
Herbert Gray College
Little Church Street
Rugby
Warwickshire CV21 3AP
(01788 573241)
Works to support marriage and family life by
providing counselling and sex therapy for
couples with relationship problems at more than
120 local centres nationwide.

Smoking
QUIT
102 Gloucester Place
London W1H 3DA
(Smokers' Quitline: 071 487 3000, 9.30 a.m. –
5.30 p.m. daily)
Advice and counselling on giving up smoking.

INDEX